The Ra

Handbook

The Radio Drama Handbook

Audio Drama in Context and Practice

Richard J. Hand and Mary Traynor

Continuum International Publishing Group
80 Maiden Lane, New York, NY 10038
The Tower Building, 11 York Road, London SE1 7NX

www.continuumbooks.com

Library of Congress Cataloging-in-Publication Data
A catalog record for this book is available from the Library of Congress.

ISBN: PB: 978-1-4411-4743-1

Typeset by Newgen Imaging Systems Pvt Ltd, Chennai, India
Printed and bound in the United States of America

This book is dedicated to: Sadiyah, Shara, Danya and Jimahl (RJH)
Peter, Molly, Connie and Mops (MT)

Contents

Acknowledgements

The authors would like to thank the following:

The University of Glamorgan's Research Investment Scheme.
Past and present students of radio drama at the University of Glamorgan.
The volunteers and staff at Khoun Community Radio for Development in Laos, who try to improve people's lives through radio drama.
The numerous audio artists and podcasters who answered all our questions with such generosity and enthusiasm.
Rik Ferrell (Managing Partner with Helicopter Marketing, Baltimore, MD, US) for permission to reproduce 'Writing Effective Radio Ad Copy: Six Steps to Successful Radio Commercials'.
Roger Bickerton and the Vintage Radio Programmes Collectors' Circle.

Part 1
A contextual guide to radio drama

1

A history of radio drama

Introduction

Why should we be interested in radio drama? Aren't its limitations blatantly obvious? Isn't radio what people had before television arrived: a TV which gives us nothing to look at? What is the point of a performance if you can't even see the actors? In playing the devil's advocate, Hugh Chignell goes as far as to argue that radio drama is a 'contradiction': 'How is it possible in such a visual age for "invisible" drama, drama without faces or scenery to exist?' (Chignell, 2009, p. 26). No one could fail to notice that we are surrounded by screens and visuals. That is what defines the advanced technological culture of the contemporary world: screens on our walls; on our desks; in our pockets; everywhere we look screens are always within sight.

These opinions are probably felt by many people, but at the same time it is true to say that *sound* is more important than people realize. Because it is literally invisible, sound is all too easy to ignore. Yet as much as people love to use their televisions and computers and mobile phones and portable game consoles, they also do other things: they drive, they do household chores, they exercise, they read and write, they sometimes even close their eyes . . . And when they do these things they often *listen*. Whether it is on their prized iPod or high-tech phone or on a radio they take for granted, they listen: it might be music, it might be news or sports broadcasting, it might be a variety of talk shows and phone-ins. But for some people it can be *stories*: audio books and even, yes, radio drama.

Sound

Before we look at radio drama specifically, let us consider the importance of sound. Even in the visual media, sound is not only more complex than what literally 'meets the eye', it is critically important. A favorite test of this is to watch a horror movie with the volume turned to mute. The carefully crafted sequences that manipulate our sense of foreboding and suspense become, with the sound off, little more than an edited succession of images. You can literally 'see the join'. Put the volume back up and you realize that the music, sound effects, voices, other utterances and mysterious noises have a calculated effect to frame the story, drive the action and sweep us along in the experience. Indeed, some people even say that although they closed their eyes in a movie theatre during a particularly scary sequence, it did not help because they could still *hear* everything. In fact, it might have made things even worse. After all, as one of the most influential producers in the history of US broadcasting (both on radio and television), Himan Brown puts it,

> The key to radio drama is sound – is imagination – is what you can do by stirring somebody. You can't do that with television. You can show them the pictures and say 'This is what it is'. But so what? So you sit there like a dummy and accept the car crashes but you can't add anything to it. *There's nothing bloodier than the blood you see in your imagination.* What are they gonna do? Pour a lot of ketchup on the television screen? It's still bloodier in your own mind. (quoted in Hand, 2006, p. 36)

In a similar spirit, Robert Arnold (executive director of Chatterbox Audio Theater) argues that 'Audio challenges the imagination in ways that video cannot. All the CGI in the world cannot create a vista more beautiful or a monster more terrifying than the one you imagine' (Arnold, 2010). Our own imaginations are the most powerful medium of all. Perhaps sound can even provide a shortcut to the deepest realm of our imagination? The formal term for this is *anamnesis*, which has been described as

> An effect of reminiscence in which a past situation or atmosphere is brought back to the listener's consciousness, provoked by a particular signal or sonic context. Anamnesis, a semiotic effect, is the often involuntary revival of memory caused by listening and the evocative power of sounds. (Augoyard and Torgue, 2005, p. 21)

Certainly, for many people, anamnesis can be extremely powerful or, indeed, *resonant*: songs and melodies, snatches of rhymes or lines from stories and poems can be evocative conduits to memory and feelings. Sometimes it is these auditory things more than the obvious – photographs or even locations – that can surprise us with their emotional potency. In Edward Bond's stage play *The Sea* (1973), the character Willy talks about the death of his close friend Colin: 'You're supposed to forget what they look like very soon. It comes as a shock. But it's hard to forget the voice. You suddenly hear that twenty years later' (Bond, 1978,

p. 145). The human voice has extraordinary importance to the communicative beings that we are. The inherent power of the acoustic and the aural was made even more profound with the invention of a piece of technology that seemed quite miraculous to many in the generation that saw its inauguration . . . radio.

The invention of radio

It may come as a surprise, but it is difficult to put a precise date on the invention of radio. This is because the technology emerges out of an international mixture of theoretical physics, practical experimentation and commercial interests. For instance, let us consider the Scottish physicist James Clerk Maxwell (1831–79), a pioneer in the area of electromagnetism. As Lewis Coe writes, Maxwell contended that 'there might be electromagnetic waves that were similar to light waves' (Coe, 1996, p. 4) and managed to prove it through advanced mathematics. Maxwell was purely a theoretician, and his ideas were explored and expanded in a laboratory context by the German physicist Heinrich Hertz (1857–94), who built equipment that functioned as an apparatus to produce and detect radio waves. The Italian inventor Guglielmo Marconi (1874–1937) was fascinated by Hertz's experiments and saw their potential for creating a practical communications system. Although Marconi would eventually be awarded the Nobel Prize for physics, it is worth noting that he was not a pioneer in the way that Maxwell and Hertz had been. What Marconi did brilliantly was develop and improve the experiments of Hertz and others in order to create a fully operational and commercially viable system of wireless technology. In this regard, Susan Merrill Squier considers Marconi's visit to the Unites States to broadcast the America's Cup yacht race in 1899, during which he demonstrated the potential of 'wireless telegraphy', to be immensely important (Merrill Squier, 2003, pp. 10–11). However, much of Marconi's research and development was undertaken in Britain, which was far more interested in the potential of wireless technology than Marconi's home nation, Italy.

The fact that the invention of radio cannot be credited to one person is most evident in numerous controversies and contestations. Other figures, including the British physicist Oliver Lodge (1851–1940), the Serbian-born inventor Nikola Tesla (1856–1943) and many other scientists and entrepreneurs, became embroiled in the arguments – and sometimes court cases – surrounding the inauguration and development of radio technology. Or, to put it more progressively, many people were part of the creation of radio and its phenomenal rise.

Wireless

For many at the beginning of its history (not least through Marconi's demonstrations), what we understand as radio was known as wireless telegraphy, which became shortened to 'wireless', a name that captures the sense of miracle that it represented. This new technology did not need to be wired in like the other monumental nineteenth-century inventions that had changed the world, the telegraph and the telephone. Lewis Coe informs us that the term 'wireless' was officially replaced by the word 'radio' at an international conference in Berlin in 1906 (Coe, 1996, p. 3), and although the usage of 'wireless' to mean radio has disappeared from American English, to this day many people in Britain still understand and use the term. Interestingly, we have lived through another global epoch that has stood in awe and wonder at the term 'wireless' once again with the explosion of mobile-phone and wireless-internet technology.

As well as instituting the name 'radio' for this revolutionary technology, the Berlin conference in 1906 also agreed on another term that would have far-reaching implications. The same conference agreed that 'SOS' in Morse code should be recognized as the international distress call (Coe, 1996, p. 16). Morse code is a system of 'dots' and 'dashes' that represent letters of the alphabet and numbers. It had been developed for the telegraph system, but effortlessly moved into radio technology. The fast-developing technology of radio was seen as particularly beneficial when it came to its potential in sending Morse code messages, especially with regard to ships. However, this system was rather ad hoc until a particularly infamous event. Although synonymous with catastrophe, the sinking of the *Titanic* in April 1912 had the immediate consequence of regulating ships' radio equipment and practice. That is not so say that radio was not in operation on the *Titanic*: although over 1500 passengers died after the ship hit an iceberg, it is true to say that if it was not for the distress signal sent by the *Titanic*'s radio operators, the loss of life would have been even greater.

Eventually, radio progressed from being a wireless conduit for Morse code, and voice transmission became possible. It was this development that would make the future success of broadcasting and mass communication unmistakably clear. As with the history of radio as a whole, there were sporadic experiments and lukewarm successes with voice broadcasting. Nevertheless, radio was initially a pastime for amateurs, hobbyists who had the time and interest to explore the 'airwaves'. As Filson Young recalls, in the early days of radio broadcasting 'Hardly anybody took it seriously; it was regarded either as a hobby or a science . . . as flying once was' (Young, 1933, p. 1). This is a powerful parallel: for us, it is extraordinary to think that human-powered flight was once seen as a slightly eccentric pastime and that radio had the same place until people gradually recognized its potential.

Radio broadcasting

A key figure in the development of radio broadcasting is David Sarnoff (1891–1971), who worked for the American Marconi Company and, in 1916, pronounced a momentous ambition: 'I have in mind a plan of development which would make radio a "household utility" in the same sense as the piano or phonograph' (quoted in Maltin, 2000, p. 2). It was this concept that would develop radio from being a hobby or an 'emergency' device (what we might call now a 'health and safety' utility) into a cultural form. Another important person in this regard is the amateur radio enthusiast Frank Conrad (1874–1941), who from around 1912 began experimenting with radios, eventually broadcasting music and the spoken word from his own self-made station in Pennsylvania. Conrad worked for the Pittsburgh-based Westinghouse Electric Company, which noticed the interest their employee's hobby was garnering. It was clear that the idea of a radio station was an extremely viable initiative. The company established the KDKA station, which started broadcasting in November 1920 with a signal strong enough to be 'heard throughout the United States under nighttime conditions' (Coe, 1996, p. 26). KDKA was a huge success, and numerous other stations rapidly emerged across the nation. In the United Kingdom, the British Broadcasting Company started broadcasting in November 1922, before it evolved into the British Broadcasting Corporation in 1926. The international rise of radio was somewhat uneven, but nevertheless many nations saw the appeal of radio broadcasting and embraced the technology with passion in the 1920s. Interestingly, and perhaps surprisingly given our sense of its ubiquity in our own time, the rise of television was a more staggered process in comparison. Although some nations, such as the United States, the United Kingdom, Germany and France, launched television in the 1920s and 1930s and returned to it with enthusiasm after the hiatus dictated by the Second World War, some nations were more reticent about this visual technology. For instance, although South Africa inaugurated radio broadcasting in 1923, it did not introduce television broadcasting until 1976.

To return to early radio, more important than any inventors, official stations or national policy regarding radio broadcasting was one particular individual: the radio listener. It was the demand of individual listeners that dictated and determined the incredible rise of radio and its phenomenal popularity. Probably a key ingredient to this is a simple invention: the crystal set radio. Factory-made radios powered by electricity were extremely expensive, although David Sarnoff's development of the 'Radiola' unit in the early 1920s would gradually push prices down. Nevertheless, even in the 1920s, many households did not have electricity at all. However, anyone had the potential to be a radio listener. At negligible cost, enthusiasts were able to buy, or even make, crystal sets for themselves. A crystal set was yet another miracle for many in an age of technological wonders: simply constructed using copper wire and a crystal detector, it required no power source, as it ran on the radio waves that it received through its antenna. Although too weak to be heard through a speaker, the crystal set could be heard through an earphone. An entire generation was converted to the wonders of radio in this way, picking up broadcasts from across the nation on these tiny inventions. If you could afford an expensive electricity-powered radio, you were fortunate, but the crystal set meant that money need not be an obstacle for participating in the burgeoning radio age. A similar leap forward happened a generation later with the invention of transistor radios in the 1950s. These portable, battery-powered radio receivers became phenomenally popular starting in the 1960s: these small and affordable radios allowed people to listen to broadcasts wherever they were and had a massive impact on broadcasting and audience, especially in relation to youth culture. The affordability of the crystal set and the transistor radio was an essential aspect to their rise and the accompanying sense of democracy. This factor contrasts very distinctly with the rise of another form of media: televisions would always be more expensive compared to the genius of the crystal set and the transistor radio. Moreover, televisions use so much power they are usually dependent on a main electricity supply. Interestingly, radio sets continue to be comparatively affordable, not least when ethical concerns have forced the issue: the British inventor Trevor Baylis (born in 1937) patented the wind-up radio in 1989. This device utilizes a hand-cranked electric generator which powers the radio receiver. Baylis developed this with a specific social purpose: to educate and disseminate information about AIDS in the developing world, especially Africa. The wind-up radio was designed to be portable and affordable. However, it is important to note that Baylis did not invent the hand-cranked electric generator: once again, we have the example of an inventor who took existing technology and saw its social and cultural potential.

Radio content

Once radio broadcasting commenced, the next question was one of content. The earliest days of radio broadcasting meant that stations were 'on air' for short periods at a time, just a few hours a day. However, the on-air time increased in response to what the audience enjoyed listening to or wanted to hear. Music was important and popular from an early time, and there was spoken word content used for news and sports results. The radio boom was immensely exciting, but it developed so quickly that it was somewhat disorientating, not dissimilar to the rapid expansion of the internet in more recent times. Radio waves were not a tangible commodity as such: who owned them? How do you regulate them? How do you control them? As Gerald Nachman puts it, the 'argument still rages over whose air – or cyberspace – it is, anyway' (Nachman, 1998, p. 19).

The impact of radio was felt through a cultural shift. Isolated communities could at last be 'in the loop'; news of current affairs and other events could be spread instantaneously; thousands of miles and disparate voices could be connected in an instant. The immediacy of radio broadcasting meant, perhaps, that everything had the potential to be 'dramatic' – not just the obviously dramatic genres. This is evident in the case of 'breaking news'. In 1927, Charles Lindbergh's departure and return on his historic transatlantic flight was captured on radio. The two world championship boxing matches between Joe Louis and the German boxer Max Schmeling at Yankee Stadium in the 1930s also became the stuff of modern legend. Schmeling was a German heavyweight boxer indelibly – yet completely unfairly – linked with the Nazi regime. In June 1936, Schmeling defeated the African-American boxer Louis ('The Brown Bomber'), which Hitler capitalized on as a victory for Aryan superiority. In June 1938 the fighters met in a rematch. This contest held significance beyond being merely a sports event, thanks, in large part, to radio. According to Hugh Chignell, 'it is estimated that two thirds of all radio sets were tuned to hear Joe Louis defeat Max Schmeling' (Chignell, 2009, p. 53). Maya Angelou vividly captures the significance of the event in *I Know Why the Caged Bird Sings* (1969). Angelou sets the scene of the local community gathering in a store in the small town of Stamps, Arkansas, well over a thousand miles away from the event itself:

> The last inch of space was filled, yet people continued to wedge themselves along the walls of the Store. Uncle Willie had turned the radio up to its last notch so that youngsters on the porch wouldn't miss a word. Women sat on kitchen chairs, dining-room chairs, stools

> and upturned wooden boxes. Small children and babies sat perched on every lap available and men leaned on the shelves or on each other. (Angelou, 1984, p. 129)

Angelou describes the commentary to the thrilling contest and the people's reaction to it, and considers if the radio 'announcer gave any thought to the fact that he was addressing as "ladies and gentlemen" all the Negroes around the world who sat swearing and praying, glued to their "master's voice"' (Angelou, 1984, p. 130). Louis's victory is conveyed instantaneously across the world by the power of radio, and Angelou describes the ensuing celebration and the realization that this was the 'night when Joe Louis had proved that we were the strongest people in the world' (Angelou, 1984, p. 132). Susan Douglas reveals another consequence of the Joe Louis boxing matches: 'his fights on the radio made boxing profitable again' (Douglas, 1999, p. 207). Radio did not just report the sports and culture of the nation, it had an instrumental role in determining and even giving a new lease of life to some activities.

One of the most famous examples of live radio broadcasting is Herbert Morrison's eyewitness account of the Hindenburg airship on 6 May 1937. The WLS radio station (Chicago) had sent its reporter Herbert Morrison and the sound engineer Charles Nehlsen to the Lakehurst Naval Air Station in New Jersey to document the arrival of the German passenger airship, the Hindenburg. Morrison speaks with evident excitement as he describes the docking airship:

> The back motors of the ship are just holding it, er, just enough to keep it from – It's burst into flames! (. . .) Get this, Charlie, get this, Charlie! It's fire . . . and it's crashing! It's crashing terrible! Oh, my! Get out of the way, please! It's burning and bursting into flames and the – and it's falling on the mooring mast. And all the folks agree that this is terrible; this is the worst of the worst catastrophes in the world. (. . .) It's a terrific crash, ladies and gentlemen. It's smoke, and it's flames now; and the frame is crashing to the ground, not quite to the mooring mast. Oh, the humanity! And all the passengers screaming around here. I told you, it – I can't even talk to people, their friends are out there! Ah! It's . . . it . . . it's a . . . ah! I . . . I can't talk, ladies and gentlemen. Honest, it's just laying there, a mass of smoking wreckage. Ah! And everybody can hardly breathe and talk and the screaming. Lady, I . . . I . . . I'm sorry. Honest, I . . . I can hardly breathe. I . . . I'm going to step inside, where I cannot see it. (Morrison, 1937)

To this day, if you listen to the recording, you can hear that it is authentic, and it abides as a remarkable example of radio history. Despite saying 'I can't talk, ladies and gentlemen' Morrison does just that: he keeps talking; although he is crying, he stays engaged with his listeners. Above all, Morrison's spontaneous phrase 'Oh, the humanity!' became one of the great quotes of the twentieth century and has often been alluded to in a variety of forums, from popular music through to the television cartoon situation comedy *The Simpsons*.

Another significant aspect of the potential of radio is in relation to political broadcasting. When Adolf Hitler wrote *Mein Kampf* in the mid-1920s, he pronounced that radio is 'a terrible weapon in the hands of those who know how to make use of it' (Hale, 1975, p. 1), and, subsequently, the Nazis were obsessed with the propaganda potential of radio to indoctrinate the German people. It seems, however, that as far as the Nazis were concerned, Hitler's appearances on radio proved less effective than his screen or 'in person' appearances. President Franklin D. Roosevelt's 'Fireside Chats' stand in contrast to Hitler's use of radio. On 12 March 1933, Roosevelt made the first of thirty live broadcasts from the White House. He opened the speech with this sentence: 'My friends, I want to talk for a few minutes with the people of the United States about banking.' This might have backfired as a cloying over-familiarity, but, on the contrary, it changed the nature of political broadcasting, and the political use of the media, forever. It may have been a gamble – after all, this was a radical departure from traditional forms of political engagement with the public – but it had a global impact and is a benchmark moment in the use of media for political broadcasting. The tone in which Roosevelt commenced his first 'Fireside Chat' is highly significant: 'My friends' is very informal. He is speaking like a neighbor, a friend in the corner of the room, not obviously the leader of your nation. The phrase demonstrates an understanding of the domestic intimacy of radio. This is in stark contrast to Hitler's attempts to exploit radio. As Julian Hale writes, unlike Roosevelt, Hitler 'wanted to arouse, not calm, his audience, inspire them, not reason with them' (Hale, 1975, p. 7).

Franklin D. Roosevelt's 'Fireside Chats' were broadcast every few months until June 1944. Around half of the broadcasts occurred after the Second World War had commenced in Europe, and twelve of them occurred during the US involvement. Although visual images of the US flag being raised on Iwo Jima, the liberation of the Nazi death camps and the atomic bomb mushroom cloud above Hiroshima are the dominant icons that define the Second World War, we should not forget how important radio was in the period. Not only had the communicative function of radio transformed the actualities of warfare and combat itself, it also had an essential role in a broader context. Listeners at home could get instantaneous news coverage, and, just as the United States could hear its president, elsewhere in the world the radio was used for propaganda purposes or resistance broadcasts.

A famous case in point is very much contemporaneous with President Roosevelt. Winston Churchill was prime minister of Britain during the Second World War, and his wartime speeches remain celebrated examples of political oration. One of his most abiding speeches was made at the House of Commons (the British Parliament) on 4 June 1940:

> Even though large tracts of Europe and many old and famous States have fallen or may fall into the grip of the Gestapo and all the odious apparatus of Nazi rule, we shall not flag or fail. We shall go on to the end, we shall fight in France, we shall fight on the seas and oceans, we shall fight with growing confidence and growing strength in the air, we shall defend our Island, whatever the cost may be, we shall fight on the beaches, we shall fight on the landing grounds, we shall fight in the fields and in the streets, we shall fight in the hills; we shall never surrender, and even if, which I do not for a moment believe, this Island or a large part of it were subjugated and starving, then our Empire beyond the seas, armed and guarded by the British Fleet, would carry on the struggle, until, in God's good time, the New World, with all its power and might, steps forth to the rescue and the liberation of the old. (Churchill, 1940)

At that time, it was not permitted to record British Parliamentary proceedings apart from in writing, but some of Churchill's speeches were subsequently recorded and broadcast by the BBC so that the public could hear the inspiring words in the Prime Minister's distinctive voice. Of course, if we read the speech, we can see that it has important propaganda value, especially in its mixture of defying Germany while calling out to the United States ('the New World'): the speech needed to be disseminated beyond a few hundred Members of Parliament, and although there would be press coverage, the spoken voice of a unique politician needed to be heard. There was a rumor that some of the BBC versions of the speeches were made by an actor imitating Churchill, and although fervently denied for decades, in 2000 proof was found in the form of a 1940s BBC record which stated 'Churchill: Speech. Artist Norman Shelley' on its label (Thorpe, 2010). Norman Shelley was a well-known British radio actor for many years, and although he had admitted that he had been approached during the war to imitate Churchill's voice, he had always downplayed the affair. The fact that it has been proved that the voice is that of an actor is now an interesting footnote: the fact that it was so controversial at the time and for many years afterwards reflects how important the issue of *authenticity* can be. People wanted to hear the voice of Churchill, not an actor imitating him. Radio, that most intimate and subtly present of technologies, speaks into our ears with disarming 'reality', like the voices we overhear in everyday life or the voice of a friend at the end of a telephone. When we learn that what we heard was not all that it seemed, we can feel duped and outraged. The most supreme example of this is *Mercury Theater on the Air*'s adaptation of 'War of the Worlds' (30 October 1938), the subject of the first case study in this book.

Other impacts of radio were apparent across the cultural industries. As Tim Crook notes, in 1921 sales of recorded music began to fall as radio broadcasted live music for free and with better sound quality than gramophones (Crook, 1999, p. 37). However, things would change again, as Gerald Nachman explains: 'At first, all the free music on radio sent record sales plummeting, but the rise of variety shows – free promotion for new pop tunes – soon had them soaring again . . .' (Nachman, 2000, p. 18). As with any new technology, when its appeal and its potential came into focus, its consequences were hard to predict and, for some, this was unnerving. This is a familiar story in the history of human invention: whether it was industrialized machinery, mechanized transport, cinema, radio, television, video recording or the internet, there are voices of dissent, and yet the progress is inexorable and adopted by the majority.

If the new-fangled invention of broadcast radio could spread information with a rapidity that was unprecedented in the history of human civilization, it could also do something else: *entertain*. From its start in the 1920s, radio was astonishingly innovative in developing new genres. If we look at radio listings or, better yet, listen to archive recordings from the 1920s and 1930s, it is amazing how recognizable the *types* of programmes are. Moreover, not only were many of the genres and formats created by early radio unproblematically adopted by television: they remain unchanged in the twenty-first century. To this end, news and current affairs coverage, political reportage and sports broadcasting have scarcely changed at all since radio invented them in the first half of the twentieth century. Likewise, the format of quiz shows, soap operas (the very phrase emerging from soap companies' sponsorship of serialized family radio drama) and situation comedies ('sitcoms') have changed very little. In addition, radio was very adept at taking on pre-existing cultural forms: vaudeville and variety shows, for instance, had a theatrical heritage, but could work consummately on the new media of radio. However, that is not to suggest that it was 'easy'. Leonard Maltin spells out the challenges very clearly:

> In the earliest days of broadcasting, there were no rules, and there certainly were no precedents. No one had ever devoted themselves to

> the purpose of providing hours of daily entertainment – and those who came closest, from the world of the theater, were accustomed to providing the *same* entertainment to a *different* audience every day, be it a play, a vaudeville show, or even a circus. A vaudevillian who perfected his act might use the same ten minutes of act for years. If the entertainer used that material one night on his local station, he couldn't very well repeat it the following evening. (Maltin, 2000, p. 12)

In addition, many theatres were not happy with their artists being broadcast. This could cost them ticket sales and, for this reason, in Britain live broadcasts of performances in theatres were banned between 1923 and 1925, and many artists had contracts that prohibited them from being featured on radio (Briggs, 1965, p. 77).

Radio drama

We saw earlier that it is difficult to unravel the history of radio and radio stations back to definitive point of origin. It is the same with specific genres, such as radio drama. In finding material to satisfy the avid and ever-growing audience for radio, stations had to harvest and develop whatever they could and whatever might work. In this respect, it is a compelling example of technology determining culture: a new medium is developed and material is needed to supply it. Leonard Maltin highlights the importance of stories being read out on the radio (what we would now call 'audio books') and gives this genre a very privileged position: 'The first radio "institution" seems to have been the reading of children's stories at bedtime. Dozens of stations seized upon this idea, and boasted of their 'story ladies' with velvety voices who would help put the toddlers to sleep' (Maltin, 2000, p. 13). One can imagine the appeal of this genre: if not technology as babysitter, at least it was modern technology helping to improve the quality of the day-to-day life of families. Moreover, after the reading of books on the air, the development of radio drama was only a step away. In fact, the importance of a genre aimed at families with children was highly influential to the evolution of the form as a whole. Describing the development of radio in Britain in the 1920s, Asa Briggs writes: '*Children's Hour*' programmes were not only very good, but introduced genuinely new radio forms and developed new radio techniques' (Briggs, 1961, p. 262).

Some of the earliest examples of radio drama in the 1920s are essentially broadcasts of stage productions. These must have seemed like 'listening in' to a play in the theatre. In fact, in some cases this was literally the situation. John Schneider mentions the live broadcast of a stage play from a college auditorium in California as early as 1914 (cited in Crook, 1999, pp. 4–5). Furthermore broadcast historians, including Howard Blue, have cited Eugene Walter's *The Wolf*, broadcast on WGY (Schenectady, New York) in August 1922, as 'the first "on air" drama' (Blue, 2002, p. 1). The broadcast historian Elizabeth McLeod puts the production into more detailed context. She reveals that a stage actor, Edward H. Smith, approached the WGY Program Director Kolin Hager in 1922 with a proposal to adapt stage plays for the radio:

> Hager liked the idea, and agreed – on the provision that none of the plays run more than forty minutes. He was concerned that the attention span of the audience might not be up to the challenge of a longer production, so new was the idea. (McLeod, 1998)

The first play, *The Wolf*, was edited down from a three-act version to a succinct, 40-minute radio show and was performed by Smith and some fellow stage actors recruited onto the project. It was so successful that Hager commissioned a series of plays, and during 1922 and 1923, a total of 43 productions (entirely based on stage plays) were broadcast. Although it was successful and led to a swath of other productions and copycat series, as Howard Blue stresses, these 'early radio plays were literal readings of famous stage plays' (Blue, 2002, p. 2). Indeed, if we look at radio listings in the early days of broadcasting, we discover Gilbert and Sullivan operettas, extracts from Verdi and Puccini operas, adaptations of popular stage melodramas, and, most of all, productions of Shakespeare.

It is a similar story in Britain. Tim Crook cites an experiment in drama broadcasting which took place in England on 17 October 1922 when an extract from Edmond Rostand's *Cyrano de Bergerac* was put on the air from a drama research station (Crook, 1999, p. 4). The BBC broadcast extracts from a selection of Shakespeare plays on 16 February 1923 with a full-length radio version of Shakespeare's *Twelfth Night* on 28 May 1923. Once again, these were essentially recited stage plays. There are other examples of such adaptations – and to this day adaptation continues to be an important and often exciting genre of radio drama. However, a key challenge was how to write *specifically* for the *medium of radio*. In an internet discussion group, radio historian Bill Jaker reveals,

> I'm always cautious about 'firsts', but I know that in 1921 a couple of agriculture professors from West Virginia University were invited to KDKA to deliver a talk on farm extension courses and showed up with a script for a playlet entitled 'A Rural Line on Education'. At first KDKA refused to let them ring a telephone bell, asserting that it would defraud the audience into thinking that they were hearing a phone call and not a radio program. The professors prevailed by

> reminding KDKA that its patriarch, Frank Conrad, had played music on his station 8XK from phonograph records, which a listener could mistake for live musicians. Not much happens in the play – it's just a chat on the phone between two farmers with an operator making frequent, somewhat comical, interruptions – but it was specially written for the audio medium at a time when the people at 'the pioneer broadcasting station of the world' had never heard of such a thing. (Jaker, 2010)

The first specific radio play in Britain was the BBC's *A Comedy of Danger* written by Richard Hughes (15 January 1924). Hughes was a young writer, but experienced in theatre writing, when he was commissioned by the BBC to write a 'Listening-Play'. The play was produced by Nigel Playfair, another figure from the theatre drawn to the BBC. *A Comedy of Danger* consciously utilizes the potential of the radio form. Hughes's play is set in a Welsh coal mine, and the opening exchange of dialogue immediately reveals that the play is exploiting the potential of the form:

> MARY. [Sharply] Hello! What's happened?
> JACK. The lights have gone out!

These lines immediately make it clear to the listener that there has been a power cut. The visual dimension – the most pre-eminently important aspect in the theatre and the cinema – is an irrelevancy on the radio. Hughes understood that radio permitted him to set a complete play in total darkness. The three principal characters in the play need to feel their way in the utter darkness and talk to each other as they do so. Their dialogue ranges from being generous and mutually supportive to, under the stress of the situation, violent. The danger of the situation is genuine, and only two of the three characters survive . . . The resulting play may be a very early example of a script written specifically for the new medium of radio, but it remains compelling and 'alive'.

As we have said, Richard Hughes was young when he wrote *A Comedy of Danger*: he was only 23 years old, and yet he was typical of the young talent that was drawn to the exciting new world of radio broadcasting. It was the same internationally: the talented could not resist the excitement that a new technology presented. They were learning as they went along and creating a new cultural form as they did so.

An important aspect to early radio is that it was an all-live medium. In our own time, we are used to radio and television being a mixture of the pre-recorded and the live: sports, news and weather updates might in large part be live, as are phone-in and talk radio programmes. In contrast, we would expect dramas, soap operas, sitcoms and other comedy formats to be pre-recorded and carefully edited. However, in the pioneering days of radio broadcasting and well into its heyday, when the radio was turned on, what the audience heard was entirely *live*. This was partly a practical issue, inasmuch as although major networks recorded programmes to be distributed on regional stations, 'only 15 minutes of sound could be recorded on large aluminium discs' (Chignell, 2009, p. 44), which made the process cumbersome. However, technical issues notwithstanding, there was also a deliberate policy on the part of the major networks to resist pre-recording. Corporations such as NBC and CBS adopted anti-recording policies which made it very difficult to pre-record: in the words of David Morton, the major networks effectively 'denounced recordings as an inferior form of culture' (Morton, 2000, p. 72). This meant that all the voices, music and sound effects the audience heard in radio drama were live. The exception was that phonograph records were sometimes used for particular sound effects and short announcements.

Although the use that small regional radio stations made of transcription recordings grew in the early 1930s, as the technology improved, the situation changed most significantly and rapidly after the Second World War when magnetic recording tape was introduced. The popular film and radio star Bing Crosby had a key role in this: his show, the *Philco Radio Time* was, according to Leonard Maltin, 'the first taped program on network radio, in 1946' (Maltin, 2000, p. 293). It was Crosby himself who precipitated this development, believing that pre-recording was much more convenient, because a whole series could be recorded in advance, rather than demanding a weekly obligation. Moreover, pre-recording could, in principle, improve the shows, as it made editing possible. As Allen S. Weiss comments, 'Practically no recording is really "live"' (Weiss, 1995, p. 36): even recorded performances tend to be cut, spliced and tidied in one way or another. Once pre-recording became standard, it must have been a small step from being *able* to edit, to it being *essential* to edit. Over all, this was a radical development: it is 'liveness' that characterizes early radio. Some aspects of this seem quite eccentric to us in the twenty-first century. For instance, the theme tune to a show would have to be broadcast live: *The Whistler* (1942–55) was a long-running thriller series which had 37 whistled notes as its theme tune. One might think that that would be pre-recorded. In fact, a lady called Dorothy Roberts whistled the 37 notes once a week for 13 years! This may seem crazy to us, but it also encapsulates one of the wonderful things about live radio: it is, in many respects, pure theatre. If one listens to archival recordings of live radio, one can almost feel the adrenaline pumping. Indeed, it was even literally theatre on occasion, which had a live studio audience of hundreds and a live radio audience of millions. This contributes to the legend of golden-age US radio in particular: a creative world that is vibrant, hectic and dynamic with so many live performers of all kinds needed to bring performances to reality, strictly on time, all fitting in with the 'on the air' light of radio.

In looking at US radio drama, the term 'Golden Age' has emerged to define the period broadly from the later 1920s to the early 1950s. The phrase is an emphatically nostalgic one – as is any other 'golden age'. However, it was certainly a rich and prolific time. The networks competed fiercely to hook and keep listeners who were enamoured with radio and had embraced it even faster than they would television. Nevertheless, by the time of the 1950s, television was regarded as the future medium, and the US networks invested heavily in this area at the expense of radio. Although a number of programmes made the step from radio into television, many shows and, tragically, many personnel, found they were at the end of the line. The majority of broadcasts were not recorded for posterity and are lost in the ether. However, what we do have is frequently fascinating.

Archive recordings from the 'golden age' of US radio – frequently called Old Time Radio (shortened to OTR) – can be purchased as MP3s and CDs, and many are available as free downloads from specific websites or via iTunes. There are also web radio stations that constantly stream classic radio broadcasts. It can be enormous fun to 'dip in' to these old broadcasts. More than that, it is still possible to learn a great deal from Old Time Radio. Jeffrey Adams is writer–producer for the web audio station Icebox Radio Theater. He has a background in stage drama, and in an interview he explains the challenge in finding a way in to writing audio drama – and the solution:

> Personally, things didn't really come alive for me until I stopped paying so much attention to the modern audio of the day (this was in the mid 1990s and much of what was being produced wasn't very good) and started paying attention to Old Time Radio. Though the recording quality wasn't as good, the writing and acting of OTR is usually superior. After all, these were working professionals practicing their craft daily. Paying more attention to OTR led me somewhat naturally into OTR-style plays, that is, thirty-minute formats with spare sound effects and music used to separate scenes. Not the only format, of course, but still a very legitimate one. (Adams, 2010)

By immersing himself in archive recordings from the classic era of radio drama, Adams has learnt the skills of audio writing and has also acquired a sense of what audio actors are able to do, equally important when one intends to produce radio drama.

As Jeffrey Adams stresses, the 30-minute format is not the only type of radio drama, but it does remain an extremely valuable one. Thirty-minute plays are perhaps easy to take in and are driven by a sense of economy and structural robustness. If we look at examples of golden-age US radio, *Suspense* (1942–62) and its sister series *Escape* (1947–54) presented many exemplary 30-minute radio plays. The repertoire of both shows broadly comprised thrillers of one kind or another, and they can still be surprisingly inventive, exciting or even disturbing. *Suspense*'s 'The House in Cypress Canyon' (5 December 1946) is a chilling tale of lycanthropy in postwar suburbia, a place one might expect to find the American Dream. *Escape*'s 'Leiningen versus the Ants' (14 January 1948) presents one man's attempts to stop a relentless horde of soldier ants as they eat everything in their path. Both plays use dialogue, sfx, music and soundscape in effective ways: although there have been countless 'werewolf' movies, and Charlton Heston stars in the role of Leiningen in the film *The Naked Jungle* (Byron Haskin, 1954), there is a genuinely unnerving intensity to the radio plays.

One of the delights of *Suspense* is that it gave famous Hollywood actors the chance to act against type. Hence we find a young Frank Sinatra playing a psychopath in 'To Find Help' (18 January 1945). In a later revived production (6 January 1949), Gene Kelly – always typecast as a song and dance man on screen – takes the Sinatra role with evident relish. Lucille Ball is best known as a much-loved 'kooky' comedienne, but in the violent play 'Dime a Dance' (13 January 1944), she narrowly escapes the hands of a serial killer. The musical star Judy Garland finds herself in a similar predicament in 'Drive-In' (21 November 1946). Other series of note that may provide rewarding listening in our own time include *Gunsmoke* (1952–61), a series set in the Old West with a variety of sometimes uncompromising adventures centred around the rugged protagonist Marshal Matt Dillon (played by a variety of actors including William Conrad). For Kc Wayland and Shane Salk, the creative team behind the 'zombie podcast' serial *We're Alive* (2009 onwards) – the subject of a case study later in this book – *Gunsmoke* is cited as the most important example of OTR drama.

If you are a fan of old Hollywood movies, *Lux Radio Theater* (1934–55) is a must, as it produced radio adaptations of classic films, frequently featuring the original movie cast. So, for example, there is an all-live broadcast of *The Wizard of Oz* (25 December 1950) starring Judy Garland recreating her legendary screen role. We mention many other OTR series in this book, but you might also like to track down extant copies of the crime series *Dragnet* (1949–57), the adventure serial *I Love a Mystery* (1939–44) and the comparatively late *CBS Radio Mystery Theater* (1974–82). As well as these sometimes outstanding examples of drama, there are many examples of comedy that still make for good listening, including *The Jack Benny Program* (1932–55) and the comedy quiz show *You Bet Your Life* (1947–59), featuring Groucho Marx as question master. Regarding UK radio, there has always been a passion for comedy, and shows such as *The Goon Show* (1951–60), *The Navy Lark* (1959–77), *I'm Sorry, I'll Read That Again* (1964–68) and *Round the Horne* (1965–68) still command a cult following and fan base.

If US radio came to an unhappy end, it was a different story in the United Kingdom. The BBC is a state-run corporation and emerged partly because of what the British government perceived as a chaotic situation of competing networks in the United States. Although the BBC would develop its own television broadcasting after the Second World War, it did so while maintaining a commitment to radio. Indeed, to this day the BBC's official magazine is called *Radio Times*, even though the radio listings within it are dwarfed by the television pages. The BBC still produces hundreds of hours of radio drama each year in a variety of formats ranging from 15-minute series to major one-off dramatizations and original plays. Sometimes the BBC monitors the success of a work on radio – especially comedy shows – before transferring them to television. To this end, the popular television comedies *Little Britain* (2003–2006) and *The Mighty Boosh* (2004–2007) both commenced on BBC radio in 2001. Other radio-only comedy shows, such as the spoof panel game *I'm Sorry, I Haven't a Clue* (1972 onwards), have enjoyed extraordinary longevity.

However, when it comes to longevity, the world's longest-running radio soap opera is unsurprisingly also the BBC's most famous radio drama: *The Archers*. As Hugh Chignell observes, 'It would be hard to overstate the iconic position of the first, and perhaps last, British radio soap, *The Archers*' (Chignell, 2009, p. 50). The programme was devised in 1950, and a short pilot run of the drama series was aired on a BBC regional station. The programme went national on 1 January 1951. Interestingly, the series was originally devised as an experimental drama with a pedagogical aim. The producer Godfrey Baseley (1904–97) endeavoured to create a drama series set in contemporary rural England which would entertain but also educate farmers by imbedding agricultural tips and advice within its storylines and dialogue. The educational aspect to the series continued until 1972.

Some BBC radio plays are commercially available or can be accessed via the BBC's online resource, the iPlayer. Some recordings can also be acquired via 'torrent' download sites. However, the BBC is not the only place that is still creating radio drama. The internet has led to a proliferation of new audio artists and dramatists producing works of spoken word drama. Indeed, the world of podcasting and downloads invites comparison with the rich era of excitement of the earliest days of broadcasting. As Hugh Chignell writes,

> Building on the success of the web log ('blog') which allowed people to communicate creatively to an Internet audience, podcasting opens up an opportunity to radio amateurs which has been largely denied to them since the birth of broadcasting in the 1920s. (Chignell, 2009, p. 43)

The web abounds with audio drama, and the majority of it is available free. For many creators, it is a labour of love, and there are exciting examples of experimentation as well as works solidly modeled on tried and tested radio formulae. A later chapter in this handbook will explore examples from the contemporary audio scene.

Radio on screen

You can detect the special place of radio not least when it appears within film. We have included a filmography at the end of this book listing some examples. There are many movies which strive to capture the glamour and passion of the era of early radio or the powerful nature of the medium as a whole. Interestingly, the genre of the films can range from comedies such as *Radio Days* (Woody Allen, 1987) and *O Brother, Where Art Thou?* (Joel Coen, 2000), to family feel-good musicals such as *Annie* (John Huston, 1982), through thrillers such as *Betrayed* (Costa Gavras, 1988) and *Talk Radio* (Oliver Stone, 1989), both of which are based on the true-life murder of the Denver Colorado radio talk-show host Alan Berg (1934–84). In addition to thrillers, radio can have a central role in full-blown horror movies: *Pontypool* (Bruce McDonald, 2009) is set in a small-town radio station while a zombie pandemic sweeps the world outside; *Dead Air* (Corbin Bernsen, 2009) centres on a radio station while terrorists detonate chemical bombs which turn people into maniacs. Both films capture a mood of terror partly by exploiting the claustrophobia of the radio studio, which is, after all, a surprisingly small environment. At the same time, the 'on air' dimension creates a limitless and open world perhaps agoraphobic in scale. In addition to these examples, wherein radio is far from being a 'nostalgic' icon, we can see that radio continues to have a special cultural place, even in 'futuristic' works: in the big-budget visions created in the science fiction film *Terminator Salvation* (McG, 2009) and the 3D movie *Resident Evil: Afterlife* (Paul W. S. Anderson, 2010), radios are used for sending and receiving messages of hope among the scattered remnants of humanity.

Exercises:

- Listen to radio – tune in or search the web for radio stations, the BBC iPlayer or podcasts. What stories, genres, voices do you hear?
- Explore examples of Old Time Radio or BBC drama.
- Speak to people about radio. What have they heard? What do they listen to? What do they remember hearing?

Case study: *Mercury Theater on the Air*'s 'War of the Worlds' (1938)

In 1937, Orson Welles and John Houseman established the Mercury Theater in New York City. This was a stage company, but the indefatigable Welles had already had significant experience as a radio actor and managed to continue to work on radio in tandem with his theatre work. In November 1937, the Mercury Theater's first production was a bold interpretation of Shakespeare's *Julius Caesar*, which received great public and critical interest, if not controversy. The opportunity for a radio series followed, and on 11 July 1938 the *Mercury Theater on the Air* broadcast an adaptation of Bram Stoker's *Dracula*. The CBS announcer who introduces the play proclaims that this new series heralds Welles's move from stage drama in order to reach a vaster audience: 'the Broadways of the entire United States'. The subsequent broadcasts continue to reveal an interest in presenting the public with adaptations of popular classics, including Robert Louis Stevenson's 'Treasure Island' (18 July 1938), Charles Dickens's 'A Tale of Two Cities' (25 July 1938) and Jules Verne's 'Around the World in Eighty Days' (23 October 1938).

On 30 October 1938 – the night before Halloween – *Mercury Theater on the Air* broadcast an adaptation suitable for the 'spooky season'. They did not choose an obviously Gothic piece (after all, the opening broadcast of the series was a version of *Dracula*), but a classic example of 'scientific romance' or what would now be described as science fiction: H. G. Wells's *The War of the Worlds* (1898). Wells's novel is a landmark of the genre, a thrilling adventure in which Martians attack planet Earth or, more precisely, the south-east of England. The opening sentences of the novel capture the tone of what will follow:

> No one would have believed in the last years of the nineteenth century that this world was being watched keenly and closely by intelligences greater than man's and yet as mortal as his own; that as men busied themselves about their various concerns they were scrutinised and studied, perhaps almost as narrowly as a man with a microscope

> might scrutinise the transient creatures that swarm and multiply in a drop of water. (Wells, 2008, p. 2)

The narrator then explains that the Martians, with 'intellects vast and cool and unsympathetic, regarded this earth with envious eyes, and slowly and surely drew their plans against us.' (Wells, 2008, p. 2) The novel is told in first-person narrative as the protagonist remembers the attempted conquest of the Earth and the ultimate defeat of the invaders. The novel's mix of adventure and speculation proved highly influential on the burgeoning science fiction genre. Moreover, on the face of it, it would be quite straightforward to take the narrative and dramatize it into a work of performance. However, when John Houseman and Howard Koch wrote the adaptation for the *Mercury Theater on the Air*, they approached the work very differently, thinking less of the fictional source text than their target medium.

Mercury Theater on the Air's adaptation of *The War of the Worlds* takes the essential concept of Wells's original novel and redeploys it for the medium of live radio. In addition, there is a key decision to cross genres: although it is a radio drama, 'War of the Worlds' unfolds like breaking news. The broadcast clearly opens with an announcement that we are listening to a radio play:

> ANNOUNCER: The Columbia Broadcasting System presents Orson Welles and the Mercury Theater on the Air in 'The War of the Worlds' by H. G. Wells. Ladies and gentlemen, the director of the Mercury Theater and star of these broadcasts, Orson Welles.
>
> ORSON WELLES: We know now that in the early years of the twentieth century this world was being watched closely by intelligences greater than man's and yet as mortal as his own. We know now that as human beings busied themselves about their various concerns they were scrutinized and studied, perhaps almost as narrowly as a man with a microscope might scrutinize the transient creatures that swarm and multiply in a drop of water. With infinite complacence people went to and fro over the earth about their little affairs, serene in the assurance of their dominion over this small spinning fragment of solar driftwood which by chance or design man has inherited out of the dark mystery of Time and Space. Yet across an immense ethereal gulf, minds that are to our minds as ours are to the beasts in the jungle, intellects vast, cool and unsympathetic, regarded this earth with envious eyes and slowly and surely drew their plans against us. In the thirty-ninth year of the twentieth century came the great disillusionment. It was near the end of October. Business was better. The war scare was over. More men were back at work. Sales were picking up. On this particular evening, October 30th, the Crosley

service estimated that thirty-two million people were listening in on radios. (CBS, 1938)

We can see here how the original novel is smoothly altered into radio speech, closely modelled on the language and tone of the 1890s original, yet with details that set it in a contemporary 1930s context (such as the 'war scare' and rising employment). It perhaps seems like a long introduction, but it certainly serves to establish firmly the central theme of the play before shifting into a style which seems unconventional compared to standard dramatic narrative. After this introduction, the broadcast moves away from being 'overtly' dramatic to become a simulation of live broadcasting, taking us on a journey from the weather, through a dance band broadcast, to a news flash:

ANNOUNCER: For the next 24 hours not much change in temperature. A slight atmospheric disturbance of undetermined origin is reported over Nova Scotia, causing a low pressure area to move down rather rapidly over the north-eastern states, bringing a forecast of rain, accompanied by winds of light gale force. Maximum temperature, 66; minimum, 48. This weather report comes to you from the government weather bureau . . . We now take you to the Meridian Room in the Hotel Park Plaza in downtown New York, where you will be entertained by the music of Ramón Raquello and his orchestra.

(MUSIC)

ANNOUNCER 3: Good evening, ladies and gentlemen. From the Meridian Room in the Park Plaza in New York City, we bring you the music of Ramón Raquello and his orchestra. With a touch of the Spanish. Ramón Raquello leads off with 'La Cumparsita'.

(MUSIC: 'La Cumparsita')

ANNOUNCER 2: Ladies and gentlemen, we interrupt our program of dance music to bring you a special bulletin from the intercontinental radio news. At twenty minutes before eight, central time, Professor Farrell of the Mount Jennings Observatory, Chicago, Illinois, reports observing several explosions of incandescent gas, occurring at regular intervals on the planet Mars. The spectroscope indicates the gas to be hydrogen and moving towards the earth with enormous velocity. Professor Pierson of the observatory at Princeton confirms Farrell's observation, and describes the phenomenon as, quote, 'like a jet of blue flame shot from a gun', unquote. We now return you to the music of Ramón Raquello, playing for you in the Meridian Room of the Park Plaza Hotel, situated in downtown New York. (CBS, 1939)

After this, the play continues to exploit an imitation of breaking news reportage regarding the Mars events, interrupting the music and eventually commandeering the broadcast. The play takes us to an interview with Professor Pierson (Orson Welles) and then on to Grover's Mill in New Jersey (a genuine location but, of course, the whole play was created live within a CBS studio) where an object has landed. With the 'on the scene' reporter Carl Phillips (Frank Readick), we are given the ingredients we might still expect in a breaking news story, namely a sense of confusion and eyewitness accounts. The brilliant scriptwriting of Houseman and Koch captures a sense of spontaneity:

> MR.WILMUTH: Well, I was listening to the radio.
> PHILLIPS: Closer and louder please.
> MR.WILMUTH: Pardon me?!
> PHILLIPS: Louder, please, and closer.
> MR.WILMUTH: Yes, sir . . .

In this example, the seemingly amateur nature of the interview is, in fact, a calculated ploy to create a greater impression of authenticity. It is carefully scripted, but it feels anything but. After this, the play gains in momentum until we are drawn into full-scale science fiction horror: we hear the cylinder creak open, and the reporter tells us that gray snake-like tentacles slither out and we then 'see' the Martian through the eyes of Phillips, in a description modelled on H. G. Wells's original account of the alien. The narrative builds in a sense of foreboding and horror:

> PHILLIPS: Ladies and gentlemen – am I on? – ladies and gentlemen, here I am, back of a stone wall that adjoins Mr. Wilmuth's garden. From here I get a sweep of the whole scene. I'll give you every detail as long as I can talk. As long as I can see. More state police have arrived. They're drawing up a cordon in front of the pit, about thirty of them. No need to push the crowd back now. They're willing to keep their distance. The captain is conferring with someone. We can't quite see who. Oh yes, I believe it's Professor Pierson. Yes, it is. Now they've parted. The Professor moves around one side, studying the object, while the captain and two policemen advance with something in their hands. I can see it now. It's a white handkerchief tied to a pole . . . a flag of truce. If those creatures know what that means . . . what anything means. Wait! Something's happening!
> (SOUND OF HISSING FOLLOWED BY HUMMING)
> PHILLIPS: A humped shape is rising out of the pit. I can make out a small beam of light against a mirror. What's that? There's a jet of flame springing from the mirror, and it leaps right at the advancing men. It strikes them head on! Good Lord, they're turning into flame!

The tone of voice that the actor Frank Readick uses in his portrayal of the reporter Carl Phillips is uncannily similar to Herbert Morrison's tone in the Hindenburg airship disaster transmission and is evidently closely modelled on it (according to Tim Crook, Readick was 'directed to listen to and study the broadcast in a CBS booth during the rehearsals' [Crook, 1999, 109]). We should remember, after all, that the Hindenburg catastrophe had happened only the year before. Soon afterwards, Phillips describes the death ray coming nearer before the broadcast momentarily falls silent and we assume the worst, even though the station announcer speaks to us calmly, commencing with a cliché that we still might hear in live broadcasting to this very day:

> ANNOUNCER: Ladies and gentlemen, due to circumstances beyond our control, we are unable to continue the broadcast from Grover's Mill. Evidently there's some difficulty with our field transmission. However, we will return to that point at the earliest opportunity. In the meantime, we have a late bulletin from San Diego, California. Professor Indellkoffer, speaking at a dinner of the California Astronomical Society, expressed the opinion that the explosions on Mars are undoubtedly nothing more than severe volcanic disturbances on the surface of the planet. We now continue with our piano interlude.

This simple speech is another example of brilliant writing. We know what we have heard: hideous aliens and a death ray exterminating human beings. Far from reassuring us, Professor Indellkoffer's bathetic dinner speech from the other end of the country only serves to makes us all the more anxious.

The terror spreads, and we hear failed military attempts to stop the Martians before the fall of New York City. We are over halfway through the play and a CBS announcer informs us that 'You're listening to a CBS presentation of Orson Welles and the *Mercury Theater on the Air* in an original dramatization of *The War of the Worlds* by H.G. Wells.' When the final part of the play is broadcast, we are taken into what is ostensibly a more conventional mode of performance. The narrative focuses on Professor Pierson with Orson Welles speaking in measured and dramatic tones and shifting between Pierson reading from his journal (taking us back to something closer to H. G. Wells's novel) and some dialogue with a stranger he meets in the desolate aftermath. Ultimately, as in the source novel, planet Earth is reprieved when the Martians are killed not by the human race, but by bacteria against which they had no defence.

In conclusion, Welles announces:

> This is Orson Welles, ladies and gentlemen, out of character to assure you that the 'War of The Worlds' has no further significance than

> as the holiday offering it was intended to be. The Mercury Theater's own radio version of dressing up in a sheet and jumping out of a bush and saying Boo! Starting now, we couldn't soap all your windows and steal all your garden gates by tomorrow night . . . so we did the best next thing. We annihilated the world before your very ears, and utterly destroyed the CBS. You will be relieved, I hope, to learn that we didn't mean it, and that both institutions are still open for business. So goodbye everybody, and remember please, for the next day or so, the terrible lesson you learned tonight. That grinning, glowing, globular invader of your living room is an inhabitant of the pumpkin patch, and if your doorbell rings and nobody's there, that was no Martian . . . it's Halloween.

With the benefit of hindsight and our awareness of the reception to the broadcast, 'Orson Welles's concluding words . . . are one of the most supremely ironic, if not completely irresponsible, statements of the twentieth century.' (Hand, 2009, p. 214). *Mercury Theater on the Air*'s 'War of the Worlds' has become a highly significant episode in the history of popular culture, which stands as extraordinary proof of the power of radio. This is because of the public reaction as the broadcast unfurled.

According to Hadley Cantril, who was commissioned by Princeton University to research the impact of the event in a work entitled *The Invasion from Mars: the Psychology of Panic*, some six million people heard the CBS broadcast, 1.7 million believed the events to be true, and 1.2 million were 'genuinely frightened' (Dunning, 1998, p. 454). It is worth noting, however, that this was a comparatively small audience: some 30 million were listening to *The Edgar Bergen and Charlie McCarthy Show* on a rival channel (NBC). Despite the fact that it was clearly announced that the broadcast was an adaptation of H. G. Wells, the damage had been done, and hundreds of thousands took to the streets in panic. In effect, there had been an invasion not by aliens from another planet, but by a drama through the technological invention of radio, which infiltrated the domestic space of millions of listeners. The combined notoriety and success of the 'War of the Worlds' broadcast was instantaneous and evident to all at CBS as soon as police officers began to flood the studio 20 minutes into *Mercury Theater on the Air*'s one-hour broadcast.

The broadcast soon became legendary, not least with remarkable follow-up broadcasts such as Orson Welles meeting H. G. Wells and discussing the broadcast on KTSA (28 October 1940), during which Welles reveals that Adolf Hitler, in a major speech in Munich, referred to the 'War of the Worlds' hysteria as evidence of the decadence and corrupt condition of democracy. In the American press, there were some 12,500 newspaper articles in the first three weeks after 'War of the Worlds' was broadcast (Douglas, 1999, p. 165), and there were frequent references to the broadcast in other radio shows of the period. The responses may have ranged from outrage to hilarity, but the broadcast had important consequences for American radio: after 'War of the Worlds', as Susan J. Douglas informs us, 'Dramatizations of simulated news bulletins became verboten' (Douglas, 1999, p. 165) while, according to Gerald Nachman, 'Many didn't believe the announcement of the attack on Pearl Harbor three years later because of the Martian landing hoax' (Nachman, 1998, p. 445). The controversy of the broadcast is somewhat ironic when one considers that *The Mercury Theater on the Air* had been commissioned by CBS 'to ward off federal investigations into radio's overcommercialization' (Hilmes, 2002, p. 104). According to Tim Crook, the 'lawsuits that followed amounted to the not inconsiderable sum of $750,000' (Crook, 1999, p. 108), which CBS settled out of court.

Although the script was written by John Houseman and Howard Koch, and performed by the *Mercury Theater on the Air* ensemble, the 21-year-old Orson Welles was indubitably regarded as the 'star', or perhaps we should say 'ring leader', of this most mischievous of Halloween hoaxes. Despite the furore and lawsuits, for Welles this was the ticket to Hollywood. Interestingly, Orson Welles's perspective on 'War of the Worlds' proved somewhat malleable over time. In a lively press conference the day after the broadcast (31 October 1938), Welles is surrounded by reporters, looking exhausted and extremely nervous:

> WELLES: You must realize that when I left the broadcast last night I went into dress rehearsal for a play which is opening in two days and I've had almost no sleep and I know less about this than you do. I haven't read the papers. I'm terribly shocked by the effect it's had. I do not believe that the method is original with me or peculiar to the Mercury Theater's presentation.
>
> REPORTER: Do you think there should be law against such enactments as we had last night?
>
> WELLES: I know that almost everybody in radio would do almost anything to avert the kind of thing that has happened, myself included, but I don't know what the legislation would be. Radio is new and we are learning about the effect it has on people. (Welles, 1938)

In contrast, in a television interview from *The Dean Martin Show* in 1970, Welles appears confident and assured, smoking a cigar:

> Back then radio was really big you know it was a big piece of furniture in our living rooms like TV today and it occupied a big piece of our lives. Radio in those days before the tube and transistor wasn't just a

> noise in somebody's pocket it was a voice of authority. Too much so, or at least I thought so. I figured it was time to take the Mickey out of some of that authority; hence my broadcast 'War of the Worlds', which informed the public that Martians had landed in New Jersey and had taken over the country. This was Halloween remember and in my middle Western childhood that was the season for pranks (...) In that notorious broadcast I said 'boo' to several million people over a full network and the pumpkin head was a flying saucer from Mars. Trouble was an awful lot of listeners forgot what day it was. (Welles, 1970)

There are many reasons why *Mercury Theater on the Air*'s 'War of the Worlds' was so effective. Welles himself argued that the resulting hysteria demonstrated that he had underestimated 'the extent of our American lunatic fringe' (cited in Nachman 1998, p. 447). However, it is worth remembering that 1938 America was a post-depression nation in a global context that was governed by paranoia due to the aggressive expansion of imperial or fascist nations (such as Japan, Germany and Italy), while the old world values of imperialist nations such as Britain jostled with the revolutionary ideology of the Soviet Union. In short, 'It was an age of anxiety, in which the idea of invasion from any quarter – even from outer space – would not have seemed surprising' (Hand, 2006, p. 7). However, aside from its exploitation of the zeitgeist, the 'War of the Worlds' is also a triumphant example of radio form, exploiting the imagination of the listener as only radio can, matching technical and documentary verisimilitude with the utilization of the formula of classic horror and suspense narrative.

Let us draw a perhaps surprising parallel for a moment: Jonathan Swift's *A Modest Proposal* (1729). In this essay, Swift outlines a plan whereby the problems of poverty in Ireland can be resolved by using the children of poor families as food. He outlines his plan in great detail and articulate argument. Of course, it is a truly horrific suggestion, and Swift knows it: *A Modest Proposal* is a masterpiece of satire. Swift uses the tone and style of the essay form to mock the rhetoric of authority, to highlight the horror of power wherein terrible actions and ideas are expounded 'rationally'. Arguably, 'War of the Worlds' does the same thing in the way it utilizes the news media form and deploys the rhetoric of on-air and eyewitness broadcasting to satirize the medium of radio and shock the audience.

The phenomenon of 'War of the Worlds' has nevertheless proved as irresistible to subsequent radio producers as a button marked 'DO NOT PRESS'. According to Crook, a version of 'War of the Worlds' in Chile in November 1944 caused such panic that 'one provincial governor mobilised his troops and artillery to repel invasion from outer space' (Crook,

1999, p. 114), while in February 1949 another version in Spanish in Quito, Ecuador, caused mass panic, which turned to fury when it was revealed as a hoax, and a mob set the radio station on fire killing 15 people inside (Crook, 1999, p. 112). In later times in the US, the occasional revival of 'War of the Worlds' on radio can – according to Robert L. Hilliard – still result 'in numerous complaints from people frightened much as the American population was decades ago' (Hilliard, 1985, p. 1).

The broadcast succeeds partly because of a consistent immediacy that conspires in an exploitation of the listener's fears: the music, sound effects, silences and hesitations throughout the play are as important as its blatant screams of hysteria and the story itself. John Houseman and Howard Koch's script is a masterpiece of radio scriptwriting in the way that it calculatedly exploits the authenticity of documentary rhetoric while utilizing the formula of horror and suspense. If we listen to the original 1938 broadcast, we can hear that Welles and the *Mercury Theater on the Air* ensemble use the Houseman and Koch script as a basis from which to deliver intense horror and suspense performances. The result is, as Jim Harmon states, an alien invasion 'more convincing than anything the movies have ever provided' (Harmon, 1967, p. 12). John Houseman himself pays special homage to Welles's performance and directorial decisions:

> The reason that show worked as well as it did was . . . nerve . . . the slowness of the show in the beginning. Those credible pauses were maintained, and Orson really stretched those. The reason the show works as it does is that the acceleration is very carefully calculated and is quite extraordinary; that is why by the time you are twenty minutes into the show you are moving hours at a time . . . and no one even noticed. (cited in Maltin, 2000, p. 81)

As Guerric DeBona argues, Welles the performer continues to make recordings of the broadcast vibrant and terrifying, well into the twentieth-first century:

> To listen to a recording of *The War of the Worlds* broadcast now is to understand Welles's ability to convey the personal urgency of a narrator who becomes witness to the horror of mass alien invasion, while inextricably connected to the terror of his listeners. Indeed, at least on one level, the mass panic resulting from that notorious broadcast owed to the intimate reality of the narration itself, personally expressing a national tragedy evolving in living rooms across America. (DeBona, 2010, p. 72)

For critics such as Erik Barnouw, the achievement of the *Mercury Theater on the Air* broadcasts may have reached its controversial apogee in 'War of the Worlds', but it is just one episode in a truly revolutionary series:

> While the public remembers the *Mercury Theater on the Air* chiefly because of the Martian invasion, the series was far more important in its general impact on radio writing. Most of the broadcasts were in the first person singular. Welles gave a series of brilliant demonstrations of what could be done with the device – and with narrators in general. He did much to loosen up the whole structure of radio drama. (Barnouw, 1945, p. 2)

Orson Welles himself talks explicitly of the 'first person singular' (*New York Times*, 14 August 1938) technique which, James Naremore contends, can be seen as the foundation of the 'oral narrative' on radio and a simultaneous acknowledgment that the radio 'was an intimate piece of living-room furniture' (Naremore, 1989, p. 13). Howard Blue argues that Orson Welles would still be remembered for his contribution to radio even if 'War of the Worlds' had not been broadcast or, for that matter, had he not done any film or stage work (Blue, 2002, p. 61). Blue quotes Arthur Miller's estimation of Welles as a genius with the microphone: 'He seemed to climb into it, his word carving voice winding into one's brain. No actor had such intimacy and sheer presence in a loudspeaker . . .' (cited in Blue, 2002, p. 61).

Case study: conclusion

Mercury Theater on the Air's 'War of the Worlds' remains a wonderful example of radio drama and a fascinating cultural phenomenon. Its impact extends far beyond radio drama. As Welles playfully reveals in the interview on *The Dean Martin Show* in 1970, that one hour of live radio in the 1930s has had an indelible impact on the perception of the cosmos and on modern paranoia:

> Now it's been pointed out that various flying saucers scares all over the world have taken place since that broadcast. Not everyone laughs at them. There are a lot of well-attested sightings by highly reliable witnesses. Not everyone laughs any more, but most people do, and there's a theory that this is my doing. That my job was to soften you up. To sell you all on the notion that creatures from outer space landing in our midst is just a hoax. That way as more and more of these unidentified objects make contact with our unsuspecting planet there'll still be a tendency to laugh. Ladies and gentlemen, go on laughing. You'll be happier that way. Stay happy just as long as you can and till our new masters announce that the conquest of the earth is complete. (Welles, 1970)

There is much to be learnt from 'War of the Worlds': the urgent performances and the meticulous construction of the adaptation as a piece of radio scriptwriting continue to make the work valuable for exploration. However, we would like to conclude with a word of gentle encouragement: 'War of the Worlds' is a monolith, impossible to ignore, and it would be a mistake to ignore it. However, radio drama is a very rich ocean: cast your net wide and see what you can discover!

Exercises

- How does the *Mercury Theater on the Air*'s 'War of the Worlds' exploit live radio drama?
- Compare the 'War of the Worlds' radio play with the original novel by H. G. Wells. How has the work of fiction been adapted into live radio? You might also like to look at some other examples of adaptations by the *Mercury Theater on the Air* (or other radio/audio drama companies) in relation to the source fiction.
- In what way does the 'War of the Worlds' radio play explore the genres of science fiction and horror?
- What can 'War of the Worlds' as radio play do that other media cannot? You might want to compare it with film versions of alien invasions such as *War of the Worlds* (Byron Haskin, 1953), *War of the Worlds* (Steven Spielberg, 2005), *Mars Attacks* (Tim Burton, 1996) or *Cloverfield* (Matt Reeves, 2008).

2

Theories of radio drama

Introduction

At its heart, drama is concerned with representation; of a story or event, a place, a person or an emotional effect. Each medium brings its own particular strength to the dramatic form. Theatre's strength is spectacle; television and film bring realism; the written word's strength is the intimacy of the relationship with the reader. Radio, too, can declare some aptitude in these, but its real strength is an ability to infiltrate the mind, to unleash the most powerful dramatic weapon of all: the imagination of the listener. However, the unique qualities of radio drama were not apparent at the outset. The first radio drama in both the United Kingdom and Unites States was strongly influenced by the theatre. In the United Kingdom, the experience of listening to radio drama was intended to replicate that of the theatre. The relationship between radio and theatre was further cemented during the blackouts of World War II, when radio became a substitute for theatre-going. As a result, the naissance of *radio drama* as distinct from *theatre for the radio* was not fully achieved until the 1950s. In contrast, radio drama in the United States soon broke free of its direct associations with theatre. Whereas the BBC was centrally regulated and funded by a licence fee, a freer commercially funded model developed in the United States. Radio stations were eager to find a medium which attracted large audiences, and they soon hit on a winning formula: radio theatre. The intense demand paved the way for great talents such as Walter Gibson, Norman Corwin, Wyllis Cooper and Arch Oboler, who cast a magic spell over radio *theatre* and created radio *drama*. Early serial productions, such as *The Shadow* (1930–54) quickly developed a successful and popular *modus operandi* and a distinctive *radio* style (Fink, 1981, p. 196). This chapter attempts to characterize those distinctive qualities of radio drama. It builds on the work of practitioners and theoreticians who have defined the essence of radio drama and have developed a vocabulary to categorize the various processes involved in creating it. The mind of the listener is as pivotal to radio drama as the screen is to cinema, so some attention will be devoted to the act of *listening* to radio drama. The words *blind, invisible* and *dark* make frequent appearances in radio drama discourse.

They seem to imply that radio is lacking in some way but, as will be discussed, radio is potentially the most *visual* medium of all. What are the magic ingredients of radio, the potions which mingle to conjure up the enchanted world of radio drama? The *vocabulary* of radio drama encapsulates the constituent parts of this captivating genre.

Listening

We may think of the radio listener as being at the *end* of the radio drama production line. First comes the script, then the production, then the broadcast and finally the listener. It may be more useful to imagine the listener as being at the *center*, the point to which all the elements in the production line refer. It is the act of listening which creates the drama. The writer and the production team provide stimuli, but the conversion of that information into drama is entirely dependent on the imagination of the listener. Donald McWhinnie, who had an illustrious career in BBC radio drama, developed an impressive insight into the nature of radio drama, which he shared in his 1959 book *The Art of Radio*. He observed that every listener must 'translate the sound-pattern he hears into his own mental language; he must apply his imagination to it and transform it'. He added a wonderful comment from the writer Tyrone Guthrie, who called on each listener to provide 'his own particular brand of moonshine' (cited in McWhinnie, 1959, p. 25). Guthrie and McWhinnie are alluding to the very personal nature of the relationship between the listener and radio drama. As Frances Gray describes it,

> Like a bedtime story, it whispers in our ear. Without visual distractions, the smallest subtleties of the voice become apparent and seize the imagination; a snatch of song or the rustle of leaves takes on a significance impossible in the theatre or on film. As soon as we hear the word in a radio play, we are close to the experience it signifies; in fact, the sound is literally inside us. (Gray, 1981, p. 51)

We may consider the role of the listener to be passive, simply a receptor, but radio drama is totally *dependent* on the listener; we are active collaborators. When watching cinema, theatre or television, we sit and absorb the drama which unfolds before us. Radio drama demands more of us, and for this reason it does not necessarily have universal appeal.

> Those who put a high premium on the creative and poetic quality of the spoken word – who do not require every question to carry with it its own answer nor every work of art to have its message written underneath in indelible ink – these will work hardest at radio, or for

> that matter at any art form, and will ultimately get the most out of it. (McWhinnie 1959, p. 63)

It is this collaboration which makes radio drama so special; we are *part* of the creative act, rather than *party* to it. It is certainly true that the relationship that the listener builds up with radio drama is unique and individual, but it is equally fickle. We rarely *just* listen to radio. Radio can be background listening in the home, something we do while driving or walking to the bus stop. Listening via computer keeps us stationary, but does not stop us internet surfing as well as listening. Hugh Chignell sums this up as 'secondariness': 'The secondariness of radio means that the listener can easily perform some other activity (work, drive and so on) while listening and paying attention to the radio' (Chignell, 2009, p. 70). 'Secondariness' could be perceived as risky for the audio artist, if not an outright weakness, but, as Andrew Crisell observes, it serves to strengthen the relationship:

> [Radio] not only combines concreteness with imaginative flexibility but enhances these qualities by not making even the visual demand upon its audience that is made by the printed word. As a secondary medium accompanying its members while they are engaged in 'primary' activities it can therefore infiltrate their view of the world in a way which is all the more powerful for being only half-conscious. (Crisell, 1994, p. 162)

The images of the early days of broadcasting suggest that listening used to be more of a 'primary' activity. The large and ornate radio was a piece of furniture in the living room, and photographs from the 1930s to 1950s show families companionably grouped around it, giving radio the undivided attention that we now give to TV. The most frequently cited view is that it was the popularity of the transistor radio in the 1960s which transformed the listening experience from a primary activity to a secondary one. However, Frances Gray (2006, p. 252) suggests that even before radio was portable, different levels of engagement were possible. Household activities, such as cooking, cleaning and reading a newspaper, could and did occur simultaneously. Her hypothesis is that radio listening has always been a secondary experience.

Blind, invisible or dark?

Radio is sometimes labelled the 'blind medium' even by some of its greatest exponents and creators, including Arch Oboler (Oboler, 1945, p. 308). The term is unfortunate, as it seems to imply that radio is afflicted with some deficiency, as though it were television without the pictures. As Martin Shingler and Cindy Wieringa point out, 'Whilst paintings, posters and photographs lack sound, their silence ordinarily goes unnoticed [...] They are complete in themselves and thus prized and for the qualities they possess rather than for their ability to compensate for what they lack' (Shingler and Wieringa, 1998, p. 75). Why then, should radio drama be characterized as deficient? One possible explanation is that *radio* drama came after *drama*. The theatre, with its emphasis on the visual spectacle, was the inspiration for the earliest experiments with radio drama, so from the outset, radio drama was disadvantaged. How could it possibly deliver that visual spectacle? If radio drama had been conceived instead as radio *poetry*, would it still be labelled 'blind'? Poetry is concerned with evoking emotional response, as drama is, but it is not seen to be lacking in any way, because it is not conceptualized in the visual domain of the theatre, as radio drama is. Tim Crook felt so strongly that radio drama is not a blind medium that he devoted a whole chapter to discussing just this point in his influential book *Radio Drama: Theory and Practice* (1999). He questions the sensory hierarchy, in which sound is viewed as the poor relation to vision, seeing no 'philosophical difference between seeing physically with the eye and seeing with the mind' (Crook, 1999, p. 54). In this sense, the supposed blindness of radio, though rather disparaging in tone, is irrelevant. Radio drama is not blind. It's just a different way of seeing.

Shingler and Wieringa (1998, p. 78) characterize radio as 'invisible', in that it cannot be seen other than inside the mind of the listener. As we have already discussed, this liberates the listener to be engaged in other activities while listening to the radio. The obvious disadvantage, however, is that radio is competing with whatever else it is that we are doing. We become distracted. In response to this, certain narrative conventions have developed in radio drama to compensate and to ensure that listeners can be 'hooked' in easily. Narrative structure tends to be uncomplicated, involving few characters, and the language is descriptive. This is the opening sequence of *The Darkness of Wallis Simpson* by Rose Tremain (2011):

> MUSIC, SFX: AN OLD-FASHIONED CAR AND CAR HORN
>
> WALLIS: (TO HERSELF) Now, let's go through them. The things I know to be true. I know I'm in Paris. Sometimes I can hear the cars making that whispering sound they make on the cobbled roads. Other times, I can't hear a darn thing. The world and everything, it just goes away.
>
> SFX: KEY IN LOCK, DOOR OPENS

> Oh God, that's probably her. 'Maitre Blum', as she calls herself. Peculiar name. Try to remember things properly. I'm in Paris. The drapes at the window are blue. The furniture looks as though it could be mine. The bed is soft. I probably had it shipped from America.
>
> SFX: FOOTSTEPS ON A WOODEN FLOOR
>
> Here she comes. My name is Wallis Simpson née Warfield. I was born in Baltimore and I can remember wind coming off the ocean.

The central character, Wallis Simpson, is in the role of narrator as well as protagonist. This device ensures that we can be made aware of important information which is not dramatized. While this could seem contrived, it is actually very successful, because the narrator is also a character in the play. We are hearing her *internal voice*, her thoughts. From Wallis, we know that we are in Paris, we know what the room looks like, that the protagonist is bed bound and possibly old and confused. We know that another character has arrived – all in under one minute. A narrator is often used in radio drama. One practical reason for this is that it is much cheaper to describe what is happening than to dramatize it, which would involve several actors and more studio time. However, provided the narrator is well integrated into the narrative, as is the case in *The Darkness of Wallis Simpson*, it can be very successful.

Although there are notable exceptions, simplicity is the key to the most successful audio drama. McWhinnie notes that 'the radio act comes out of silence, vibrates in the void and in the mind, and returns to silence.' (McWhinnie, 1959, p. 93). Characters and events live in the moment, and we forget them as soon as we can no longer hear them. For this reason, radio drama works best when it is not cluttered with characters or events which are not directly relevant. The extract under discussion contains reminders of what has occurred so far and *signposts* to hint at events to come. For similar reasons, sound effects tend to be iconic, rather than naturalistic. These conventions are not designed to patronize, but rather to liberate all listeners to take part in the experience, with whatever level of engagement they can give.

Radio may not be a blind medium, but it is nonetheless characterized by *darkness*. For Jim Harmon, radio drama is unprecedented in its ability to explore and exploit 'that purity of darkness, that blank slate of imagination' (Harmon, 1967, p. 80). McWhinnie is lyrical in his description of the imaginative power of radio:

> For the world of visual detail which the listener creates is a world of limitless dimension; they exist in a world which is largely *dream*. The radio performance works on the mind in the same way that poetry

> does; it liberates and evokes. It does not act as a stimulus to direct scenic representation; that would be narrow and fruitless. It makes possible a universe of shape, detail, emotion and idea, which is bound by no inhibiting limitations of space or capacity. (McWhinnie, 1959, p. 37)

Shingler and Wieringa have deconstructed this rather nebulous quality of radio drama, subdividing it into radio's 'spatial and temporal flexibility' and its 'access to the inner recesses of the mind' (1998, p. 88). We'll apply these definitions to *The Voyage of the Dawn Treader* (one of the *Chronicles of Narnia* series, 2005) by way of illustration. C. S. Lewis wrote a series of seven books for children, *The Chronicles of Narnia*, between 1949 and 1954. In the books, he conjures up the magical world of Narnia, a land of adventure and talking animals, with the lion, Aslan, as deity. The writing is richly descriptive and evocative and, through it, generations of readers have discovered Narnia. There have been many attempts to recreate Narnia, first through the illustrations in the original books, then through radio, animation, theatre and film. However, there is only one version which had the official approval of the writer himself: radio. Writing to Lance Sieveking, producer of the first radio adaptation of *The Chronicles of Narnia* in 1959, C. S. Lewis showed his approval of the radio adaptation and his dislike of an animation which had just been released:

> Anthropomorphic animals, when taken out of narrative into actual visibility, always turn into buffoonery or nightmare. At least, with photography. Cartoons (if only Disney did not combine so much vulgarity with his genius!) [would] be another matter. A human, pantomime, Aslan [would]. be to me blasphemy. (Lewis cited in Brady, 2005)

Of course, if C. S. Lewis was alive today, he may well have enjoyed the Disney/20th Century Fox film adaptations (2005–10). However, at the time of writing, he clearly approved of the radio version because he appreciated radio's capacity to liberate the words he had so carefully written, to set them free in the minds of listeners. In *The Chronicles of Narnia*, the central characters are children, transported from Britain to the magical land of Narnia, in an epic shift of time and space. In *The Voyage of the Dawn Treader*, the children enter Narnia through a picture on a bedroom wall:

> What they were seeing may be hard to believe when you read it in print, but it was almost as hard to believe when you saw it happening. The things in the picture were moving. It didn't look at all like a cinema either; the colours were too real and clean and out-of-door

> for that (. . .) Eustace jumped to try to pull it off the wall and found himself standing on the frame; in front of him was not glass, but real sea and wind and waves rushing up to the frame as they might to a rock. (Lewis, 1952, p. 13)

The writer has already indicated that we need to draw on our own imagination to create this image. Above all else, his words have the power to stimulate that imagination, but surely radio comes a close second. This transcript of the *Focus on the Family* 2005 radio version shows how Lewis's words are adapted, through careful use of dialogue, music and sound effects to express these enchanting images:

EUSTACE: Why do you like it, Lucy?
EDMUND: For heaven's sake don't answer him, or you'll get him started on art and all that.
LUCY: I like it because the ship looks like it's going somewhere, as if it's on a great adventure on the high sea. It looks as if it's really moving and the water looks as if it's really wet and the waves look as if they're really going up and down.
EUSTACE: Oh. That's your expert artistic opinion is it, 'that the waves look like they're are going up and down!' Hah!
LUCY: But they do look as if they're going up and down.
SFX: MUSIC, SEA AND WIND (CONTINUES THROUGHOUT)
EDMUND: Oh, I say, Lucy, you're right.
EUSTACE: Barmy, you're both barmy.
EDMUND: No, we aren't. Look!
EUSTACE: I'm not falling for that old trick.
SFX: WIND AND SEA
EDMUND: Do you feel that Lucy? The wind's kicking up.
LUCY: I feel it!
EUSTACE: This is absurd. Close the window.
LUCY: The window is closed. Can't you smell the sea, Eustace? It's magic. Oh, Edmund, is it possible?
EUSTACE: Stop it. It's some silly trick you're playing on me. Stop it or I'll tell Alberta.
SFX: SPLASHED BY A WAVE.
EUSTACE: This can't be happening.
EDMUND: Watch out, here comes another wave!
SFX: SPLASHED BY A BIGGER WAVE
LUCY: What are we supposed to do?
EUSTACE: I'll smash the rotten picture. That's what I'll do.
EDMUND: No Eustace. Don't go near it!
SFX: VERY LARGE WAVES
LUCY: Edmund, be careful!
SFX: THEY ARE THROWN INTO THE SEA

The dialogue reveals the narrative and shows the relationship between the children; the signposts hint at excitement to come ('Oh, Edmund, is it possible?'). It provides descriptive elements, which, alongside the sound effects and evocative music, work with the imagination to create 'spatial and temporal flexibility' (Shingler and Wieringa, 1998, p. 88). The scene makes us believe the unbelievable: that we can enter a parallel universe through a picture on a bedroom wall.

The words 'blind', 'invisible' and 'dark' seem negative, because we perceive vision to be the most important sense. Perhaps we are mistaken in trying to link radio drama to any one sense. Certainly, our *reception* of radio drama is dependent on the sense of hearing, but surely our *appreciation* of it calls on all our senses. In this sense, radio drama is extrasensory: a heightened and extraordinary experience.

The vocabularies of radio drama

Having devoted some time to a discussion of the unique qualities of radio drama, we will now turn to its structure; how those unique qualities are actually communicated. On the face of it, the constituent parts of radio drama are simple:

- Words
- Sounds
- Music
- Silence

However, each of these elements communicates particular meaning, depending on its relationship with other elements within the play, with the listener and with the world around us. In this section, we will examine each constituent part, discussing its particular contribution to the radio drama form.

Words

> Speech may be the primary code of radio, but, nevertheless, non verbal codes, such as noise and music, are still integral to the medium. They evoke radio's moods, emotions, atmospheres and environments. They provide a fuller picture and a richer texture. Without words, radio would be seriously disadvantaged, rendered obscure, ambiguous and virtually meaningless.
>
> *(Shingler and Wieringa, 1998, p. 51)*

There are many examples of the superlative use of sound and music in radio drama, and even examples of drama constructed entirely from sound, such as *The Revenge* (1978). Nevertheless, the supremacy of the spoken word in the hierarchy of radio drama remains unchallenged. Its function is communication: communication of information, emotion and imagination, and of inner thoughts. We will examine each in turn, drawing on the expertise of radio theoreticians and practitioners to elucidate the purpose of the spoken word in radio drama.

Michel Chion created a very detailed vocabulary of sound design for cinema, which Tim Crook (1999, p. 81) has adapted for radio. He categorizes words in radio drama as,

- 'theatrical', which can best be described as dialogue
- 'textual', which is most commonly achieved by narrator
- 'emanation', where words can be heard, but not understood, such as the words of a distant crowd.

McWhinnie (1959, pp. 49–59) has a slightly more detailed version of similar categories to deconstruct the strengths and weaknesses of the spoken word in radio drama. He believes that the communication of factual information and ideas is of primary importance, though he argues that radio's ability to achieve this is limited. Notwithstanding the opportunities we now have to listen to radio drama multiple times via the internet, the spoken word is fleeting. We hear it and it is gone. This means that, in comparison with the written word, its ability to communicate complicated or abstract information is limited. For example, on 17 November 2010, a radio news headline announced the wedding of Prince William, heir to the British throne, and Kate Middleton. The headline lasted a few seconds and gave minimal information, compared with the substantial written coverage available in newspapers and on the internet. Radio had the 'edge' in the immediacy of the communication, but for providing the detail, the written word was more effective. The implications of this transitory nature of the spoken word for radio drama is that abstract ideas can only be communicated successfully 'by making them palatable, that is to say, by cheapening them to some extent' (McWhinnie, 1959, p. 50). This may seem like a derogatory statement, but the selection of exactly which information should be communicated in the radio drama script is a fine art which challenges each generation of radio drama writers.

Andrew Crisell recognizes this point, but argues that the spoken word also needs to carry 'extra freight' because dialogue in radio drama needs to communicate additional information which would be visible to a cinema or theatre audience. He takes a semiotic approach when discussing speech in radio drama. Words, he argues, fulfil a vital function beyond dialogue: they are 'primary signifiers'. When an object cannot be seen, then it must be heard, and if this sound alone does not communicate, then the function of words is to offer explanation. Crisell calls this 'transcodification' (Crisell, 1994, pp. 146–9). McWhinnie provides a wonderful elucidation of the process of 'transcodification' by using what one might expect to be the 'obvious' signifier of footsteps:

> I would defy anyone to judge by ear alone whether the feet in question are crossing the street or walking up the side of a house, or even to be quite sure that they are feet at all – they might, for example, be the sound of a methodical workman stacking bricks into heaps. 'Fade in the sound of Euston Station': the picture is clear enough to writer and producer, but to the listener it might well be Beachy Head during a storm; it certainly will not be Euston Station unless someone says so. (McWhinnie, 1959, p. 80)

The communication of information may be important in radio drama, but when the spoken word is used to convey emotion and imagination, it is at its most potent. This does not necessarily mean that the communication needs to be overly descriptive. Norman Corwin, a pioneering writer and producer of US radio drama, perfectly describes how 'less can be more' in the best radio writing:

> First, radio is a stage with a bare set. This is not a deprivation, but an advantage, for a bare proscenium should be as inviting to a radio playwright or director as a bare wall is to a muralist, as a silent organ was to Bach. Not to be grand about it, but the features and dimensions of a place, of a room, of a landscape, are not, in a good radio script, described in so many words. They are perceived by characters and brought out by speech, sound, by allusion. Obliquely. (Corwin, 2003)

The careful selection of language to evoke emotion and imagination is not limited to radio drama. Descriptive language is a clear way in which all manner of radio programmes take on the characteristics of radio drama. Radio advertisements frequently use descriptive language for dramatic impact and, since they are usually under 30 seconds long, succinctness is of the essence. A particularly powerful example is the following advertisement, to encourage listeners to train in first aid. It begins,

> If you've ever thought you were too busy to attend a first aid course, we suggest you listen to the following recording of a 999 call. It's between a paramedic and a young mother who's just discovered that her baby has stopped breathing and turned blue.

We then hear the recording: a traumatic and harrowing conversation between the paramedic and the mother as she attempts to revive her sick baby. He calmly explains various techniques to try revive the child, each of which fail, until finally we hear the baby cry and the ordeal is over. The advertisement ends with the following announcement: 'Call the Red Cross on 0245 490090 and ask about a short first aid course near you. (*Pause*) Unless, that is, you're still too busy' (Red Cross Emergency, 2009).

This advertisement is a particularly interesting example because it demonstrates that dialogue does not have to be pre-determined to be of dramatic value. It is the clever contextualization of the recording from real life (sometimes called 'actuality') which turns the recording from a piece of factual information into audio drama.

The power of the word, both written and spoken, to communicate the 'secret states of mind, the inner world and private vision of the speaker' (McWhinnie, 1959, p. 57) is surely its most unique attribute. Often described in radio as 'internal voice' or 'inner monologue', this technique is sometimes used in TV and film, but lacks the dramatic tension that can be achieved on radio. This is possible because, as we discussed earlier, the listener has a particularly intimate relationship with the radio, which insinuates itself in the psyche. The following example is taken from *Another World* (1936), written by one of the preeminent figures of golden-age US radio, Arch Oboler. Interestingly, Oboler does not follow the more usual convention of the character herself vocalizing the inner monologue. He chooses instead to use a second voice. This clever device adds to the dramatic tension: is the voice real or not?

CARMEN: So! Now you know where I am, don't you?
JOAN: I – no! It can't be true.
CARMEN: It *is* true. I speak from within you.
JOAN: No. No, it's someone speaking from the outside. Someone trying to frighten me. I won't listen to you.
CARMEN: (IN COLD AMUSEMENT) Yes – cover your ears.
JOAN: (MOANS)
CARMEN: Yes – you still hear me.
JOAN: (DAZED) In my head.
CARMEN: Yes – in your head.
JOAN: (TEARFUL) Madness!
CARMEN: (SHARP) You little fool! It's reality! Stand where you are and listen – you *must*!
JOAN: (DISBELIEF) In my head.
CARMEN: (ANNOYED) Yes, yes, in your head! That's where I am, and that's where I've been all these years.

Sound

During the process of constructing radio drama, producers subdivide 'sound' into three separate categories:

- sound effects (sfx)
- acoustics
- perspective

'Sound effects' are 'live' or pre-recorded sounds, usually juxtaposed with dialogue, which signify an event (such as making toast) or a location (such as a beach). 'Acoustics' is the nature of the space in which the drama occurs: the natural ambience of environment. 'Perspective' indicates the spatial relationship between characters within the drama: distant or close, to left or right. We will discuss these definitions in a little more detail, beginning with sound effects, a term which is usually abbreviated to 'sfx'. Reflecting on sfx in cinema, Filson Young comments: 'The sounds seem true, because the eye is assisting you to recognize them. But shut your eyes, and how many of the noises of the sound screen explain themselves without the help of vision? Only a small proportion' (Young, 1933, p. 147). In radio, the process by which sounds 'explain themselves' without vision has been the subject of much debate. Crook (1999, pp. 70–89) presents an overview of the work of several expert radio drama theoreticians and practitioners. He gives considerable attention to Lance Sieveking, the talented BBC radio producer who, as we mentioned earlier, won C. S. Lewis's approval for his production of *The Chronicles of Narnia*. Sieveking was a key figure in the BBC between the 1930s and 1950s, a fascinating time during which radio drama was in the process of breaking free from the traditions of theatre to become a dramatic form in its own right. Sieveking devised a vocabulary to categorize the different uses of sound effect in radio drama, which is as valid today as when it was first conceived.

This is a summary of Sieveking's vocabulary of sound effects. You might like to listen to a radio drama yourself and categorize the sfx according to this vocabulary:

- *The realistic, confirmatory effect*: for example, if a character has introduced the idea of a storm, the sound of 'a ship laboring in a storm' will confirm the idea.
- *The realistic, evocative effect*: for example, a rural, rustic atmosphere of church bells, bees buzzing, creating a sense of peacefulness.

- *The symbolic, evocative effect*: The purpose is to represent or express confusion in a character's mind, so we could describe this as a symbol of mood or feeling.
- *Impressionistic effect*: Sieveking likens this effect to the world of a dream.
- *The conventionalized effect*: for example, objects and phenomena such as cars, trains or horses. This is a sound which is instantly recognizable.

John Drakakis describes sfx as 'sound signs' which 'both [listeners and producers] agree will conventionally represent particular kinds of experience' (Drakakis, 1981, p. 30). His definition draws on the notion of a mutual understanding of what particular sounds represent. If the sfx is 'a meadow on a summer's day', his definition is probably uncontested, as that sound effect would signify something similar to all of us. However, as Crisell (1994, p. 46) argues, some sfx have an 'extended signification'. They have a meaning beyond what they literally signify. For example, sfx of a creaky door signifies literally that the door needs some oil *and* has an extended signification that a sinister figure is entering the room. As we have discussed earlier, it is the process of 'transcodification' which illuminates the precise meaning for the listener.

In her advice to radio writers, Rosemary Horstmann (1997, p. 41) suggests that 'sound effects (…) should be used with discretion to create atmosphere rather than as a primary vehicle of information.' McWhinnie, too, had come to this conclusion and gives a persuasive example of 'less being more' in radio sfx:

> A match strikes, breath is exhaled: but we do not hear – and could not keep mental track of – the creak of the chair, the sound of the matchbox being replaced, the match dropping into the ashtray, the scrape of the foot across the carpet. Sound Radio cannot aim at realism but only at the most persuasive illusion of reality: since every sound that comes out of the loudspeaker is significant the radio producer needs to look always for the most typical and evocative detail in order to build his sound picture: otherwise the ear is distracted and the image blurred. (McWhinnie, 1959, p. 79)

It is a lesson that the radio dramatist Tony Palermo learned the hard way. In his extremely helpful radio drama web resource *Tony Palermo's RuyaSonic Site* (2010), Palermo speaks with refreshing honesty about a failed radio play that reveals a great about the challenges and risks of sound effects:

> So how far can you go with the illusion presented by sound effects in audio theatre? To illustrate the danger in relying too heavily on sound effects, I'll explain a failed comedy radio show I produced.

> While experimenting with mic setups in the [. . .] radio production studio, we did a run-through of a script of *The Lone Ranger*, but the sound effects we had on-hand were from *Superman*. Since this was just a mic test, we did part of the show with the wrong effects – ray guns instead of six shooters, cars instead of horses, etc.
>
> It was hilarious! I thought I'd found a way to do comedy radio workshops for kids – something notoriously hard to pull off because comedy requires timing and vocal inflection – which is difficult for amateurs, especially students. So, I decided to write a special script that used the 'wrong sound effects' gag – timing and inflection wouldn't matter.
>
> I wrote a 1953-style soap opera, complete with all the typical soap sound effects of the era – baking cookies, pouring lemonade, the phone, the doorbell, etc. (Soaps were a dull gig for a sound effects artist – nothing much to do.)
>
> As a plot device, the star of the show receives a mysterious voodoo doll, pricks her finger and faints. In a dream, she re-lives the previous scene, but now all the sound effects are wrong: dropping the cookie tray is now the sound of a bomb dropping; the phone ring is now a jackhammer; she answers the door and it's a train wreck, etc. What a brilliant conceit!
>
> But the whole thing *flopped!* The kids doing the show didn't get it and it didn't work when we listened to it upon playback.
>
> I found that even setting up the scene with dialogue like 'I'm expecting Sam's phone call [. . .]' SFX: jackhammer, 'Oh, That's him now [. . .]' didn't 'read' right. The audience merely accepted the jackhammer as some type of noisy phone sound.
>
> On the *I Love Lucy* TV show, this kind of gag would have you in stitches, but without the visual disparity of image and wrong sound, this gag just didn't work in radio.
>
> So, as much fun as sound effects are, don't over-rely on them. At some point they just get in the way and become noise. While the lack of visuals allows radio to do many things (plane crashes, medieval wars, prison breaks), it does impose some limitations too. (Palermo, 2011)

As Palermo's experience demonstrates, a careful selection of sfx will stimulate the imagination of the listener to complete the required image. In a similar way 'acoustics' and 'perspective' can be used to suggest the natural ambience of an environment and the spatial relationship between characters. We will take an aesthetic look at acoustics and perspective here, but the Production chapter later in this book takes a slightly more scientific approach, which readers will find useful.

The way that sound waves resonate in a space determines how they sound. For example, if you yell at the top of your voice in a cathedral (not advisable, admittedly), your voice will bounce off the walls and ceiling to create an echo effect. If you yell in your living room, your voice is less likely to echo because the room size restricts the 'bounce' and the sound waves will be absorbed in the soft furnishings (unless you happen to live in the White House, of course). In radio drama, the different ambient properties of various environments (acoustics) can be recreated and used very effectively to communicate spatial dimension. Shingler and Wieringa explain:

> (If) sounds are produced in a studio and all resonance is deadened then these sounds seem to occupy the same space as that of the listener, replicating the acoustic qualities of most people's homes [. . .] However, if the sounds on the radio are highly resonant [. . .] then these sounds seem to come from a quite distinct space beyond the listener's own environment. (Shingler and Wieringa, 1998, p. 56)

The Production chapter goes into some detail on how the radio drama producer can contrive more or less resonant acoustics in the studio by using acoustic screens to absorb sound waves or hard surfaces to reflect sound waves. The effect can be enhanced by adding reverberation during post-production. These effects simulate acoustics that, for the listener, are reminiscent of particular locations, such as the cathedral. The addition of a sound effect, such a distant organ playing, completes the sound picture.

While acoustics play a vital role in determining the spatial nature of radio drama, 'perspective' is needed to elucidate how characters interact within that space. Drawing on the work of Michel Chion in relation to film, radio academic and practitioner Alan Beck (1998) describes a 'point of listening' in radio plays. The 'point of listening' represents both the physical position of the characters in relation to each other, as well as the significance of each character within the scene. Beck argues that, unlike vision, sound has 'wandering and centrifugal tendencies'. The ear is not naturally drawn to a focal point in the way that the eye is drawn to an image presented in a film. The radio listener must be guided towards an aural focal point – a 'point of listening'. The main way in which this is achieved in radio drama is by creating a hierarchy of sound whereby the most important sounds in the narrative become the loudest and closest; the equivalent of a 'close-up' shot in cinema. A 1998 BBC production of *Sherlock Holmes: The Hound of the Baskervilles* demonstrates the hierarchy of sound very effectively. The scene takes place on a blustery moor. Dr Watson (Michael Williams) and Sir Henry (Mark Leake) are on the moor, investigating a strange light which they have seen flashing from the house. They hear a ghoulish howl in the distance. At first, they think they have misheard, but the howling is getting gradually closer. They hurriedly return to the house.

Here is the Hierarchy of Sound in this scene:

1. Dr Watson and Sir Henry
2. Their footsteps through the undergrowth
3. Hound
4. Atmosphere; blustery moor

Dr Watson and Sir Henry are the central characters. Their voices are the loudest and closest sounds we hear. Their footsteps are slightly quieter and further away; our focus is on the faces of the characters, rather than their feet. The hound is quiet and distant at first, but throughout the scene it becomes louder and closer. Luckily for Dr Watson and Sir Henry, the sound of the hound remains quieter and more distant than them, indicating that it is not yet dangerously close to them. The atmosphere of the blustery moor is lowest in the hierarchy. However, the sound is quiet, rather than distant. This indicates that the characters are actually within the location, but not dominated by it. The hierarchy of sound also provides an indication of which characters or events are 'in' or 'out' of the scene. Dr Watson and Sir Henry are 'in'. The hound is 'out'; to use a theatrical analogy, the hound is 'in the wings', awaiting its entrance.

Stereo recording is usually utilized in radio drama to add further perspective. To distance and volume can now be added left and right – and movement between left and right. If we add a stereo dimension to our hierarchy of sound, it might look something like Figure 2.1. This diagram demonstrates that the use of stereo can create a sense that the hound is moving from left to right, to indicate that it is circling the characters. This example demonstrates that stereo can provide an enhanced perspective in radio drama, but its use is contentious. Stereo requires the listener to be at a fixed point between the left and right sources of sound, which is not a natural listening condition for radio. Stereo listening is best achieved on headphones, but this not

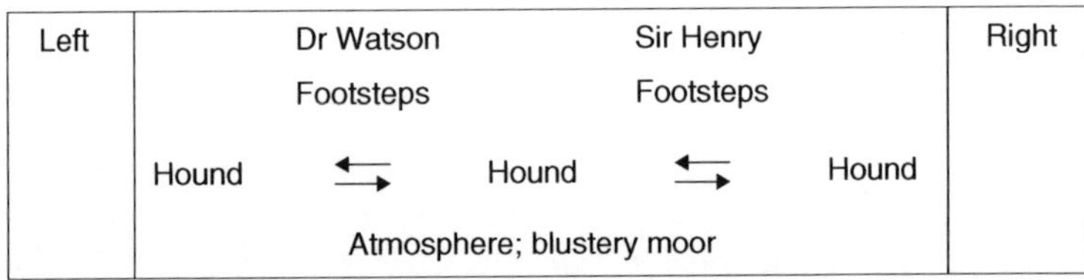

Figure 2.1 Hierarchy of Sound with Stereo in Sherlock Holmes: the Hound of the Baskervilles (1998)

always practical or desirable. Some producers are not convinced that stereo enhances drama at all. Radio writer Jonathan Raban finds it restrictive:

> Some plays are enhanced by it but for many stereo is a straight jacket. It tends to impose a mechanical naturalism on everything it records. It keeps sounds 'out there' making it very hard to create the special 'in there' quality that was once the hallmark of radio drama. (Raban, 1981, p. 82)

Raban feels constrained by stereo because, as we have discussed, one of the unique strengths of radio drama is the extent to which it is revealed in the mind of the listener. Our mind's eye does not 'see' any limits, so why should we restrict our 'vision' to left and right perspectives? In this sense, the use of stereo is reductive. It prevents us from forming our own, bigger and better perspectives. The creator of the 'zombie podcast' *We're Alive* believes that recording in stereo gets in the way:

> I think it's just distracting. It's not like a TV where the left and right balance isn't as noticed . . . When we first did . . . the left right thing . . . [it] only took us a few episodes to realize it wasn't necessary. We went back and re-did the voices to mono-centered. (*We're Alive* Forum, 2010)

Thanks to Digital Audio Broadcasting (DAB), the sound spectrum need not be limited to stereo. A small number of radio stations in the United States, China and Germany broadcast music in surround sound, though not drama, as yet (Slavik, 2010). Other forms of distribution for radio drama, such as the internet, podcast and DVD, often make use of a wider sound spectrum. 3DHorrorfi makes excellent use of 3D technology, which is an enhanced form of binaural stereo, in its horror radio plays. (see the Production chapter for more information on binaural stereo) The creators describe their productions as

> a hyper sound quality in the very smallest performing spaces and equally, in the biggest cathedrals. And, we don't write and direct as you would a radio play. We always think in terms of screenplays – so no surprise one reviewer has said 'This is like cinema in your head.' (3DHorrorfi, 2010)

The cinema analogy is fascinating, and accurate. The intensive experience created by the high-quality sound, the tightly focused script and tense performances do turn this into a cinematic experience in the sense that it is immersive. However, it is doubly affecting, because the listener is isolated and alone in the 'cinema'. Another production which makes equally good use of the sound spectrum is a surround sound version of *Under Milk Wood*, broadcast online in 2003, and simultaneously on FM in stereo. This superlative BBC production, produced by Alison Hindell, remastered the original narrator 'First Voice', played by Richard Burton, and mixed it with contemporary performances and music. Surround sound was extremely effective in evoking the dream-state of Llareggub, sweeping us effortlessly from character to character and location to location.

Music

The power of music in radio cannot be underestimated. After all, it is central to the vast majority of radio output. Shingler and Wieringa (1998, p. 61) point out that radio is a highly appropriate vehicle for hearing music, because we do not need images to make sense of it: our relationship with it is direct and personal. As a dramatic device, it has particular strength because of its emotional power. Music performs many functions in radio drama, which have been articulated by a succession of radio drama producers and theoreticians. Crisell (1994, pp. 51–2) describes these functions particularly effectively, and we summarize them here:

- *Music as a link*: In radio generally, an example of this might be a musical jingle or signature tune. Used in this way, music provides continuity and identifies the radio station or show. In radio drama, it represents the curtain falling between scenes. It marks a boundary between one scene and the next.
- *'Mood' music*: This can be heard in radio documentaries, features and commercials, as well as in radio drama. It is music which in some way evokes the feelings or thoughts of the character.
- *Music as a stylized sound effect*: This is particularly used in radio drama. Sometimes it is impossible or undesirable to create a naturalistic sound effect, and music can be used to evoke, or partially evoke, that sound. For example, the sound of a thunderstorm might be better evoked with the use of some percussion instruments than a naturalistic recording of the event itself.
- *Music as an indexical function*: This is music as it would occur in the world around us. In radio drama, a scene set in the London Underground might include a busker strumming a guitar. A news report about a children's orchestra would include some music created by that orchestra. Use of music in this way in factual broadcasting is usually called 'actuality'.

As we have seen, music has several distinct functions within radio drama, but its power is not limited to drama. Music is a clear way in which dramatic elements are introduced within other kinds of radio programme, such as news and documentary. We will begin with the most unlikely of examples, current affairs. BBC Radio 1 is particularly aimed at 16- to 24-year-olds. Its format is music and speech, with regular news bulletins called *Newsbeat*. Music is used in *Newsbeat* for emotional effect, just as it is in radio drama. For example, the 5 January 2011 edition featured 'mood' music during a news story about a murder, which was clearly designed to evoke an emotional response from listeners. The newsreader 'links' and many of the stories were accompanied by urgent, driving music, again to evoke emotional response. Linking music in the form of jingles is used between stories; this music forms a boundary, which is evocative of a scene change in the theatre.

Music can be very effective in helping us to create images. We are familiar with the eerie sound of whale song from wildlife recordings, but a BBC production of *Moby Dick* (2010) calls for a more malevolent and vengeful whale, 'a portentous and mysterious monster' (Melville, 1952, p. 6): a sound that could not easily be found in nature or replicated using sound effects. In this production, Stuart Gordon creates a wonderful soundtrack to evoke the quintessence of the whale Moby Dick, using music as a stylized sound effect. The resulting tones are almost human: mesmerizing and full of pathos, capturing the essence of the great white whale and its strange power over Captain Ahab in a way that could not be achieved through the use of sound effects alone.

The method of creating stylized sound effects has its roots in the *musique concrète* technique established in France in the 1940s. The method involved manipulating recordings of everyday sounds to create new ones. In the early days, this manipulation was limited by what could be achieved with the tape technology available but, later, thanks mainly to the pioneering work of the BBC Radiophonic Workshop, the technique was enhanced with electronic effects and grew musical 'wings'. The Radiophonic Workshop offers a fascinating example of the link between music, sfx and drama with an important place in the development and conceptualization of audio drama.

The story of the BBC Radiophonic Workshop

The Radiophonic Workshop was a department within the BBC which was dedicated to producing original sound effects and music for radio and, later, television (most famously creating the theme tune to the science fiction series *Doctor Who*). Like so many great inventions, the Radiophonic Workshop was born out necessity. In 1946, the BBC established the Third Programme, a national station that, according to Sir William Hayley, the then director general of the BBC, aimed to provide programming for the cultural elite: 'an audience that is not of one class but that is perceptive and intelligent' (Hayley, 1946). The new station was the perfect medium for the work of emerging avant-garde writers such as Dylan Thomas, Samuel Beckett and Giles Cooper. These writers were fully exploiting radio's potential to stimulate the imagination with works such as *Under Milk Wood* (Thomas, 1954), *All that Fall* (Beckett, 1956) and *The Disagreeable Oyster* (Cooper, 1957). Writing to a friend in 1956, Beckett provides us with a glimpse of the demands that these highly innovative writers were placing on the radio medium: 'Never thought about radio play technique but in the dead of t'other night got a nice gruesome idea full of cartwheels and dragging of feet and puffing and panting which may or may not lead to something' (Cited in Knowlson, 1996, p. 428). Before the Radiophonic Workshop was established, it was the job of the BBC studio manager to interpret the often highly surreal ideas of this new breed of writers and realize them in the form of sound effects and music. However, in the 1950s, the technology available to achieve such audio wizardry was extremely limited. Most sound effects were either produced 'live' in the studio as spot sfx or were pre-recorded on vinyl discs. It was very difficult to make layers of sound, since multitrack technology was not yet in use. However, studio managers were highly resourceful and creative individuals, and simply manipulated and even rebuilt the technology available to them to get the job done. Dick Mills, who later joined the Radiophonic Workshop, describes a particularly taxing historical radio drama scene consisting of a stage coach arriving at a wind- and rain-blown crossroads on the moor. The studio manager had to engage in an elaborate juggling act to recreate this deceptively simple scene. It involved playing three or four vinyl discs simultaneously, which also had to be restarted mid-scene, because the discs themselves lasted only two and a half minutes each. This is how radio drama was made until one studio manger had the bright idea of recording all the sound effects first on to a relatively new invention, a reel-to-reel tape machine, and then playing the recording in the background while the actors recorded their lines (Mills, 2010). The inventiveness of these early pioneers of sfx, such as Mills, Daphne Oram and Desmond Briscoe, was ground-breaking and inspired. Their efforts established a real need for a dedicated resource to cope with the technical demands of radio drama and, in 1958, the Radiophonic Workshop was born, with studio managers Oram and Briscoe at the helm.

Brian Hodgson, who joined the Radiophonic Workshop in 1962, was unimpressed by the commitment made by the BBC to the workshop:

> In the very beginning, Desmond (Briscoe) had been given £2000 and the key to 'redundant plant' [the BBC's junk pile] and that was it! The place kept going for years on what we called 'fag-ends and lollipops'. 'Fag-ends' were the bits of unwanted rubbish that other departments had thrown away; 'lollipops' were the much rarer treats that were occasionally sent down to keep Desmond quiet. (Hodgson, cited in Marshall, 2008)

Nevertheless, the studio mangers did what they had always done, and worked with the facilities available to invent innovative sound and music. Oram was particularly interested in *musique concrète*. The technique, pioneered by composer Pierre Schaeffer in 1948, involves manipulating original sounds to make new ones. With the limited technology available at the time, this was achieved by recording an original sound onto tape (such as a knock on a door), slowing the tape down or speeding it up to alter its pitch, turning it back to front, upside down and splicing it in weird and wonderful sequences to create new sounds. Before joining the Radiophonic Workshop, Oram used *musique concrète* techniques to produce 'Still Point' (1950), which consisted of pre-recorded instrumental sounds and *musique concrète* effects – all achieved using the basic technology of the time. Hugh Davies (2003) asserts that it is almost certainly 'the earliest composition to specify the real-time electronic transformation of instrumental sounds' – a pioneering breakthrough. Oram and Briscoe applied *musique concrète* techniques to a production of *Embers* by Samuel Beckett for the BBC Third Programme in 1959. The central character, Henry, sits on The Strand in London, tortured by the sounds of the omnipresent sea which has taken a loved one from him. Oram and Briscoe's interpretation of Henry's relationship with the sea is eerie and haunting. The echo of a distant car passing seems to resonate with the rhythmic lapping of waves on a shingle beach. The strain of a car horn is reminiscent of a fog horn at sea; different pitches are layered and the sound is extended and dies away with the receding waves. This ghostly blending of locations perfectly mirrors the confusion in Henry's mind. The rhythmic rise and fall of the sounds provides an uneasy, threatening rhythm track which insinuates itself into the fibre of the narrative. Henry evokes voices and sounds from the past to try to suppress his obsession with the sea. The sounds are intentionally crude and disjointed, to illustrate how they appear in Henry's confused psyche. The sound of a horse is created by coconut shells recorded in stark isolation. A slight echo has been added (achieved by opening the fader on the recording machine slightly to create controlled feedback) which emphasizes the surreal, discordant and disturbing effect.

The services of the Radiophonic Workshop were not limited to high-brow radio drama on the BBC Third Programme. The British comedy series *The Goon Show*, which was broadcast on the BBC Home Service between 1951 and 1960, also called on the services of the Radiophonic Workshop. Perhaps the most famous *Goon* sound effect created was 'Major Bloodnok's Stomach': an impressive cacophony of rumbles, gurgles, burps and twangs which leaves the listener with a deep sympathy for Major Bloodnok and his unruly digestive system. Mills (2010) recalls that Goon member Spike Milligan was so enthusiastic about the workshop that he had to be banned from entering, for fear that the demands for ever more wacky sfx would completely monopolize the workshop staff.

The Radiophonic Workshop was primarily established to provide sfx for BBC drama but, in the minds of the studio managers at least, their remit extended to the creation of sound in its broadest sense, including music. While *musique concrète* techniques offered some limited opportunities to create what could loosely be described as music, it was the use of oscillators which allowed the early pioneers to experiment with the creation of electronic music for the very first time (Marshall, 2008). Oscillators, which produce an electronic sound, were widely in use in the BBC to test equipment. The studio managers acquired several oscillators and set them to generate different electronic sounds and electronic musical notes. Delia Derbyshire, who joined the Radiophonic Workshop in 1960, combined oscillator-generated sounds and *musique concrète* techniques very successfully in the 1964 piece *The Dreams* by Barry Bermange. Described in the opening of the composition as an 'invention for radio', the piece combines sound and voices recorded from life with electronic sound, in five movements. The contributing voices describe dreams in a matter-of-fact, almost reportage style. Meticulous editing is used to emphasize particularly poignant moments (such as the repetition of the phrase 'and I was running and running and running; running and running and running'). Sometimes the contributors describe common dreams and the mystical quality of their collective subconscious experiences is again enhanced by skilful editing. Oscillator-generated tones are juxtaposed to create dissonant and disturbing chords which are intercut with the voices. The overall effect is unsettling, dreamlike and mesmerizing. The sophistication of the piece is such that only the voices, with their slightly twee British accents, situate this composition as a product of the 1960s.

Through the 1970s and 1980s, as the technology developed, the Radiophonic Workshop continued to lead the way with experimental electronic music. Synthesizers were introduced, and their evocative names tantalize us with a glimpse of their audio delights: Wobbulator,

Crystal Palace, Arp Odyssey and Fairlight. Though the Radiophonic Workshop was increasingly diverted by the demands of television, the studio managers still found time to make a major contribution to what is perhaps the most famous BBC radio drama serial of all: *The Hitchhiker's Guide to the Galaxy* (1978). The production called for such challenging effects as 'the sound of an office building flying through space in the grip of seven powerful tractor beams', genius audio sculptures which continue to resonate with each new generation of listeners (Briscoe and Curtis-Bramwell, cited in Hendy, 2007, p. 192).

The first 25 years of the BBC Radiophonic Workshop were its glory days, but as the technology required to devise electronic sounds became more accessible outside the BBC, the demand for the talents of the Radiophonic Workshop declined (Hodgson, 2010). There was no final blaze of glory, no audio inferno. The workshop simply could not survive the cuts that were made to BBC budgets during the 1990s, and it finally closed in 1998. It is gratifying to note that today the web shows that the Radiophonic Workshop has finally achieved the recognition it so richly deserves. The studio managers, particularly Oram and Derbyshire, who received no production credits at the time of broadcast, have posthumously achieved cult status. Their work is regularly cited as having influenced new generations of musicians, from Pink Floyd in the 1970s to Orbital in 2010, a fitting tribute to these 'alchemists of sound' (BBC4, 2005).

Experimental Sound

Though the Radiophonic Workshop was focused primarily on music and sound for radio and TV, its work had considerable influence on the development of experimental sound more generally. Unfortunately, programme formats in radio generally tend to be quite rigidly delineated into specific genre such as 'drama', 'music, and 'documentary', so experimental sound, which often crosses genre, does not have an obvious natural outlet. However, there are several examples of experimental sound within radio documentaries and features. For example, the wildlife sound recordist Chris Watson has produced an amazing documentary exploring the sound of water, called *Water Song* (2006). The radio medium was perfect not only for Watson to air the extraordinary music he had created from the sounds recorded above and below water, but also to explain his motivations and recording techniques. The dramatic narrative of the work is incredibly powerful because of the combination of beautiful sounds and Watson's own description.

Experimental sound is far more common on radio in Germany, where there is a proud tradition of experimental work which can be conceived as drama or music or, more usually, something between the two.

German sonic artist Andreas Bick attributes this freedom of approach to paranoia about the power of radio, following Germany's experiences under the Third Reich during World War II. He describes the experimental slots available on German radio as 'a kind of laboratory for what radio would be if it could be different from the mainstream' and finds working in sound, rather than music, extremely energizing: 'From a musical perspective, it frees you of the "limitations" of musical instruments; the whole sound world is your treasure trove' (Bick, 2011). Bick's treasure trove includes field recordings (sound recordings of particular environments) ranging from a cable car descending from the Mount Etna volcano to biblical locations at the Sea of Galilee to water taxis in Venice. Fascinatingly, these works seem to have a dramatic narrative. For instance, Bick set up a microphone in the Holocaust Tower at the Jewish Museum in Berlin. One can hear the eerie void of the space with distant echoes of the world outside the deliberately unnerving structure. Bick describes what is captured in his recording:

> I left the recording equipment inside the tower and waited outside to capture the 'sound of emptiness' without me being present in the recording. Some museum guests enter the room occasionally; most of them didn't stay for a long time due to the uneasy atmosphere of the place. Finally you hear the steps of a visitor approaching the recorder who was attracted by the red and yellow LEDs in the dark. He ran into my microphone, put it back in place and left the tower immediately, passing me by with a somehow sorrowful expression on his face. I thought if I would have to describe the German guilt complex towards the holocaust, it would have looked somehow like that. (Bick, 2010)

The collision with the audio equipment could be comical: a slapstick moment in such a sombre environment. In fact, it is literally both disruptive and disturbing. The museum guests become part of the sound space and, because of this, the work has more poignancy and emotional depth. Bick's work seems to have resonances with traditional radio drama in the way that it uses sound to explore narrative, place and emotion, but his approach to the creative process is firmly in the musical tradition: 'I tried to always look at the composition of the sounds first, how they interact with each other, how the sounds blend and how 'musical' dramaturgy can be applied, dynamics, peaks and tension and so forth' (Bick, 2011). This blend of dramatic intent with musical technique, coupled with the opportunities for distribution offered by the internet, is causing an evolution in audio drama – or should that be *revolution*? The democratization of both genre and mode of distribution are blurring the boundaries between audio drama and music, allowing new forms of expression to emerge. This presents tremendously exciting and liberating opportunities for the audio producers of the future.

Silence

> If we have a hope of improving the acoustic design of the world, it will be realisable only after the recovery of silence as a positive state in our lives.
>
> *(Schafer, 1994, p. 259)*

We are all familiar with the expression 'as silent as the grave': our life begins and ends in silence, so perhaps it is not surprising that we surround ourselves with noise. Nevertheless, Canadian composer R. Murray Schafer argues, if we are to realize the value of silence, then we must view it as a positive, rather than negative, force. John Cage understood the positive value of silence, or rather the value of *lack of noise*, as evidenced in his composition *'4'33"* (1952), which consists of the pianist sitting silently at a piano for four minutes and thirty-three seconds. What the audience experienced is not silence at all, but the ambience of the location in which the work was 'performed'. In radio, silence usually has a negative connotation. Something must have gone wrong, we have 'dead air'; but John Cage's composition makes a virtue of silence. It becomes a positive expression of the location. In radio drama, however, it is the contextualization of silence which makes it positive, as McWhinnie explains:

> Silence, as a calculated device, is one of the most potent imaginative stimuli; prepared for correctly, broken at the right moment, in the right context, it can be more expressive than words; it can echo with expectancy, atmosphere, suspense, emotional overtones, visual subtleties. (McWhinnie, 1959, p. 88)

In radio drama, silence between scenes marks a boundary. It represents a lapse of time and, sometimes, a change in location, but the more aesthetic qualities of silence, which McWhinnie alludes to above, are the most potent. Corwin (2003) describes these as 'dread silences and spooky silences and heavy silences and restful silences. There's a whole vocabulary of silences alone.' Here are some brief examples to illustrate the use of silence in radio drama:

Silence engenders irony or humor:
MOLLY: How does my hair look today?
Pause
JAKE: Lovely, darling.

The use of the 'Pause' precipice can also create dramatic tension:
MUGGER: Give me the money.
VICTIM: No.
MUGGER: I'm not messing. I'll count to three and then it's all over. *Pause* One *Pause* Two *Pause* Three!

Exercise

This is a section from a radio play called *The Dark* by Arch Oboler, broadcast in 1937 on NBC. Where would *you* add pauses to create dramatic tension?

SAM: Here, Doc. The lamp.
DOC: Okay. Hold it high.
SAM: Yeah. (SHARP GASP) What . . .?!
DOC: Oh, mother in Heaven!
SAM: What . . . On the floor – what is it?
DOC: It's . . . a *man*.
SAM: Ohhhh, no! It can't be, I tell you, it can't be.
DOC: Oh, yes. It's a man. A man – and he's been turned inside out.
WOMAN: (SHRIEKS WITH LAUGHTER)
SAM: *Inside out*?
WOMAN: (SUBSIDES)
DOC: Here. See for yourself. It's a man. But the skin is the inside; the raw flesh is the outside. Organs . . . Hanging . . .
SAM: (SHUDDERS) Yeah.
DOC: It's a miracle – a man turned inside out. Like you'd turn a *glove* inside out.

In conclusion, there's no better way to learn about radio drama than actually listening to it. Most of the audio examples used in this chapter are available free on the internet or for purchase on CD or DVD. While the act of listening is hugely rewarding in itself, it can only be enhanced by listening with an analytical ear. This chapter has drawn on the work of great radio theorists and practitioners to provide an overview of the distinctive qualities of audio drama and a vocabulary which can be used to deconstruct its constituent parts. Apply this knowledge to your radio listening, and you will develop an enriched understanding of the audio drama genre and its far-reaching influence on radio.

Case study: *The Revenge* (1978) and *A Pot Calling the Kettle Black* (2010)

The crucial supporting role of sound effects in radio drama has been the subject of debate since the earliest days of radio, but how does it fare when it is thrust into the limelight? This case study focuses on two radio pieces made without words, to discuss the extent to which radio can be successful without speech. While there are many wonderful examples of sound playing a vital subsidiary function in audio drama, there are far fewer in which it is the star. The most famous example of a radio play without words, *The Revenge* (1978), has been selected as the first example for discussion. The second example is provided by the internet, rather than conventional radio. The internet is an ideal means of mass distribution for experimental forms of audio drama, some of which could perhaps be more accurately described as 'sonic art'. Though sonic art often makes a virtue of subverting the conventions of traditional radio drama, the two genres share a common purpose of stimulating listeners to construct meaning. There are many examples of sonic art composed without speech, but a particularly fascinating example, *A Pot Calling the Kettle Black* (2010), has been selected for discussion. Unusually, the two selected pieces offer the opportunity for close study of sound alone: its vocabulary in radio drama, its scenography and how these elements synthesize with the imagination of the listener to construct meaning.

The Revenge, written and performed by Andrew Sachs and produced by Glyn Dearman, was first broadcast on BBC Radio 4 in 1978 and has been repeated many times since. The play is composed entirely of sounds, without any audible dialogue. Somewhat ironically, the inspiration for the play came from a master of the spoken word, playwright Tom Stoppard. Stoppard suggested that it ought to be possible to make a play with no dialogue whatsoever, an idea that appealed to Sachs: 'Very often in radio plays people seemed to never stop talking and I thought it would be quite nice to have something other than talk that tells a story' (Sachs, 1978).

It is the story of a prisoner who escapes to exact revenge on a man who has wronged him. The narrative is revealed through a series of naturalistic sound effects, non-verbal human sounds and a strong hint or two in the play's introduction and title. The structure is that of a traditional radio play, with a linear narrative, subdivided into five scenes.

Like *The Revenge*, *A Pot Calling the Kettle Black* has no direct speech. It consists entirely of sound effects: the kitchen provides the inspiration for a fanciful journey in which the everyday sounds of kettle boiling or an egg frying are mischievously subverted by electronic manipulation. The work was composed by Andreas Bick as a commission from SilenceRadio, an audio-based website 'dedicated to showcasing work and artists who demonstrate audio excellence and who exploit radiophonic expression to its full potential' (SilenceRadio, 2010). The work explores 'how sounds could be mirrored in other sounds and how the meaning of sounds shifts depending on context' (Bick, 2011). The result is a whimsically evocative piece, during which the listener is transported away from the humdrum kitchen to a spectacular parallel universe, one which is created in the imagination, a universe unique to each listener.

Neither piece is an 'easy' listen and can require several intensive sessions in order to decipher and make meaning. In radio terms, this is contradictory. We do not normally give radio such undivided attention. Typically, we have one opportunity to listen, usually while we are simultaneously engaged in something else. It is interesting that, even in the early days of radio, producers such as the BBC's Donald McWhinnie recognized the value of multiple listening opportunities, though they were rarely available:

> I do believe that any artistic experience worth having can only be enriched by a second acquaintance, and the more profound the content the more closely you need to study it, as you come back again and again to a painting or a piece of music to discover new perspectives, new shades of meaning. (McWhinnie, 1959, p. 43)

Of course, it has long been technically possible, if not entirely legal, to record radio programmes and listen over again, but it is the internet that presents the most flexibility for listening to audio drama. In particular, sonic art has benefited greatly from this mode of distribution. Nebulous and esoteric work such as Bick's is enhanced by an intensive, self-determined listening experience and the supplementary written information that can be provided via the web.

Lance Sieveking's early articulation of sound vocabulary, which we discussed earlier, proposes clear distinctions between the functions of sound in radio drama (cited in Crook, 1999, pp. 70–4). His vocabulary can be applied to both pieces, but is perhaps more applicable to *The Revenge*, since it is the traditional radio drama genre which Sieveking, among others, helped to establish as a producer in the BBC.

> *Sound Effects: The Revenge, Scene 1.*
> *Throughout*: rural atmosphere, moorland birds.
> *Specific sounds*: protagonist breathing (at various times out of breath, nervous), siren, running through undergrowth, wading in water, indistinct shouting, dogs barking.

Sieveking's sound vocabulary assumes that speech is the main element of the drama and that sound effects take place in relation to speech. Though there is no speech in the play, we are aware of a central character, the protagonist. It could be argued that, though we cannot hear his words, the protagonist fulfils the role of a speaking character in the play. The sound effects are accurate in relation to him: the dogs approach and he breathes nervously; he breathes heavily as he wades into the water. Sieveking categorizes these sounds as 'realistic, confirmatory'. The rural atmosphere in Scene 1 is the equivalent of the backdrop in a theatre. It sets the scene, conjuring up an idyllic image of the countryside, a feeling of calm and serenity, which is categorized by Sieveking as the 'realistic evocative' effect. Sieveking's vocabulary can also be applied to some extent to the opening section of *A Pot Calling the Kettle Black.*

> *Sound Effects: A Pot Calling the Kettle Black. Section 1: 0 – 20".*
> *Specific sounds:* protagonist breathing excitedly, roar of a gas flame, clock chiming randomly, water glugging in a sink, fizzing.

In this piece, the protagonist does not provide a fixed point of reference for the sounds, which seem to appear as if at random. Bick was inspired by 'Alan's Psychedelic Breakfast' (Pink Floyd, 1970), during which 'Alan' prepares his food, with a suitably spacey musical accompaniment. Bick intends his protagonist to be similarly playful, as is clearly evident from the juxtaposition of the sounds presented. Sieveking categorizes sounds such as these, which reflect the protagonist's state of mind, as 'symbolic evocative'.

As we discussed earlier, some sounds have what Andrew Crisell (1994, p. 46) calls an 'extended signification' and there is an example of this in *The Revenge*, in the form of a clock ticking and chiming. On a fundamental level, the clock indicates that a clock is in the room. It chimes to tell us what time it is. A scene ends with a 'fade-down' on the ticking clock. The next scene begins with a 'fade-up' on the ticking clock, signifying that time has passed and that we are in the same location; an example of 'extended signification'. Bick does not intend any particular meaning from the ticking sound in *A Pot Calling the Kettle Black*. However, he articulates the notion of 'extended signification' in a fascinating way: 'There is a way to hear sounds apart from their actual source and attached meaning. It is more the physicality or materiality of the sound, which makes them compositional matter and also a playground of ambiguity of meaning' (Bick, 2011). For Bick, sounds are important for their audio qualities as well as for what they may signify. From a radio listening perspective, it is a generally understood convention that a ticking clock signifies the passing of time, so it is possible that a listener will draw this conclusion, regardless of Bick's intention. This would not create a difficulty for Bick, who clearly enjoys teasing and intriguing the listener: 'I was thinking after finishing the piece that there are some sounds from a narrative perspective, that should not be there, but I kept them because it also adds some absurdity and openness. Something not rational' (Bick, 2011). Perhaps it is the vocabulary of sonic art which offers the best opportunity to categorize the sound effects in *A Pot Calling the Kettle Black.*

Schafer (1994, pp. 9–10) provides a succinct vocabulary, closely related to musical terminology:

- keynote sounds
- signals
- sound marks

Taking another sequence of sounds from this piece as an example, it can be seen how this vocabulary can be applied:

> *Sound Effects: A Pot Calling the Kettle Black Section 2:21" – 2'36".* Electronic fizzing, electronic interference, ignition button, flame ignites, gas flame burns, egg breaks into a pan, frying, altered frying sound, altered breathing sound, ticking clock, winding clock, bells, frying, panting with anticipation, glass of water poured, altered bubbles sound, gulping, electronic fizzing.

The 'keynote' is 'the anchor or the fundamental tone and although the material may modulate around it, often obscuring its importance, it is in reference to this point that everything else takes on its special meaning' (Shafer, 1994, p. 9). The naturalistic sounds of the kitchen form the 'anchor' in *A Pot Calling the Kettle Black*. The frying, the water, the kettle filling are rooted in reality and are the keynote sounds around which the piece is structured. The 'signals' are what Schafer describes as 'foreground sounds . . . listened to consciously' (Schafer, 1994, p. 9). In Bick's work, the 'signals' are the electronic sounds, fizzing and electrical interference, the clock and bells, which seem to point to a change in mood, pace or direction. A 'sound mark' is 'unique or possesses qualities which make it specially regarded or noticed'. (Schafer, 1994, p. 10). There are potentially many sound marks in the piece, but the one that is the most striking is the human 'voice', panting and breathing. The strange human sounds are at the same time intriguing and alienating; the listener can recognize the sounds as human, but cannot easily make meaning from them.

Though the 'keynote' sounds of the kitchen are easy to identify, it is impossible to locate the origins of many of the 'signals' in *A Pot Calling the Kettle Black*. These wonderful 'acousmatic' sounds are doubly affecting, because they defy identification. Writing on the subject of acousmatic sound, an early pioneer of experimental sound, Pierre Schaeffer, draws on the original Larousse dictionary definition of 'acousmatic': 'a noise that one hears without seeing the cause of it' (Schaeffer, 1966, p. 76). An acousmatic sound has a 'life' of its own which is distinct from how it was created. For example, a familiar sound such as a cork popping becomes a piece of evocative audio, unrelated to the sound of a bottle being opened. Acousmatic sound is pure and simple audio, free of any associations it might have with its original source. Though it is rarely possible to recognize the original source of the 'signals' in *A Pot Calling the Kettle Black*, Bick identifies them as 'volcanoes, gardens, Venice boats, dripping patterns of rain, tweaked and edited, so they appear to be more in the surreal realm' (Bick, 2011). Their dreamlike qualities are heightened by their juxtaposition with easily identifiable 'keynote' sounds of the kitchen:

> The kitchen noises turn into abstract sound worlds which may arise from her imagination and memory – but perhaps they are just sounds that have been released from their chemical bond with a specific meaning and which, when heated, recombine to form new molecular structures. (Bick, 2011)

Meaning

Through the vocabularies of Sieveking, Crisell, Schafer and Schaeffer, it has been possible to categorize the sounds in both pieces, but how then can the listener make meaning from them? Crisell notes that to begin to construct drama, visual codes (images) must be replaced with auditory codes (sounds, including speech), a process we mentioned earlier: 'transcodification'. He draws particular attention to the role of speech in the process of transcodification, postulating that description is generally the most effective way of compensating for the lack of visuals (Crisell, 1994, p. 146). In the case of our two examples, there is no direct speech and no verbal description. *A Pot Calling the Kettle Black* is not conventional drama, and there is no predetermined image to describe, so the process of transcodification has little relevance. However, in *The Revenge*, it could be argued that the protagonist plays a role in the process of transcodification, even without the benefit of speech. The sound of his running footsteps and anxious, laboured breathing signify that the dogs and policemen are actually chasing him, rather than just coincidentally present.

The selection of sound effects is significant in *The Revenge*. They are used sparingly, to hint at environments and events, rather than to replicate every possible nuance of the scene. The reason for this is that the producer wishes the audience to create an image which is consistent with his own vision. The real world is a constantly fluctuating soundscape, consisting of noises that are relevant to us and those that are not. Theoretically, we can hear all sounds that are within audible reach of us, but we do not actually *listen* to all those sounds. Stop reading for a moment and listen to the sounds around you. There's a very good chance that you will notice noises of which you were not aware a few moments ago. This is because your brain is selecting sounds which are relevant to you and filtering (or attempting to filter) extraneous sound: this is the act of *listening*, as opposed to the indiscriminating act of *hearing*. In *The Revenge*, the producer is helping us to *listen* by selecting the important sounds for us. In the case of *A Pot Calling the Kettle Black*, the intention is not to guide each listener to create the same image from the sounds presented, but rather to provide stimuli for the creation of unique, individual images. Nevertheless, the choice of sounds is equally significant. They have been carefully selected by the creator as the launch pad for the flight of imaginative fancy which they evoke.

Scenography makes a significant contribution to the way we interpret drama. When we visit the theatre, the visual boundaries of the play are physically determined by the stage in front of us. For example, we can see that the scene takes place in a drawing room in 1920s London because the set, with backdrop and props, shows us. On screen, the camera follows the protagonists, simultaneously revealing the location and drama in a naturalistic manner. Some films make a particular feature of this, such *The Blair Witch Project* (Daniel Myrick and Eduardo Sánchez, 1999) and *Cloverfield* (Matt Reeves, 2008), in which we experience the drama in 'real' time, along with the protagonists, via the shaky, handheld camera. In radio, there are no visual points of reference to anchor us. The radio scenography is nebulous. It is up to the producer to provide the locations and boundaries within which the radio drama takes place. In order to define boundaries, we must first have a point of focus. Alan Beck (1998) describes this as the 'point of listening'. In conventional drama, the point of listening is fixed at a location from which the drama is best revealed (called the 'sound centre' by BBC radio drama producers). Normally, the microphone is positioned in the sound centre. In *The Revenge*, our central character does not speak. Nevertheless, all the sounds emanating from the character are at the sound centre of our listening experience. In Scene 2 we are 'with' the protagonist as he walks quickly toward a village. We hear the distant merrymaking in the local pub as he passes by. We are there when he attacks a biker, stealing his motorbike and jacket. The police pursue us, at first at a distance and then closing in. We are party to the protagonist's snigger of delight as he manages to hide and elude the police. The main audio indication that the protagonist is at the sound centre is the volume of his voice in relation to the other sounds around him. In the hierarchy, he is loudest and therefore the most important. This hierarchy is also apparent in *A Pot Calling the Kettle Black*, in which the breathing and muttering sounds of the protagonist take sound centre, drawing the listener's attention to her.

The hierarchy also helps us to determine where our 'stage' begins and ends. Which events are within our main field of 'vision' and which are peripheral, behind-the-scenes. Scene 1 of *The Revenge* provides a good illustration. The protagonist is at the sound centre and is the principal focus of attention. In the hierarchy, he is loudest and very close to us. There is significant peripheral action in the form of the police officers and dogs who are tracking the protagonist. We know that they are peripheral because they are quieter, more distant, in relation to the protagonist. As they catch up with the protagonist, the sounds become louder and insinuate themselves more into the scene – they are less peripheral now. When the protagonist hides underwater, the sounds become louder, indicating that his pursuers are now dangerously close. However, the sound is distorted, as it would seem to the protagonist under the water. We are assured that the protagonist is still safe, because the prison officers and dogs have not entered the sound centre. When he surfaces, the sounds are receding, and he is safe. This very effective representation of scene boundaries and peripheral activity has been achieved in the main by a simple variation in volume.

The use of stereo is also a useful determinant of boundary and peripheral action. *The Revenge* is particularly successful in this regard since it has been recorded in binaural stereo, which, when listened to on headphones, gives the impression of behind as well as left to right. In scene 5, the victim returns home. We hear the car approach from behind and to the left. The protagonist hears the arrival and hides. The victim approaches the sound centre, but remains slightly distant. He is in the scene, but has not discovered the protagonist. He moves to the right, becoming more distant as he climbs the stairs to the bathroom. We can hear the victim's movement at all times, as he sings to himself. Stereo is also used to excellent effect in *A Pot Calling the Kettle Black*, but as a means of subverting spatial awareness rather than determining it. Should the listener dare to become comfortable in the soundscape, the sounds shift randomly to disorientate, spinning the listener round as if caught up in a game of 'blind man's bluff'.

Though we have gone into some level of detail on sound vocabulary and treatment, to limit an overall appreciation of radio drama to its constituent parts is reductive. The glorious smell of perfume fills the air, yet the basic ingredients are civet musk, petrified excrement and lavender oil, which have fused and morphed to create the magical scent. Similarly, radio drama transcends its raw ingredients: the catalyst is the imagination of the listener, who turns the base metal into gold. By way of an example, here is a personal interpretation of Section 2 of *A Pot*

Calling the Kettle Black, the raw ingredients of which have been outlined earlier:

> *A Pot Calling the Kettle Black: Section 2*
>
> I am transported from the frying pan to a Jurassic park-style swamp and I realize I'm not alone; a velociraptor has joined me, growling ominously. I'm sucked out and parachuted gently onto a volcanic island. The volcano is rumbling and cicadas tell me that I'm in a rainforest. Now I'm inside a clock, temporarily calmed by the gentle rhythm. Soon I'm hurled once more to the frying pan for a spell of reality, before being launched once more into another world. This time I'm in a rocket, heading for the stars.

How on earth can I have made such incomprehensible images from the audio provided? Bick (2011) warns us that the noises become 'abstract sound worlds', but why did I construct this particular set of images? Clive Cazeaux, writing on phenomenology and radio drama, offers an explanation for this. He believes that, though hearing is clearly separate from sight, touch and smell, all the senses are interlocking. The ear is a 'world opening', a gateway to all sensory experience (Cazeaux, 2005, p. 163). Cazeaux draws parallels between sound and a work of art. A painting is more than mere brushstrokes. Every word that is spoken about the painting, every word that is written 'contributes to the work and sustains it as a coherent whole through a series of "beckoning" or "opening onto" relationships with other elements in the work and with elements in the world.' (Cazeaux, 2005, p. 167). Thus, when I listen to *A Pot Calling the Kettle Black* I am constructing my own response with reference to all my knowledge and experiences, meaning that my interpretation of the work is widely informed, but is unique and personal to me. It is for this reason, coupled with Bick's intention to challenge and stimulate, rather than guide me to a fixed conclusion, that my listening experience is so extraordinary and powerful.

In contrast, a personal response to *The Revenge* is less imaginative, less unique and likely to be similar to that of other listeners:

> *The Revenge: Scene 1*
>
> It's a peaceful Saturday morning on a summer moorland. The idyll is broken by a loud siren, an alert that a prisoner has escaped from a nearby prison. The escapee is panic-stricken. Policemen and dogs pursue him and he runs, submerging himself in a river to hide. When the danger passes, he emerges from the river and wades to the edge, pulls himself out, checks that he cannot be seen and walks away.

The limited creative satisfaction I experience is not necessarily negative, as the aim of the production is to enable me to understand a narrative without the use of speech, rather than to challenge and stimulate me to create new narratives or meaning. *The Revenge* is successful in achieving its aims. The sounds are effective in conveying the narrative. As a listening experience, it is more complex than radio drama with speech: the listener has to work hard to construct the images and narrative, and in this sense it is immersive and rewarding. However, perhaps the play's defining feature is, at the same time, its greatest downfall. It is a play constructed *without* speech, rather than a play constructed *with* sound. Sachs has removed one of the most important components of radio drama – speech – and not replaced it. The experience is lessened as a consequence. The narrative is simple and linear, and the locations are straightforward and heavily signposted, because this is all that is possible without speech. The listener can fill in the gaps with imagination, but, in effect, our capacity to develop the raw materials we have been given to create complete and satisfying images is seriously restricted. This is particularly the case with characterization. In radio drama, it is speech which fleshes out the characters, clothes them, ages them, makes them live. In *The Revenge*, there is a character. We hear him react, breath and move, but in terms of making him live, we have very little to go on. If it were not for the title of the play, we would not understand his motivations or, arguably, even the narrative. It seems that those involved in the production understood this, as the introduction to the play is laden with reminders that we are following one character's journey and that the title of the play has great significance (Mason, 1978). *A Pot Calling the Kettle Black* has a central character, too, described in the accompanying text as 'a woman who is inspired to vocal experiments by her daily routines'. Similarly to *The Revenge*, it is difficult for the listener to construct a 'real' person from the audio clues and without the benefit of speech. Arguably, this lack of clarity is less of a drawback in this case. We do not depend on an understanding of the woman's motivations to be able to construct meaning, because her motivations are not central to the piece. She is the conductor of a magnificent orchestra of sound, summoning, manipulating and unleashing it for listeners to interpret as they wish.

In conclusion, *The Revenge* and *A Pot Calling the Kettle Black* are impressive examples of the use of sound and demonstrate that drama *can* be successful without speech. However, the extent of that success is determined by how the drama is conceived. *The Revenge* is conceived very much as a traditional radio drama and, as such, is limited to its conventions of narrative structure. These conventions normally depend heavily on speech for a very good reason, as McWhinnie points out: 'The radio writer may deploy his words musically, surrealistically, impressionistically, intellectually – what you will. If he uses his materials successfully the sound complex he creates will not have any easy equivalent' (McWhinnie, 1959, p. 62). The soundscape of *The Revenge* is enjoyable and effective but deficient, because speech is *supposed* to be there. Turning to *A Pot Calling the Kettle Black*, the term 'convention' is almost anathema. Bick is not particularly concerned with the mode of distribution and places more importance on the work itself (Bick, 2011). For this reason, the work is not subject to the boundaries of time and space imposed on the more traditional broadcast form of radio drama. The judgements to be made about *A Pot Calling the Kettle Black* are much more subjective and depend largely on how much we individually appreciate or benefit from the listening experience. In this sense, it is unfair to compare the relative merits of the two plays. Both have much to teach us about the power of sound alone to convey meaning, evoke emotion and free the imagination, and therefore make a tremendously valuable contribution to the audio drama field.

3
Radio drama in the contemporary world

Introduction

The era of the crystal set feels like ancient history now. In addition, the term 'radio drama' can still conjure up images of an arcane past: formally dressed performers clustered around microphones with scripts in hand; audiences gathered around huge, furniture-like radios, looking like they are just waiting for television to be invented. However, audio drama has not only continued since those early days, but in our contemporary world it is also thriving in many respects. The digital revolution and the information age have allowed dissemination through the internet and the efficient creation and packaging of audio materials. Archive and historical recordings are digitized in remastered quality that can be even better than when the programs were first broadcast. As well as the wonders of the digital age – technological developments equivalent in impact and potential to the dawn of radio broadcasting – radio continues to have a vital function in the developing world as a means of education and outreach.

Audio drama in the digital age

Established in the 1920s, the BBC has existed for nearly the entire history of radio broadcasting. Even with the rise of television, the BBC maintained its commitment to radio, and in our own time there continue to be more BBC radio channels than television channels. BBC radio features national channels specializing in spoken word, popular music, classical music, news and sports broadcasting. In addition, there are numerous regional stations, while the BBC World Service is its most consciously 'international' channel. Although music and current affairs might be dominant, audio drama is a significant form. It is an essential ingredient in channels such as BBC Radio 4, which broadcasts drama on a daily basis. Radio drama can also be found on stations such as the BBC World Service and BBC Radio 3. In responding to the digital age, the BBC launched a number of digital-only channels, such as BBC Radio 7 (launched in 2002 and renamed 'BBC Radio 4 Extra' in 2011) which specializes in drama and comedy, featuring classic recordings and all-new commissioned works. As well as launching new channels, the BBC has responded to the internet and endeavoured to use it in effective and even radical ways. The internet is the most significant development for radio since the transistor radio. Recent research in Britain has revealed that around one-third of the population has listened to the radio via the internet, and the majority of these have accessed a BBC iPlayer 'listen again' or podcast service (Plunkett, 2010). In some ways, the experience of listening to radio via a PC is reminiscent of the early days of broadcasting. Similar to those images of the old-fashioned radio in the living room, the PC is a focus of attention. In terms of the technical quality, listening online can enhance the experience, because we often listen on headphones, which is by nature much more immersive than listening via loudspeakers. Headphone listening particularly enhances the reception of stereo, which requires listeners to remain at a fixed point between two sources of sound.

Radio applications such as 'listen again' and podcasting, and access to these services via smartphones, have revolutionized the listening experience. Radio listeners themselves can control what, where and how to listen, rather than being at the mercy of the scheduling whims of radio stations. This is a significant development for radio drama. Now you can choose to listen to a horror drama alone in the dark . . . if you dare. While this choice is tremendously liberating, the disadvantage, it could be argued, is that the listener is less likely to 'discover' radio. My most pleasurable listening experiences have not taken place by choice, but when my radio just happens to be on. I lived through every second of radio presenter James Naughtie's excruciating gaff on BBC Radio 4 on 6 December 2010, when he accidentally turned the name of a British government minister into an unbroadcastable expletive. My cereal spoon hovered halfway to my mouth as the drama unfolded; there was no one in the studio to save him as he attempted, in vain, to disguise his giggles as a coughing fit and struggled through the news headlines. I was part of that drama, an ally, urging him to 'get a grip' and cheering when his ordeal was over. Though the internet offers the opportunity for everyone to listen to this hilarious clip, nothing could possibly be better than the experience of hearing it 'live'. The joy of radio is its immediacy, and the internet, though it offers many other possibilities, does not enhance that fundamental quality.

An advantage of the internet is that it can provide new depth to the listening experience by presenting supplementary information. The long-running BBC radio soap *The Archers* serves as an excellent example of this. Its website supplies a whole new dimension to the drama by providing extensive information designed to extend and enhance the listening experience. Through the site, you can catch up with previous episodes, take part in the *Archers Quiz*, play *Fantasy Archers* or join an online community of so-called Archers Addicts. These aspects of the website enhance the listening experience and are particularly helpful for new listeners, who can fill themselves in on the storylines of the previous 60 years, should they be having trouble sleeping at night. Other aspects are equally entertaining, but perhaps do not actually enhance the listening experience. For example, an interactive map allows you to zoom in and out of the fictional village of Ambridge, where the play is set; information on the characters is available, including a picture of the actor who plays that character. This supplementary information could be regarded as subverting one of the most powerful aspects of radio drama, its ability to stimulate the imagination of the listener to create his or her own images. After all, as Donald McWhinnie says, 'The radio listener . . . will clothe the sounds he hears with flesh and blood; and since he has to find his images in his own experience and imagination they will be images which belong to him in a special way' (McWhinnie, 1959, p. 26). The *Archers* website also gives listeners a forum to discuss all issues relating to the drama. A particularly exciting development has been the addition of the microblogging application *Twitter* which allows 'tweeters' (contributors) to 'tweet' (comment) on events, real or fictional, as they unfold. A special 60th anniversary of *The Archers* generated 10,000 'tweets' from listeners discussing the drama as it unfolded (The Archers 60th Tweetathon, 2011). This is a particularly interesting development, as it allows producers to gauge the overall listener response at the time of the broadcast, which has hitherto been out of reach. Without this kind of interactivity, Frances Gray observes that an *audience*, as distinct from individual listeners, is not normally formed until after the broadcast:

> In the 1940s and 1950s *ITMA* or *Dick Barton* [BBC radio drama serials] arguably achieved true collective response when discussed the next day in the workplace, or when their catchphrases or distinctive voices passed into common currency. The willing entry into a radio fiction by the individual was, even in its so-called golden age, the key moment in the communicating process, the one thing needful to prompt the listener to metamorphose the next day into part of a responding and discussing 'audience'. (Gray, 2006, p. 252)

For radio drama producers, this ability to understand the impact of the drama at the time of broadcast is a potent tool, but does 'tweeting' mean that listeners have input into the development of radio drama? In most cases, probably not. 'Tweeting' is the modern day equivalent of shouting at the radio, an impotent, rather than empowering, activity. However, other interactive features have been utilized to encourage listeners to influence radio drama storylines. *Chain Gang* (2009) is a drama series which calls on listeners to text or email their suggestions for the next episode, which are then incorporated into the script.

Sometimes the BBC has been particularly ambitious in its attempts at 'interactivity'. Nick Fisher's *The Wheel of Fortune* (2001) is regarded as BBC radio's first interactive drama. It comprised three simultaneous versions of the play in radio and online form, enabling the listener to 'channel hop' between different versions of the play. Another BBC experiment in interactive audio drama was Mike Walker's *The Dark House* (2003). This play featured three separate characters within the same story (they are all trapped in a haunted building) and after a fixed, opening five minutes to establish the story, the listeners were able to vote via phone or text message for the character they wanted to focus upon. Every three minutes, the votes were collated and the character who received the most votes became the protagonist until the next democratically elected 'shift'. The play was really three simultaneous scripts, but on the day of broadcast was crafted into a single, experiential drama by the listeners. In 2010, BBC Radio 3 broadcast Graham White's adaptation of B. S. Johnson's *The Unfortunates*. Johnson's novel was published in 1969 in the form of a box with loose chapters inside. Although the first and last chapter need to be read in their specific location, the other 25 chapters can be read in any random order. *The Unfortunates* takes place in a single day (like another masterpiece of experimental writing, James Joyce's *Ulysses* (1922)) and is about a football journalist who arrives in a strange city to report on a match, only to discover that he knows the place well, as it was here that he met a now deceased friend. The necessarily randomized structure permits a switching between past memories and the present. The radio broadcast played the adaptation in a fixed sequence (albeit one that was decided at random prior to broadcast) but the online presence after the broadcast permitted the adaptation to come into its own in a way that returned to Johnson's original intention. Once it was placed online, the listener could choose the adapted chapters in whatever order they preferred, although the titles of 'First Part' and 'Z Final Part' were clear signposts as to when they should be listened to. The voice of the narrator (Martin Freeman) dominates, and yet there are highly effective sequences of dialogue and a constant awareness of environment and setting through a meticulous sound design and Mary Peate's well-paced direction. Overall, however, the BBC's forays into interactive drama are fairly sporadic.

There have been other examples of online audio interactivity aside from the BBC. For example, the online music streaming site Spotify (launched in 2008) offers a vast collection of recordings that can be selected and queued individually or as part of a 'radio' function. Although predominantly music, there are some examples of spoken word tracks, including historical speeches and classic examples of radio drama. In 2010, Spotify was used as a forum for an innovative type of drama best described as an interactive audio novel. The British novelist Joe Stretch and the music group Hurts co-created *Don't Let Go* in which the actor Anna Friel narrates a story accompanied by a backing soundtrack and song extracts by the band. The 'chapters' are effectively short tracks – rarely over two minutes – and the listener makes choices regarding which path to follow by typing specific codes into the Spotify search engine. The choices may seem mundane (e.g. whether to wear a gray three-piece suit or a turquoise dress; or whether to play the party game *Twister* or enter a carnival Tunnel of Love) but there are always consequences to the decisions taken. The work is an evocative thriller in which you, as the protagonist, are attempting to save the human race from the diabolical Guy Lockhart, who is attempting to destroy existence as we know it with his 'heartbreak cocktail'. There are many ways to die in *Don't Let Go* and this generic choice of the thriller is important as a way to keep the listener engaged enough to keep listening and to keep typing in the codes. Obviously, *Don't Let Go* belongs to a tradition of interactive games (especially computer-based) in which the participant is required to make informed choices or downright lucky guesses in order to progress through what is usually designed to be a compelling and dynamic narrative.

Similar to *Don't Let Go*, and yet more blatantly a game, is *Soul Trapper*, an iPhone game produced by Realtime Associates in 2009. The advertising blurb for the game states,

> Sure, you're good at video games, but how are you at audio challenges? *Soul Trapper* is a unique, richly produced interactive audio drama that's going to challenge your memory, stereo perception and pattern recognition skills by asking you to master audio minigame sequences interwoven into the narrative. (Realtime Associates, 2009)

Soul Trapper strives to make us re-evaluate the 'invisible' sense of hearing, so often taken for granted. Our culture is visually dominated, and yet sound, too, is ubiquitous. In contemporary gaming, sound is an extremely important feature, but often as a way to create atmosphere, depth and rhythm or, at worst, as a kind of 'filler' for the visual spectacle. After all, traditionally, games are visual. The *Soul Trapper* game tests our aural sense inasmuch as the game is about *listening*.

Small-scale audio drama companies

Despite these examples of interactive experimentation, perhaps the essence of audio drama in the digital age is not to be found in the work of corporations. Writing in the late 1990s, Tim Crook stated, '(The) Internet expands the democratic potential of freedom of expression in writing and art in broadcasting. It clearly extends public access to mass communication and participation in the public sphere' (Crook, 1999, p. 41). If anything, the truth of Crook's statement has become more evident in our own time. The culture of downloads, file sharing and podcasts has created a wealth of access to audio art, whether collections of historical material or all-new works for listeners. Moreover, as Crook suggests, the internet has created a forum for the creation and consumption of audio drama. There are countless small-scale groups and companies that are producing a new generation of radio drama, many of which can be listened to as live streams via their own websites or as freely downloadable podcasts. For audio creators at the vanguard of this, such as Robert Arnold of Chatterbox Audio Theater, it is a thrilling time:

> I would like to see nothing less than the revival of audio theater as a popular art form. For the first time since the advent of TV, there's a real possibility of that happening. The internet has blown the doors wide open. It's a wonderful time to be a creative artist. We can reach people directly and communicate as though they're in the same room with us. (Arnold, 2010)

Hugh Chignell warns that there is a 'danger that all that is produced is the work of the highly esoteric amateur' (Chignell, 2009, p. 43), and although there are some poorly produced (and even troubling) materials available, there is much that is gold dust. To an extent, it is like a return to the early era and golden age of US radio, as there is a prolific amount of work being produced, some of it conventional and some of it experimental.

Significantly, one of the key challenges in the contemporary audio industry is financial. The majority of downloadable audio drama tends to be free. In fact, for many creators this is a necessity, given the volume of work available; it is difficult to expect a listener to pay when there is a vast amount of equivalent drama that is freely available. For this reason, many free audio companies are driven by a passion for the form; in interviews, producers of free audio drama frequently talk about how 'fun' it is to create their work. It probably has to be, as there would be little incentive otherwise. However, the financial challenge often becomes a very real one for audio companies, and a variety of solutions have been attempted. Some have attempted to charge for all downloads or restrict acquisition to CD-only format. Other companies feature 'donation' or 'members only' options or have attempted to sell merchandise (such as T-shirts) promoting the audio drama from their websites. It is also clear that some companies are even hoping to sell their work as film or television adaptations building on the success of the audio versions. As Mariele Runacre Temple (artistic director of the Wireless Theatre Company) explains, the 'free' dimension to the podcasters' work is simultaneously the sector's best friend and worst enemy. She also outlines the future direction of her company's website, essentially a mixture of free and purchase-only recordings:

> It is probably our biggest attraction, and also our biggest problem. Our passion for spreading the word of radio drama is what made us decide to make our plays free, and it has certainly been a big factor in making us so popular. However, it also means we don't generate an income! We have a donations button, which some people are generous enough to use, but not many, and we make some money from our live recordings [some recordings take place in theatres with a paying audience], but as you can imagine there isn't a huge amount of money coming in (and lots going out!). So, our kid's site's downloads unfortunately will not be free, and we will be launching a small paid section of plays on the Wireless Theatre Company website. We will still be known for free radio drama, but hopefully with a small income we can make even more radio productions for everyone's enjoyment. (Runacre Temple, 2010).

Donations are limited, and although some revenue is brought in through audiences attending performances (in other words, through combining audio drama with another art form: live theatre), the outgoing costs of producing audio drama and running the website have compelled a mixed mode of mainly free, but some paid, plays. David Accampo (of Habit Forming Films, LLC and co-creator of the podcast audio drama *Wormwood*), strikes a similar note when he discusses the future plans for his company:

> As producers, we'd like to find a way to keep telling stories and entertaining our audience, but to be brutally honest we also have to really consider the cost. We used the internet because we knew we could reach everyone with our stories. The trade-off is that creating dramas for 'small-scale internet radio' is essentially a hobby. I don't mean that as a slight to any of the great producers out there, but the reality is we've yet to successfully monetize this creative venture, and that's something we'll have to consider as we move forward. (Accampo, 2010)

Small-scale audio drama is seen here as a 'hobby' dependant on the passion of its creators. Certainly, the web has plenty of examples of audio drama that has foundered, forced to terminate despite the high ambitions for longevity boldly asserted in the extant episodes. Often, one assumes, this is because of financial reasons or because the creators discover how demanding it can be to deliver one episode, let alone a long-running series. If the problem is an economic one, the risk is that for many in the sector, audio drama will have to remain a sideline, not a 'day job', until a financial solution is discovered. Julie Hoverson, director of podcast drama company 19 Nocturne Boulevard, describes the current nature of the industry as she perceives it:

> There are plenty of people who dabble a toe, or try an amateur production or two (and then realize how much work it turns out to be and run away), or who are 'just in it for the fun'. There are, however, a number of us who are trying to pull away from the 'amateur' label, despite being unpaid (since that is one of the criteria for being an 'amateur') and bring this genre back to its professional roots. Not that there's anything wrong with amateurs – this is a lovely fun thing to do as a hobby – just that we all tend to get lumped in together, and all seen as some variety of vanity press. (Hoverson, 2011)

As Hoverson stresses, there are a number of companies who are striving to change the perception of the form so that it is not regarded as being quirkily amateur or even, most negatively, as an example of 'vanity press'. Despite the economic and 'perceived status' challenges, Kyle Hatley of Chatterbox Audio Theater is more optimistic, and he highlights the rich period we are in: 'as long as people are downloading and using the internet, we'll be fine' (Hatley, 2010). Jeffrey Adams of Icebox Radio Theater also draws our attention to the era we are in:

> Many new technologies are being dumped on the public at an ever-increasing rate. More media means more pictures, but it also means more audio. I have far more options for listening due to podcasting and internet radio than I did say twenty years ago when my listening choices were limited to local radio and recordings (CDs and tapes). And what pop culture image says '21st Century' more than an iPod? Yes, I know, most of them feature visuals now, but I think the iPod is still, first and foremost, a music player. (Adams, 2010)

Among contemporary producers, the consensus seems to be that the great coup is to get people to realize the advantages of audio drama. We cannot always be watching screens, and sometimes listening to music is neither appropriate nor desirable. It is therefore a question of getting listeners to understand, as it were, that their iPods are not just music players, but can contain audio drama, too. Certainly, many in the contemporary podcast scene feel that there is a growing interest in audio drama. This will, inevitably, lead to a higher profile for the form and for the companies that produce it. The growing ambition and confidence of small-scale audio drama groups is reflected in initiatives such as *Transcontinental Terror: An Express Train to Audio Horror* in October 2010. The project was a collaborative effort by six international audio companies (the Wireless Theatre Company; Electric Vicuna Productions; FinalRune Productions; Chatterbox Audio Theater; Icebox Radio Theater; and the Willamette Radio Workshop). Each company produced an hour-long audio play, resulting in a six-hour stream of audio drama appropriate for Halloween. The companies approached the genre of horror audio in their own ways, which ranged from pre-recorded and edited plays, to fully live performances. The project thus retained each company's preferred style (and even ethos), while being part of a complex collaboration.

It is also worth noting that the small-scale audio drama community can find a valuable and beneficial niche which can challenge the traditional models of the industry. Tim Heffernan is the organizer of The Drama Pod, a website dedicated to producing and disseminating free audio podcasts with a special interest in audio readings. Heffernan's account of the immediate plans for The Drama Pod give us an interesting insight into the free audio drama industry:

> We have recently contacted visually impaired centres that provide audio entertainment for their clients. We hope to offer them not only some of our original work, but we will also engage in classic literature as well. I have made many contacts with other podcasters who specialize in audio entertainment, and we will be able to provide thousands of hours of high quality audio for free. We also hope to turn professional and provide high quality audio books at low prices. I find it quite ridiculous that several audio books are being sold at a higher retail price than the books themselves. (Heffernan, 2010)

We see here that one company from the free-audio-drama industry is interested in increasing its social impact by providing the visually impaired with new audio and adaptations of classic works. It is also interesting that they are planning to move from amateur to professional status and challenge the audio book industry, which Heffernan perceives as being overcostly.

It is worth mentioning at this point that not all audio drama companies approach the medium in the same way. Indeed, one of the exciting things about the contemporary podcast scene is the range of approaches to drama one can find. The diversity of genre and form to be found in traditional radio is fully reflected in podcasts – and more besides. In addition, the issue of practice and methodology is an interesting one. The science fiction audio drama *The Leviathan Chronicles* has succeeded in recruiting an international cast, partly through the use of the remote recording of performers. The voices of the various actors are then edited together in the creation of the drama. Shows such as the 'zombie podcast' *We're Alive* also emerges out of many more hours in the postproduction suite than in the recording studio. However, the show is always recorded 'theatrically' inasmuch as the ensemble is recorded together in the same studio: in fact, this has become a governing principle of the programme. However, the subsequent complex and lengthy editing process adds detailed layers of sound design to the show. Other companies deliberately approach the production of audio drama following the paradigm of the early days of radio. Consider how Jeffrey Adams, the director of Icebox Radio Theater, describes his company's methodology:

> I think we are, perhaps, a bit old-fashioned in our approach to production. My background is in newspapers and journalism, and I find deadlines to be very stimulating. So the Icebox Radio Theater has been designed more like an old time radio show, which had to meet the deadline of production or suffer real consequences. In truth, we probably could miss a podcast deadline or two without many consequences, but the Show Must Go On, and that's how we approach production. In this way, I think we aim to capture the spirit and feel of live theater while still producing a work of recorded art which can be enjoyed again and again. (Adams, 2010)

Essentially, the adoption of the pioneer model equates to a more theatrical approach, which includes the primacy of the deadline and the compelled focus and adrenaline rush that accompany that. Robert Arnold of Chatterbox Audio Theater extols the virtues of ensemble production: 'We enjoy the thrill of performance that comes from everyone working together. Our actors can play off one another, and that often creates a real magic in the room' (Arnold, 2010). His colleague Marques W. Brown further emphasizes the importance of 'liveness':

> We at Chatterbox always try to present all of the sound effects and music live, in the moment, rather than editing them in post-production. This can make for messiness at times, but it also forces us to rehearse, explore, and edit throughout the creative process. We use many old stand-bys of classic radio sound-effect productions and

> Foley artists, but are also always exploring with new sounds and ideas to create the perfect effect for the given need. Also the use of live musicians, whom we typically use live and in the studio, adds another element and depth of collaboration and creation. (Brown, 2010)

From these perspectives, liveness is not only about deadlines; it also has a direct impact on aesthetics, forcing a great deal to be achieved at the point of production/creation. By implication, this can sometimes make the production process difficult, but it is instrumental in creating audio drama that meets the standards the company is aiming at. We should also note that Chatterbox Audio Theater is not entirely 'purist' about practical methodology: as Brown reveals, the company is perfectly happy to explore new methods if that will optimize the work.

The UK-based Wireless Theatre Company is another contemporary audio drama group that combines the advantages of the theatrical approach with the benefits of pre-recorded sound technology, as the company's artistic director explains:

> The Wireless Theatre Company works in a traditional way, in a studio. Unlike the heyday of radio drama production, realistic sound effects are much more readily available as pre-recorded MP3 files, which does mean a lot of our fx are added in post-production. Some people feel that this perhaps removes some of the magic of radio drama (the Foley guy carefully treading out the footsteps in a tray of gravel in the studio) but I disagree – there is still a lot of magic to be created by mixing and changing sfx in post. In our live recordings, for the visual enjoyment of the audience, we do perform as many of the fx live as we can – although there are certain things (like explosions, pirates attacking, things turning to stone – to name but a few) that simply can't be created live. With the advances in editing, we also have advances on the fx possible with radio drama. We can create anything through sound! (Runacre Temple, 2010)

Part of the Wireless Theatre Company's activities includes offering workshops for schools. This is an important aspect to the work of many contemporary audio drama companies and can presumably assist with enhancing profile and, in some cases, revenue. Chatterbox Audio Theater has even created the specific role of education director. The current post-holder, Marques W. Brown, articulates his aspirations:

> I want to see audio drama become a more popular tool for teaching. The potential to use this form of media to enhance the curriculum of schoolchildren is beyond limits. Even in a world of technology that allows us to see other people's creations in high definition, multi-dimensional quality and enhancement, the world of audio is still one

> that intrigues, grabs hold, and allows the mind's eye to create and comprehend. The theater of the mind is powerful, and I would argue that the classroom of the mind has great potential as well. (Brown, 2010)

In addition to a specific educational function, some audio drama groups emphasize their community role. One such example is Icebox Radio Theater, established in International Falls, Minnesota, in 2004 by the writer Jeffrey Adams. The Icebox Radio Theater has produced a large body of work available as podcasts across a range of popular and traditional genres, including comedy, superheroes and horror. In its mission statement, the company explains,

> The Icebox Radio Theater exists as an education and charitable and literary group dedicated to the study, practice and production of radio theater and the related arts to include, but not to be limited to script writing, production, acting, sound effects, music composition and directing. We strive to provide quality radio theater programs and related events for the greater enjoyment and appreciation of the people of International Falls, its surrounding communities and the general public. (Icebox Radio Theater, 2011)

The mission statement reveals a dynamic whereby the work of the company has an impact on the local community as well as being accessible to a wider, potentially international, audience. Audio drama can have the ability to function locally and globally at the same time. As well as having outreach into schools, there can be other social and participatory impacts. After all, community participation does not just mean being part of an audience; it can mean playing an active role in the creative process. As Chatterbox Audio Theater's Robert Arnold reveals,

> Chatterbox is a community theater, and we rely heavily on our community. The final recording is the most important thing, but it's not the ONLY important thing. The process is part of the experience. We like to bring in creative people and challenge them to do something they've never done; to perform in a new medium, to interact with others using an interesting voice (or three or four), to contort themselves to perform multiple sound effects at the same time. It's a large part of the charm of what we do, and a large part of the fun. You can't get that in an isolation booth – at least not to the same extent. (Arnold, 2010)

As we have seen, contemporary audio drama can be high-tech or traditionally theatrical, and sometimes it can mix both. It can have a direct impact on its local community (including through direct participation) and can build an audience within the studio, the local community or globally. The educational and social impact of audio drama is perhaps most powerfully evident when it comes to radio drama-for-development.

Radio drama-for-development

Drama has a great propensity to tell us something about our own lives. It allows us to engage with 'real', sometimes difficult, issues of everyday life, but in a detached way; we can observe, judge, or speculate about how we would react, and apply these insights to our own situation. Soap opera is an instantly recognizable example. The glossy ABC television soap opera *Desperate Housewives* (2004 onwards) portrays the lives of the women of Wisteria Lane, an impossibly perfect suburban street where, paradoxically, the characters lead extremely imperfect lives, blighted by bankruptcy, alcohol addiction, child neglect, domestic violence, unwanted pregnancy and infidelity. The scenarios presented often contain subtle, or unsubtle, moral messages for the audience: don't drink too much, or your family and friends will despise you; don't live beyond your means, or you will lose your house and become an internet porn star (yes – really!). Clearly, *Desperate Housewives*' main purpose is to entertain, rather than provide information. But it is easy to see how drama can be manipulated as a means of influencing behaviour to bring about positive social change.

Throughout radio's history, radio drama has been considered to be an efficient and effective way of informing listeners in an entertaining way. The question is who decides what information listeners need to receive? From the outset, state and public service radio have been manipulated by governments, religious groups and aid organizations to disseminate information deemed to be for the 'good' of listeners. While recent radio innovations, such as community radio, are more democratic and participatory in nature, in many cases they struggle to break free from the top-down modes of production which persist in radio. The growth of radio drama as vehicle for development must be positioned within the wider contexts of the evolution of radio, generally, and the shifting approaches to development communication that have taken place over the course of the twentieth and twenty-first centuries.

The earliest nation–state radio stations, such as the BBC in the United Kingdom, were strongly committed to the betterment of listeners – to educate, entertain and inform them – and this ethos persists to this day. Though US radio stations were less centrally controlled, a similar ethos existed (About the BBC, 2010 and About NBC, 2010). Early radio stations were paternalistic in style and, particularly in the case of the BBC, were frequently a mouthpiece of the respective government. Throughout the world's troubled colonial history, radio has often been used as a means of imposing the philosophy of the dominant power on colonized nations. By the mid 1940s, the BBC was broadcasting in 34 languages worldwide (BBC World Service History, 2010), a clear signal that the British government wished to promote its ideologies directly to its colonies in Africa, India and Asia. As well as expanding broadcasts from London, the BBC supported the development of radio stations in the colonies themselves, which improved the dissemination of messages from Britain, but also had clear remit of contributing to the 'betterment' of indigenous populations:

> It was the colonial governments of the dependent territories, with their large black and brown populations who showed greatest interest in imperial broadcasting. Bearing no electoral obligations, they could indulge in the luxury of theorising over the dissemination of British values, consolidating the Empire through a set of aural symbols and using the medium to spread such benefits to education, hygiene (and) good agricultural practices. (MacKenzie 1987, p. 37, quoted in Kerr, 1998 p. 113)

This rather 'top down' approach, sometimes called 'cultural imperialism', characterizes how media was used for development in the first half of the twentieth century (McPhail, 2009, p. 24). Cultural imperialism was much in evidence in Africa in the 1940s, where radio was controlled by the British Administration and used to broadcast programmes, including radio drama, with clear moral messages. Commenting on the development of the Central African Broadcasting Services (CABS), Kerr argues that the new radio stations which had been established in the colonies generally followed the top-down information dissemination approaches practiced by the BBC. However, he goes on to describe a model for radio drama-for-development which, in some ways, has yet to be bettered. The CABS had an enlightened policy of employing Africans alongside Europeans. African approaches to storytelling and entertainment were interwoven with European methods to produce radio drama containing development information, but which were also accessible because they drew upon the cultural traditions of the audience. One example of this is the radio drama *Mwa Shimwamba Kapolo*, which was heavily influenced by the BBC radio soap opera *The Archers*. Between 1950 and 1972, *The Archers* was essentially drama-for-development, with a remit to inform listeners of the latest farming techniques (About *The Archers*, 2010). In a wonderful subversion of cultural imperialism, the producer of *Mwa Shimwamba Kapolo* 'read the scenarios to the cast under a tree outside the studio, where the play itself was created through improvisation' (Kerr, 1998, pp. 113–70).

These enlightened approaches were difficult to sustain when the colonies gained independence and direct European support for the emerging nations' media decreased. McPhail (2009, p. 2) identifies the Second World War as the turning point at which the 'economic and cultural elites based in the Northern Hemisphere' took up the cause to 'improve the lives and lot of inhabitants of the peripheral regions of the world'. Harry S. Truman, president of the United States between 1945 and 1953, is credited by McPhail with leading the push to assist in the development of poorer nations: 'More than half the people of the world are living in conditions approaching misery . . . Their economic life is primitive and stagnant. Their poverty is a handicap and a threat to them and to more prosperous areas' (Truman, 1949, p. 5, quoted in McPhail, 2009, p. 4). It is clear from this statement that the motivations of the superpower governments were not entirely philanthropic. The perceived lack of productivity in poorer countries was seen as a threat to developed nations as well as to poor ones. Radio was a key way in which the citizens of poorer countries could be 'educated' to become more productive.

Direct European government intervention in newly independent countries waned, but its influence persisted through the work of European aid agencies and non-government organizations (NGOs), who also disseminated their development messages through radio. To begin with, this approach was generally unsuccessful. For example, in India, development messages about productive farming techniques were broadcast without any attempt to make them relevant to audiences – and had no impact, as a result (Jayaprakash and Shoesmith, 2007, p. 45). Gradually, an alternative to this kind of overt cultural imperialism emerged; a model which was more receptive to the needs of audience itself, rather than the 'owner' of the message. This model is known as 'entertainment-education', sometimes called 'edutainment' or E-E.

E-E: Entertainment-education

'Entertainment-education' is described by Arvind Singhal and Everett M. Rogers thus:

> The process of purposively designing and implementing a media message both to entertain and educate in order to increase audience members' knowledge about an education issue, create favourable attitudes and change overt behaviour (Singhal and Rogers, 2004, p. 5).

One of the most widely acclaimed examples of E-E is *Soul City*, a multimedia project which includes a TV and radio series. The project is run by the Soul City Institute for Heath and Development Communications, 'one of the world's most influential social and behavioural change programmes' (Soul City Institute, 2007, p. 12), based in South Africa. The series was established in 1994 and claims to reach (through multimedia) an impressive 87 per cent of the population of South Africa. Each series is themed to cover various health and development issues 'with the aim to empower audiences to make healthy choices – both as individuals and as communities' (Communication Initiative Network, 2010). The project is particularly successful because the story lines are not message-driven and have been developed in an inclusive way, with strong input from listeners as well as health professionals. Susan Goldstein et al. (2005, p. 481) claim that the model which has been employed in *Soul City*, drawing on theories of health promotion, policy environment, community action and services, has strengthened and broadened the intervention. There are numerous other examples attesting to the success of the E-E model and an indicative sample follows. In Vietnam, radio drama was one of the methods used to encourage farmers to use less pesticide sprays on crops, resulting in 50 per cent reduction in pesticide use (Heong et al., 1998, p. 413). In 2000, the government of Botswana worked with the United States Centers for Disease Control and Prevention to develop a radio serial drama to encourage safer sexual practices and HIV testing. The hypothesis was that if listeners identified with the characters in the drama, they would be more likely to be influenced by their behaviour. One of the main characters in the drama had undertaken a HIV test and the research uncovered that the listeners who named that character as their favourite were twice as likely to take a HIV test themselves (Pappas-DeLuca et al., 2008, pp. 486–503). David O. Poindexter's excellent chapter on the history of E-E in *Entertainment Education and Social Change: History, Research and Practice* gives a comprehensive historical overview and many more examples of the E-E model in action (Singhal et al., 2004, pp. 20–37).

Entertainment-education is widely regarded as a successful model, but there are limits to its successful implementation. It is relatively expensive to produce radio drama, and it could be argued that other radio formats, such as interviews or a straight 'talk' on the subject, could be just as successful in terms of disseminating the development message (de Fossard and Riber, 2005, p. 19). The choice and treatment of the message, too, can be difficult to negotiate. Some topics, such as reproductive health, may be too sensitive within some cultures to broadcast on radio at all. The prominence of the message within the drama can be contentious, as was the case when an E-E drama was established at a BBC local radio station in the United Kingdom. For the health professionals, the message was of paramount importance. For the broadcaster, the quality of the programme took precedence and the message was of less importance (Dickinson, 1995, p. 421). Furthermore, it can be complex to measure the impact that radio drama has on development. Funders may expect to see tangible results that can be attributed to the radio drama intervention. Exactly how many people have taken a HIV test because of a particular radio campaign? As is the case with *Soul City*, radio is often just one part of a much bigger campaign to raise awareness of the development issue. In addition, effective radio drama-for-development stimulates debate within communities, which is an important by-product of the intervention and ensures that it has wide resonance. Such variables can make it extremely complex, if not impossible, to make a direct causal link between the radio drama and any behaviour change that occurs as a result.

While entertainment-education is by far the most widely articulated and successful model for the production of radio drama-for-development, it does not propose a particular role for listeners, beyond the consumption of radio drama. Singhal attributes this to the 'one way nature of mass media interventions' (Singhal et al., 2004, p. 397). He calls on media producers to draw on the work of development communications researchers and practitioners who, since the 1970s, have been advocating more participatory approaches. Paulo Friere, a Brazilian politician and educator, was a leading critic of the top-down, paternalistic approach to development. He argued that positive social change is best achieved by empowering communities to identify and deal with their own problems (Friere, 2006). A key way in which communities can take control of their own development is through community radio. Though community radio defies a single definition, it can generally be summarized as serving a relatively small audience which shares a common geographical location or interest, democratically managed, not for profit and with a remit of actively encouraging participation from the community it serves (AMARC, 2010). Radio drama-for-development has new possibilities in this context. Whereas a radio drama on a national radio station is necessarily geared to majority mass audience, community radio drama can be very specifically oriented towards the development needs of a minority group. This might include covering issues that are very particular to a community or producing radio drama in minority languages. For example, a community radio drama in Burkino Faso covered issues related to HIV and polygamy, which made it culturally relevant to that country. The drama was also produced in the local indigenous language, rather than French, which made it more widely understood in that community (Fisher, 2009). Some community radio drama projects are founded on consultation with their listeners, responding to the issues that listeners themselves raise. For example, the storylines for *Urunana* (*Hand in Hand*), a radio soap opera in Rwanda, are informed by informal interviews with audience groups (Kyagambiddwa, Uwamariya, 2004). Story Workshop, an organization that works in Malawi on radio drama initiatives, uses several methods to maximize audience involvement. It runs over 60 radio listener clubs in the country, which contribute to story ideas and evaluate the effectiveness of its radio drama. Its 'action research' team gathers feedback from rural communities by letter, focus-group discussion and interview to ensure that the needs of the most remote communities are reflected in the drama (Story Workshop, 2010). The International Institute for Environment and Development has developed a 'Powertool for Interactive Radio Drama'. It discusses further ways in which listeners can be encouraged to participate in policy planning through radio drama, such as contributing to a 'phone in' with a panel of experts following the drama (Apte, 2005).

Despite the increase in community radio and its opportunities for participation, these examples show that audience involvement does tend to be limited. Listeners can offer their views both before and after the drama has been produced, but there is little evidence that they take part in the processes of production. The opportunities for listeners to be empowered by their participation in radio drama are therefore restricted. This can be explained by the dominance of 'professional' radio drama production techniques within community radio. For instance, the BBC model for radio drama involves a writer, producer, actors and technicians. The production process is hierarchical and complex; the script is prepared in advance, rehearsed, recorded in a specialized studio and edited before broadcast. Despite the obvious drawbacks, this model is often replicated in radio drama-for-development. It is disappointing that a democratic and participatory model for community radio drama production has not yet emerged. Radio drama does not need to be complex. Scripting is not necessary, as drama can be improvised. Much of the technical complexity arises because radio drama is recorded in advance of broadcast, but it is perfectly possible to produce radio drama 'live', including using 'live' sound effects and music. These minor adjustments to the production process would maximize opportunities for participation at all levels.

In contrast, participatory approaches to theatre are well developed and have been effectively documented. For example, Zakes Mda (1993) describes the evolution of theatre-for-development from an African perspective. Traditional storytelling and entertainment have been incorporated into 'popular theatre' involving the whole community and utilized as a means of communicating development messages. Mda goes on to discuss how Friere's participatory model enabled audiences to identify development issues for themselves and to articulate and propose solutions to the challenges they faced. This model informed Augusto Boal's 'forum' theatre approach, which broke down the barriers between producers and audiences (Mda, 1993, pp. 10–18). Forum theatre is perhaps the ultimate example of participatory drama. Actors become 'spect-actors' and can stop the drama at any point, taking over the role of a character and influencing the direction of the storyline. In this way, spect-actors take control of events in the drama, an act which resonates with everyday life and empowers them to manage real situations more effectively (Boal, 1996, pp. 224–33).

Ironically, it appears that new modes of distribution for radio drama-for-development have created the best opportunities for participation. The structures and production methods of traditional radio can be radically subverted in an online environment, and there are many examples of participatory audio drama-for-development. For example, in the United Kingdom, a group of prisoners took part in improvised radio drama as a rehabilitation project called *A Journey Through Drugs* (English Wordplay, 2010). A further example is *Out Of The Gate* (2009), an online audio soap opera created by young scriptwriters, some of whom are ex-offenders, from different parts of London, which aims to illustrate the problems faced by a young person leaving prison. Mobile phones are also proving to be a good means of distributing drama-for-development. *THMBNLS* is an interactive soap which aims to reduce teenage pregnancy and sexually transmitted diseases in 15- to 18-year-olds. It calls on the audience to interact with the cast, which is drawn from youth groups in London (Department for Children, Schools and Families, 2009). Though *THMBNLS* is visual as well as audio, it provides a model that could easily be adapted to audio only.

These drama-for-development projects have great value and will certainly contribute greatly to debates about the evolution of drama-for-development. However, mobile and internet technologies do not yet effectively penetrate the world's poorest countries. For example, in Rwanda, only around 4 per cent of the population has access to the internet, and 24 per cent subscribe to a mobile phone (UN Data, 2009). Radio is still the most widely accessible media in the world and in times of crisis, such as the Haitian earthquake in 2010, forms the most immediate connection between victim and aid (Radio Conventions, 2010). For the foreseeable future, radio drama has an important role to play in development. Singhal is optimistic that entertainment-education will 'evolve, grow and reinvent itself, [and that] participatory strategies for empowering the underdogs will increasingly find a more central place in the E-E discourse' (Singhal et al., 2004, p. 397). The challenge for the radio drama-for-development producers of the future is to create a truly participatory model for radio drama: a model which overturns the top-down tendencies of radio, an enhanced entertainment-education model which is informed by the successes of participatory approaches in theatre.

Exercise

- Explore the web and forums such as iTunes and iTunesU to see the kind of audio drama that is available. What kind of styles and genre does podcast drama explore and what does this imply about audience? How do companies or artists describe their own work in 'mission statements' or 'program descriptions'? Can you use this to categorize current work and approaches?
- Write a plan for a fully participatory radio drama-for-development project which will have an impact in your local area. Remember that participation can take place at all levels, from identifying the development issue, through all aspects of radio drama production, to listener feedback.

Case study: *We're Alive: A Story of Survival* (2009 onwards)

Modern Myth Productions' *We're Alive: A Story of Survival* is aptly described by its creators as 'The Zombie Podcast' and is an audio drama that is available as a podcast via iTunes and through a variety of other audio forums on the show's website (http://www.zombiepodcast.com). This serialized drama is set in an apocalyptic Los Angeles where a disparate group of survivors struggle to keep alive in the face of a multitude of zombies as well as other living rivals fighting for the remnants and fragments of a crumbling civilization. From that short description, it is evident that *We're Alive* emerges from the popular culture industry of zombie horror which has seen a wealth of films and other cultural manifestations. The milestone achievement in the modern zombie genre is George A. Romero's *Night of the Living Dead* (1968), a simple and low-budget film which remains the quintessential survival horror movie: a group of people thrown together by circumstance try to survive in an isolated house which is besieged by the reanimated bodies of the recently dead who want to cannibalize the living. *Night of the Living Dead* develops a tremendous level of suspense, not simply because of the deadly menace beyond the crudely barricaded doors and windows, but also because of the complex interrelationships and conflicts between the survivors themselves. Romero's paradigm has been further developed in various sequels, remakes, tributes and parodies. Nevertheless, it is worth stating that the scenario of the doomed siege finds a precedent in legends such as the siege of Troy; pre-existing fiction such as Richard Matheson's vampire novel *I Am Legend* (1954) and André de Lorde and Eugène Morel's Grand-Guignol stage play *La Dernière Torture* (*The Ultimate Torture*, 1904); and even, of course, genuine historical events such as the 'against all odds' attempts to defend the Alamo (1836) or the grain silo in Stalingrad (1942). However, Romero's introduction of flesh-eating zombies into the siege narrative is a key moment. In addition to countless films which would be hard to imagine existing without the achievement of *Night of the Living Dead*, the influence can be traced through other media away from cinema, including popular fiction, comic books, and games (whether digital, role-playing or board). In our time, the 'living dead' zombie has become one of the most eminent icons of horror, pervasive in contemporary popular culture.

We're Alive is an example of zombie culture in the realm of audio drama. There have been precedents for this in the golden age of horror radio in shows such as *Lights Out* and *The Shadow*. In the fertile territory of podcasting, there have been examples of zombie audio such as Necropolis Studio Productions' five-part *Age of the Zombies* (2009–10) and *One Eighteen: Migration* (2008 onwards), which is essentially a richly constructed audio prose fiction about survivors of the zombie pandemic. Although the principle of a first-person narrator reading out from a detailed 'journal' dominates each episode of *One Eighteen: Migration*, the program can feature a mixture of voices to articulate dialogue, and the program utilizes a detailed soundscape, including the sound of the pen scribbling the journal entries, music, heartbeats and sound effects. *We're Alive* is more authentically an audio drama. Like *One Eighteen: Migration*, *We're Alive* has achieved longevity. While films might be anything from 90 minutes to two hours in duration, and if there are sequels there might be months or years in between, *We're Alive* has established a disciplined and consistent output and presence. The first series commenced in May 2009 and concluded in April 2010. The drama was structured into twelve chapters, each divided into three parts (except the final chapter – 'The War' – which was in four parts). The parts of each chapter varied in duration from 13 minutes to 27 minutes. The resulting 37 chapter 'parts' creates an epic saga that is many hours in duration. The economic partition of each chapter permits a tight focus and a dramatic pace designed to keep the listeners hooked. Furthermore, the comparatively short parts typically utilize cliffhangers designed to ensure that the audience listens to the next episode. To this end, the nearest parallel to *We're Alive* in contemporary zombie culture is Robert Kirkman's epic comic book series *The Walking Dead* (2003 onwards), which was adapted into a successful television series (2010 onwards). *We're Alive* is a distinctive achievement in audio drama, and the regular output and quantity of the show has created a body of work rich for analysis.

The core creative team behind *We're Alive* comprises Kc Wayland and Shane Salk. Interestingly, neither was trained in radio before inaugurating *We're Alive*. Wayland was educated in film production, and Salk was trained as a theatre actor and has used his training for stage roles, stand-up comedy and screen work. Wayland has created numerous films as writer, producer and director, including a feature-length documentary, *365 Boots on Ground* (2005), about his time serving in the US military during the Iraq War (2003–10). The combination of Wayland's writing/directing skill and Salk's acting experience proved to be a compelling mixture when they moved from screen and stage modes into, for them, the new forum of audio drama. However, it is worth noting that although Salk did not have professional experience of audio drama, he was an avid listener of vintage radio drama recordings, citing *Gunsmoke* (1952–61) as a particular favourite. This gave him an instinct in the developmental stage of *We're Alive* as to what would 'work' as audio. This is especially important given that Wayland (as lead scriptwriter) has an idiosyncratic approach to writing audio drama:

> I write it exactly like I would a screenplay. Some people go for older formats like they did for radio – very line by line. But I find that to get a really good flow of the scene, script format for films and feature films is the best technical way of getting those things across. (Wayland, 2010)

Evidently, even if the scripts begin like this, they are carefully refined into audio drama. Although Salk has a key role in achieving this, he nonetheless sums up *We're Alive* as 'a movie that you listen to' (Salk, 2010). This phrase is reminiscent of the description of *3dhorrorfi* as 'cinema in your head' that we saw earlier.

Although Wayland mentions that he admires classic radio such as the *Mercury Theater on the Air* 'War of the Worlds' adaptation and his co-creator Salk's favourite *Gunsmoke* series, his own key influences are not audio works. The film director Wayland most admires is Frank Darabont, and especially his work *The Mist* (2007) – the screen adaptation of Stephen King's 1980 novella – which Wayland regards as one of the greatest horror movies ever made. Significantly, *The Mist* is not about zombies, but an array of increasingly grotesque and indistinct creatures that lurk in the mist of the title. The desperate human survivors hole up in a supermarket, and although they are sporadically attacked by the monsters from the mist, in time their all-too-human fellow survivors prove to be just as lethal. Basic parallels between *The Mist* and *We're Alive* are evident, and yet the scope that a long-running audio series affords has permitted Wayland to develop the scenario into a broader and deeper narrative. Interestingly, since *We're Alive* launched, Frank Darabont was appointed as the director of the television adaptation of *The Walking Dead* (a series which, perhaps for unsurprising reasons, Wayland has decided to avoid watching, given the similar theme (Wayland, 2010)). The other influence that Wayland acknowledges is perhaps more surprising: J. K. Rowling's *Harry Potter* series (1997–2007). For Wayland, *Harry Potter* is 'one of the best stories ever told' (Wayland, 2010), and it is clear that the sense of narrative function and development could be an influential paradigm for anyone developing a long-running audio drama series. Rowling's book series comprises seven novels which develop a single story with many subplots. Numerous characters can come and go while retaining a core 'ensemble' at its heart. Although in some examples of fiction series with recurrent protagonists (whether it is Arthur Conan Doyle's Sherlock Holmes or Richmal Crompton's William Brown), the central characters can remain comfortingly 'fixed' over many years, Harry Potter is permitted to age and change. This is extremely apt in relation to *We're Alive*, in which key characters can develop and evolve radically through the trials of their desperate situation and the various stresses this puts on their physical and mental well-being.

It is clear that Wayland and Salk developed *We're Alive* meticulously. Part of this was an awareness of audience. Wayland knew that it would prove a particular challenge to secure a youth audience who live in a visually-dominated culture and are arguably less attuned to listening (beyond music). The consequence of this is that they may not have the reliance to 'come up with the visuals' themselves and thus have to learn to 're-experience something inside their heads and inside their minds rather than being spoon-fed something (Wayland, 2010). For Salk, the very notion of 'audio drama' risks branding a work as 'arcane':

> It's difficult at first, because people think it's from the 1920s or something, but once people understand what's going on with radio drama, they stick with it. That's to say, they take a risk with it, they check it out and then they get into it. TVs are everywhere, but audio drama is something you can do while jogging, while driving . . . You could call it an 'i-Entertainment'. (Salk, 2010)

To this end, Modern Myth Productions is an interesting example of the new generation of contemporary production companies working in audio podcasting who, resistant to creating audio drama as a kind of museum piece, are endeavouring to pioneer digital audio drama as an 'i-Entertainment' which creates 'movies that you listen to'. Certainly the project seems to be gathering momentum, and after a very modest uptake at the beginning of the series, the website announced that, as of January 2011, *We're Alive* has hit the two-million downloads mark. It is also interesting to note that beyond the show, there is a detailed website which hosts all the episodes for download as well as episode synopses and a discussion forum, and which sells merchandise. In 2011 a fan community podcast (*We're Not Dead*) launched. According to his own informal audience research, Kc Wayland states that *We're Alive* has attracted radio drama aficionados and horror fans who search out anything 'zombie', but apart from these, as it were, 'specialist' listeners, the show has succeeded in securing a growing audience among US high school students more used to Hollywood's big budget 'high-volume special effects' (Wayland, 2010). Audio drama can be extremely cost-effective – as Shane Salk puts it 'You can produce a *lot* of it without a lot of money' (Salk, 2010) – but that is not to say it has to 'sound cheap'. On the contrary, Modern Myth Productions works extremely hard on high production values creating a richly textured soundscape and performance.

We're Alive: The first episode

Chapter 1 of *We're Alive* ('It Begins') uses the character Michael Cross (Jim Gleason) as focalizer. A former sergeant in US military intelligence who undertook tours of duty during the Iraq War, Michael has returned to study at college and remains the key protagonist throughout the series, although, interestingly, on occasion he disappears from the immediate action or exposition of the story. This is particularly significant when in Chapter 8 ('Where Do You Go When You Sleep?') Michael disappears from the plot and does not reappear until Chapter 10 ('Purgatory'). Michael is so integral to the plot it is possible that during this hiatus he has been killed: *unlikely* but nevertheless *possible.* It is possible because *We're Alive* uses a transferring system of narratives. Although Michael leads the saga off, over time we hear from various characters' journals, making them the protagonist at that moment and privileging their point of view. As Shane Salk explains, the device of transferring narratives has strategic and logistical advantages:

> We were really happy when we came up with that. Part of the reason is that the audience is never really *safe*. If Michael was narrating the whole thing it would mean that Michael can't die. It resists letting the audience say 'Michael's my rock'. It gives the audience a sense

> of fear. It also allows for flexibility within the cast, especially as this is a long-running drama. An actor might say I'm moving to Guatemala for eighteen years and we can say 'Okay, we can kill your character off!' (Salk, 2010)

This is Michael's first narration in Chapter 1:

> As I recall, the months leading up to when this all began weren't much to remember. My unit returned home earlier that year from our tour in Iraq. I'd spent 365 on ground working as Military Intelligence. Our group came up with those playing cards you saw on the news: 'The 52 Most Wanted'. I was a hard-charged PFC back then. But that was the first tour. After our third, I was the tired and depressed sergeant. Nothing scared me back then. I didn't fear death or what might be on the other side, if today was my last day. That was then. And this is now. I write this not for anyone to read, but for my own sanity. Maybe if I go over it again from the beginning it might make more sense to me. And then again, maybe not.
>
> SFX: outside, footsteps and voices
>
> I was 27 at the time, and in my fourth year in college. I started my freshman year in 2001: almost eight years ago now. I remember the day as if it was burned into my head. May 8th, 2009.

In less than 200 words, Michael's back story is established in a mixture of both broadly generic and extremely precise detail. We learn his age and the fact that he is just one of many former military personnel returning to ordinary life back home in the United States. However, we learn that he was in military intelligence, and reference is made to a set of playing cards which had photographs of the most wanted figures from the deposed regime: this is a strong visual reference to a genuine historical item that became one of the icons of the Iraq War. Michael's background in the military – and in Iraq specifically – will often be an important point of reference to the narrative as a whole. We are also given an insight into Michael's state of mind: he is jaded and perhaps disillusioned, while his lack of a fear of death reflects that he is tired of life. He also admits that his sanity is being challenged. If he is to be the 'hero' of this saga, he is perhaps an unlikely one. It is also worth noting how the narration establishes the story as 'contemporary': the first episode was broadcast 4 May 2009 and Michael cites 8 May 2009. For a few days, the downloadable episode was about the 'future', but after that it settles into the context of a temporal world parallel to our own.

Immediately after this we are in Michael's college class, and some small talk with classmates reveals that, although Michael is evidently likeable, he keeps his distance. When a female student invites him to a party, he declines, which offends her, to which Michael responds 'I was being direct. How's that being a jerk?' This simple exchange establishes a sense of Michael as both honest and a loner. Soon after he has entered his class, we hear a distant but nonetheless massive explosion resonating through the air. His professor states it is probably just construction work, but Michael knows that the sound is more than that: we, the listeners, have connected with Michael, and knowing his background, we *trust* his reaction to a large detonation. This has all happened in less than 150 seconds of the episode beginning. This represents a remarkable economy, and yet in that short period of time so much has been established about the focal character and the central conceit: enough to propel the show through the months to come. Admittedly, no zombies have emerged yet, but we know that the explosion can only be ominous: 'a bombing or another attack on US soil' as Michael puts it. He and his fellow students catch a television broadcast and see that across Los Angeles and San Diego men and women are attacking and biting each other. Michael is called by Lieutenant Angel (Shane Salk) who summons him to the Army Reserve Center. Caught in a traffic jam on the freeway, Michael sees a pack of 'people' attacking the gridlocked motorists, and when they pull a victim through a shattered windshield – 'like a pack of wild dogs they tore him apart' – we are firmly launched into zombie culture, although the assailants are still described as 'rioters'. In extreme economy, we have moved from Michael's narrative, a class, a news report, to genocide on the freeway. We have been drawn in by Michael's personal account, and now the panorama has become epic.

On arriving at the Army Reserve Center, Michael, Angel and Saul Tink (Nate Geez) argue about what is happening, and the straight-talking Saul causes consternation by describing the rioters as 'zombies': at around seven and half minutes into the series, the word has finally been said, and we are in the territory of 'zombie horror'. The most senior officer – the suitably officious Angel – wants to wait for the Commander to arrive, but is overruled by Michael and Saul, and they access the armory. The alarm is activated and the noise draws a horde of zombies to the base, and the three soldiers are forced to barricade themselves into a vault. This sequence features what will become the distinctive echoing wail of the zombies, followed by snarling zombies on the attack and gunshots and screamed dialogue between the survivors:

MICHAEL: Aim for the head! Come on, Angel, what the hell are you doing!?
ANGEL: It's jammed!
MICHAEL: Yeah – no shit!

The men shut themselves into the echoing vault (establishing the theme and motif of entrapment which recurs throughout the series), and the following sequence in which they try and make sense of what is happening is accompanied by the blaring armory alarm in the distance. The men try to make phone calls, but these result in 'no connection' signals. These sound elements enhance the tension and alienating atmosphere. They realize they are not secure in the vault and argue about where might be a safe resort. Angel suggests his girlfriend's apartment block and the men agree to head there, although the very act of leaving the vault is evidently extremely perilous: this is the 'hook' to secure the audience for the next episode, as it is here that the first part of Chapter 1 ends. The episode has been less than 20 minutes in duration, but has achieved a great amount. The formidable economy of the writing has been mediated through a carefully designed soundscape and moderated performances, above all the measured tone of Jim Gleason's assured narration, which belies the rapid pace of the unfolding drama, presenting the social fabric of Los Angeles deteriorating into dystopia.

In the next part of Chapter 4, Michael, Angel and Saul survive gruesome peril and head to the apartment block. En route, they rescue two women – Pegs (Elisa Eliot) and Riley (Claire Dodin) – who are stranded on the roof of a flower shop. The characters are distinctive in voice and sentiment, and are an effective complement to the three soldiers. Pegs was the proprietor of the flower shop and is somewhat pacifistic, while the French character Riley has some experience handling weapons. By the end of Chapter 4, the gang is installed at the apartment block – The Tower – along with a number of other effective characters. Once it has been cleared and 'made safe', The Tower becomes the dominant location of the first season of *We're Alive* and is the equivalent to Troy in classical legend. Like Troy and so many tales of siege ever since, The Tower is at one and the same time a haven and a prison. The inhabitants certainly stay alive, and their life there defines their humanity as they develop a microcosmic civilization. However, there are inevitable conflicts within as well as the deadly enemies outside (zombies and rival survivors). There are disagreements over strategy and conduct, and at the same time they are forced to make forays into the world outside.

Like any good soap opera, *We're Alive* explores the interrelationship of a range of characters with long-running subplots or direct crises. This can be traditionally 'dramatic', such as in the form of the slow blossoming of romance between some characters or sudden violent conflict between others. However, one of the advantages of a long-running series is the other 'textures' and details that can be brought into play. For instance, one character suffers from celiac disease (severe gluten intolerance) which has a significant impact on the provisions needed; and in another chapter there is a discussion about the difference between types of engine fuel when a foray group are searching for gasoline. In a one-off drama or film, these details might easily seem overstated, superfluous or even confusing, but in a long-running series these can establish rich detail and realism. To signpost a character with celiac disease could be heavy-handed if this becomes defining too quickly (beyond dictating that the survivors will need a broader range of food types to survive). However, on a long-term basis of weeks, this could be an engaging subplot. It also serves to add detail to character and may bring to mind what other health issues and needs might impact the survivors. The fuel distinction serves to establish a realistic level of detail about life as a survivalist, but also to sow a potential dramatic seed (i.e. will all the characters remember the difference? Could the failure to remember this prove disastrous?) When asked about these aspects, Kc Wayland explains,

> Sometimes we want to explain to the audience the schematics and function of the world. They go to a fuel station and they're going to choose between a diesel and an unleaded truck, I want the audience to understand why there's a difference between the two. And for a character who doesn't know the difference it's nice to have that 'Oh, what is the difference?' Other things in the show like celiac disease: some people are not aware of the conditions some people live with and some of the constrictions that might happen. Or the flipside of that is that it might make people aware of survival techniques. I have heard people say after episodes 'You know, I don't have spare water stored in my home . . .' It is a little educational. (Wayland, 2010)

In this respect, *We're Alive* belongs to a tradition of radio as instructive medium reminiscent of the agricultural pedagogy in *The Archers* and KDKA's 'Rural Line on Education', or contemporary entertainment-education.

Narration and characterization

The over-reliance on narration can be a mistake in effective audio drama. As Shane Salk explains, the *We're Alive* creators realized that 'Narration isn't necessary, but it can be an extremely helpful device' (Salk, 2010). The principal writer Kc Wayland adds,

> Narration has to be placed very carefully. If you put it in the wrong spot, you lose the entire momentum of the scene. And that's rough sometimes – you want to describe what's happening, but the entire action of the scene will be lost. (Wayland, 2010)

To this end, narration in *We're Alive* tends to be pithy and yet character driven. The use of narration in *We're Alive* can serve to establish context and exposition – it can 'describe what's happening' – but just as importantly, it is used to consolidate a sense of character and point of view. The decision to avoid a fixed narrator throughout the saga frees up the plot to differing points of view and may even help to keep the audience hooked. We have already seen how the first speech in Chapter 1 succinctly creates Michael's back story and state of mind, as well as the 'where/what/when' issues. As another example, here is the narration of Burt (Scott Marvin) at the beginning of Chapter 6 ('The Remains of Eastern Bay'):

> Like always, the Marines are mopping up the mess made by the Army. He he. Saul, Lizzy, and I are headed back to The Tower as I write this. We decided to take a route closer to the coast to try and avoid the congested parts of the city. Didn't help much, considering there were still lots of abandoned cars, but maybe less here than most of the other areas. (beat) Saul and I keep switching driving since Lizzy can't seem to handle the whole concept of a clutch. Educated idiot if you ask me, can't function in the real world. Saul, gotta hand it to him, has been doing well considering what he went through last night.

In a little over 100 words, we are presented with a precise account of what is happening (returning to The Tower), which also captures a sense of the desolate city. In addition, we are given a sense of Burt's back story and feelings about the other survivors with him: he's a former marine and admires Saul, but has no time for the 'Educated idiot' Lizzy (Blaire Byhower). It is a narration as economic as any of Michael's, and yet very different in language and mood, befitting the tough-skinned Burt.

We're Alive utilizes distinct characters with distinct voices. The audience finds it easy to differentiate between the smooth voice of Michael the deep gravel tones of Burt, the French accent of Riley, delicate-voiced Pegs, the formal register of Angel, the streetwise Saul and so on. The carefully wrought and delivered monologue/dialogue in *We're Alive* makes the voice actors seem to achieve that most desirable quality in any audio performer: the ability to talk from the mind. The discipline with narration and dialogue, the fact that *We're Alive* is not 'over-wordy', can also be used to advantage in relation to ambiguity. For instance, there are many 'gaps' in *We're Alive*: these can be major themes, such as the fact we are never sure how the zombie pandemic commenced, and the clues we are given simply heighten a sense of intrigue. But they can also relate to the back stories or actions of specific characters, including the untold story of Michael's escape in Chapters 8 through 10.

Intensity of interrelationship

We're Alive is characterized by an intensity of interrelationship between the characters. This is undoubtedly facilitated by an ensemble approach to production. In creating audio drama, it is possible to record actors at different times and edit them together. However, Kc Wayland insists on what could be seen as a more 'theatrical' approach:

> Get everyone in the same spot . . . You have to have the actors interact with each other. Otherwise you lose so much power over what's going on. There's so much that could be said for development of characters between each other. In just getting up the energy for scenes there's no other way to do it than have the people there together. Otherwise, what's going to happen in the long run is you'll have a drama that's mismatched all over the place and people will not be able to follow the flow of the scene. (Wayland, 2010)

The survivors in the world of *We're Alive* have passions, resentments and hidden agendas when it comes to each other, and it is probably no surprise that the actors have been recorded in the same space and time. One of the consequences of *We're Alive* being a long-running series is upon rehearsal:

> When directing my actors, I don't rehearse them. A lot of people think that's a mistake. Initially, when we first started I ran actors through rehearsals and then after they had a sense of who they were I felt that getting their first impressions to a scene on the microphone with each other you get some really interesting interactions. Then giving simple directions will take them to a new level. (Wayland, 2010)

This is corroborated by Jim Gleason, the actor who portrays Michael, who starts with a tribute to Wayland's refined script:

> It was written so clearly it was very easy to 'get into'. When we first started recording, we would come as a group and actually read through the script in its entirety and then go away and record it. Now we don't do the read-through anymore. It is not necessary. We know who we are. We know what the situation is. We know where the story's going. (Gleason, 2010)

Working as characters in a long-running drama, the *We're Alive* actors have evidently found that it gets easier as time has gone on: they have gotten to know their characters intimately. It also seems that Wayland, as director, makes a particular effort to rectify efficiently any problems and also to place the scene in context. As Elisa Eliot (Pegs) explains,

> What we'll do is go through a scene top to bottom and then we'll go back and fix anything we need to. Kc is really good about giving us direction in what we *don't* see. So if we've gone through a scene he'll remind us what the physical context is: he's great at bringing the 'other' audio, the audio we *don't* hear, to life in the studio for us so that we can bring that into the acting as well. (Eliot, 2010)

In terms of 'fixing' the script, this might be reattempting a line of the script which was inauthentically delivered, or it might entail small adjustments to dialogue for the sake of clarity or more comfortable delivery. For instance, in the unpublished script of Chapter 6, Saul hears a noise and says, 'I hear it too! Can't tell where, though.' In the recording of the episode, the character says, 'I hear it too! Can't tell where it's coming from though.' It is a very slight change, but it undoubtedly becomes a more emphatic utterance. Elisa Eliot makes it very clear how Wayland, as a director, endeavours to ensure the actors 'tune in' to the environment of the play, elucidating what the play will sound like when edited with sound effects, music and soundscape.

The fact that there is so much that the actors 'don't hear' is a point worth remembering. *We're Alive* is characterized by its strong ensemble, but this is just one component of it as a work of audio drama. The show uses a carefully constructed soundscape. Despite its sequences of high action, full-blooded adventure and extreme violence and horror, the series is equally characterized by a surprising subtlety. Music is important, but is never overstated; it is more likely to offer a subtly evoked mood to a particular sequence, sometimes merging into soundscape or ambient sound. On occasion, the general ambience works together with very specific sound effects to create a detailed sense of 'layers', i.e. different actions occurring simultaneously. In one particularly ambitious sequence in Chapter 6, we hear a frantic Saul attempting to start his motorbike while being shot at by a group of rival survivors, with a pack of snarling zombies fast approaching. At the same time, we hear Michael's voice at the end of a radio receiver as he tries to contact Saul. It is a complex auditory sequence, and yet we manage to 'hold' the frantic scene in our minds. It succeeds in constructing a complex yet robust 'hierarchy of sound'. At other times, *We're Alive* exploits silence or near silence. In one sequence, Michael stands on top of The Tower, surveying the scene. A slight breeze in the void becomes 'painted' for the listener as the panorama of a desolate Los Angeles, enhanced by Michael's observation: 'Nothing. No planes. No cars. Nothing.' As well as creating a mood of existential angst, silence – that simplest of devices – can be an extremely suspenseful technique. As Shane Salk explains,

> Silence is scary on radio, but it can have a huge, huge impact on any scene. After all, you don't have to have talking all the time. Also, having a character just walk down a hallway can be riveting. You can also have a group of characters in a room and someone say 'Quiet! I need to hear if they're still there!' followed by five seconds of dead silence. The longer the silence is, the more listeners lean in to their computers or radios, wondering what's about to happen. It can really get people into it. But as ever, there's a balance: don't overdo it or people will get bored. (Salk, 2010)

In conclusion, we can find in *We're Alive* an ambitious and meticulously constructed example of contemporary podcast audio drama. It compounds a number of effective ingredients of audio drama in relation to narrative, writing, performance and production. The *modus operandi* of *We're Alive* includes the manipulation of suspense, action and horror; it uses post-production to develop a rich hierarchy of sound; and is partly an assimilating adaptation of broad horror themes and motifs (zombies, entrapment and survival), combined with highly detailed characterization and performances.

Exercises

- How and why have the creators of *We're Alive* made the series 'a movie that you listen to'?
- Select an episode of *We're Alive* and analyze the creation of character and context through the use of narration, dialogue and soundscape.
- Contrast the use of violence and the use of silence in *We're Alive*.
- Compare *We're Alive* with other examples of 'zombie horror' from the screen, comics, fiction or audio. In which aspects is *We're Alive* challenged and in which aspects does it excel?

Part 2
A practical guide to radio drama

4 Writing

Audio drama: Constrained and limitless

Writing drama for audio is simultaneously the easiest and most difficult type of performance writing. It is easy inasmuch as, on the face of it, the writer only needs to consider the aural dimension. However, it is difficult at the same time, for the very same reason. Radio drama may have existed for the better part of a century, but it is a form that is still perceived as having an essential ambiguity. There is a peculiar dichotomy in audio drama between its *constraints* and its *limitlessness*. On one side, it is easy to become fixated by audio as a visionless form. In other words, the tiresome myth of its 'blindness' can become an obstacle, especially for an aspiring writer. This is partly because for the majority of creative writing, the traditional mantra is '*show*, don't *tell*'. In other words, the writer should not be heavy-handed with narration or dialogue, but should permit the reader or audience to *interpret* and even *experience* the inherent drama in a work for themselves. Most people hate being told what to think or what to make of a situation. Part of the pleasure of experiencing a creative work is for us to infer or 'read between the lines' for ourselves. If we think of some of the best examples from screen or stage, we will probably find that there is very little narration. The dialogic exchange may be more minimal than we might remember and a great deal is conveyed by nonverbal context, subtext within the actors' performance and our own role as 'receiving' interpreters.

On first approaching audio drama, it may strike us that we cannot 'show' easily. For instance, when Kc Wayland – the lead writer on *We're Alive* – came to audio drama from a background in film, he immediately had a rude awakening when he began to write audio scripts:

> The first thing I had to learn when writing for this medium was how exactly to *tell* rather than *show*. Having a background in film I was inundated with 'you need to *show* them how this scene progresses and use subtext between the actors rather than doing it with words'. Now it's a flip. It's a complete 180 degrees. You basically have to tell

> your audience everything and then use extremely subtle cues with writing and the way someone says something, but also with sound effects, soundscape and things like that. (Wayland, 2010)

Other audio writers take a slightly different perspective. Scott Hickey and Robert Madia insist that '"Show, don't tell" is the rule for all good writing', but fine-tune this for audio drama by explaining that 'Dialogue is showing for the ear. Narration is telling.' (Hickey and Madia, 2007, p. 212). This is certainly a helpful differentiation, and it serves to spell out one of the perils in writing audio drama: the overuse of the narrator. However, Wayland's experience when first coming to audio drama is worth further analysis. Wayland discovered that words are the principal resource of audio drama. Wayland is one example of the new generation of artists who have been drawn away from the screen industry to the domain of podcast audio drama. Another example is David Accampo, co-creator with Jeremy Rogers of the serialized audio mystery *Wormwood*, who explains, 'Both Jeremy and I had written film scripts prior to *Wormwood*. When it came to scripting for audio, we established fairly quickly that the two most important aspects were the dialogue and the call-outs for sound effects' (Accampo, 2010). In the visual-dominated performance media of screen and theatre, we see carefully designed decor and *mise-en-scène*, costume and make-up, body language and the deployment of subtext: a wealth of visual codes and languages which assist us in interpreting as much as what is actually *spoken*. The audience will not be able to glean meaning from what they can *look at*: radio drama has to put everything into the aural form.

We will look at approaches to audio writing in due course, but let us return to the concurrent *constraints* and *limitlessness* of the audio drama form. As we have said, for decades this dichotomy has been an obsession of those approaching the form. For example, Rosemary Horstmann writes,

> The writer cannot call on the resources of scenery, lighting and costume to reinforce his message. The silent visual coup de theatre is denied him. But the other side of the coin is pure gold – he doesn't have to give the audience anything to look at, and this means nothing less than total freedom in time and space. This is the theatre of the mind, and the writer can move his characters instantly backwards through the centuries or forwards into the future. He can set the first scene on an airliner and the next at the bottom of the sea. If he chooses to send his protagonist to the South Pole we can go with him every step of the way. This is liberation indeed. (Horstmann, 1997, p. 37)

Audio drama has the potential to be limitless to an extent which would challenge any other medium. Exotic locations and elaborate set pieces could propel a film budget into multi-millions. Even what we might expect to be a 'quick fix' with CGI can be technically demanding and expensive. It may be the greatest sequence ever envisioned, but practical or financial reasons make it utterly prohibitive. However, audio drama has the potential to realize anything. In the same spirit, Shaun MacLoughlin is another writer who reveals the dichotomy inherent to audio drama:

> In radio you can have a cast of thousands and you can span centuries and continents. You can make the equivalent of a film like *The Lord of the Rings* for a thousandth of the cost. You can also enter the recesses of a person's mind. It can be the most intimate of media. It is a wonderfully liberating medium, yet the craft of writing a radio play is one of the hardest to master. (MacLoughlin, 2008, p. 14)

The freedom that radio permits has been recognized since its earliest days: it is another potential of this 'miraculous' invention. In the first full-length study of the form, *Radio Drama and How to Write It* (1926), Gordon Lea makes the straightforward observation that when it comes to finding a setting, radio plays 'can actually take place anywhere' (Lea, 1926, p. 37), later adding, in a phrase that captures the supreme limitlessness of radio: 'There are no restrictions whatever' (Lea, 1926, p. 40). Radio drama at its best has always recognized this. We have already referred to Richard Hughes's *A Comedy of Danger*, a play set in complete darkness, and other plays also utilize audio drama to the optimum. Another classic of radio drama is Lucille Fletcher's 'Sorry, Wrong Number' which was performed, always live, on the *Suspense* show eight times between 1943 and 1960. The play concerns a bedridden woman, Mrs Elbert Stevenson (Agnes Moorehead), who overhears a crosswire conversation on the telephone in which a murder is planned. This terrifying play presents the woman's desperate attempts, through a number of phone calls, to alert the authorities or to get help. The play is about telephones, overhearing and listening, and works consummately in the ears that belong to us, the listeners. Although the 1948 film version of the play, directed by Anatole Litvak and starring Barbara Stanwyck, might be a classic of film noir in its own right, it can never capture the claustrophobic terror of this quintessential example of radio drama. More recently, Clare Bayley's *The Container* (2011) is about a desperate group of illegal asylum seekers travelling in the oppressive conditions of a lorry. Although *The Container* was originally a stage play, the work is extremely well suited to radio, not least because BBC Radio Scotland were bold enough to record the play inside a container lorry.

In the classic US radio series *Quiet, Please* (Mutual, 1947–49), the writer-director Wyllis Cooper uses an extraordinary range of settings for his 30-minute plays: the audience is taken to a dizzying array of locations, including Egyptian tombs, oil wells, battlefronts, the planes of Hell, scientific labs, the lost city of Atlantis, the open road, mineshafts and so on. In our first case study, 'War of the Worlds', we learnt that many listeners believed that they were hearing the end of human existence live on air, complete with death-rays and mayhem. The opening episode of *The Hitchhiker's Guide to the Galaxy* (BBC, 1978) certainly pulls no punches either: it presents the complete and utter annihilation of planet Earth within the first 15 minutes.

Audio drama does not always have to be apocalyptic in order to demonstrate its potential. *Under Milk Wood: A Play for Voices* (BBC, 1954), by the poet Dylan Thomas, remains one of the triumphant achievements in radio drama. The play is centred on a seemingly mundane small community in Wales. Thomas presents us with the humble day-to-day lives of the inhabitants in the fictional Welsh village of Llareggub, but we also experience the profundity of their memories, fantasies and dreams. We are led on a journey through the social and inner life of Llareggub with writing that can be lyrical, humorous and emotive. *Under Milk Wood* follows the tradition of a modern classic such as James Joyce's *Ulysses* (1922) – an epic novel about the events of one ordinary day in Dublin – whereby the presentation of the unremarkable lives and inner realities of a small group of people, living in a particular place and time, becomes a profound exploration of human existence as a whole.

Story and plot

The BBC website provides an extremely beneficial resource for would-be radio writers, and it begins quite playfully, by spelling out the most important requirements for good audio drama:

> We are looking for three crucial things:
> - Story
> - Story
> - Story
>
> (BBC Radio 4: Writing for Radio 4, 2011)

A work of drama presents the listener with a 'plot' at the heart of which is a 'story'. In effect, stories are the linear works that lie at the heart of a dramatic work, which are reworked and restructured into artistic plots. Although an audio drama could begin at the very beginning of a story, more often the plot might open with a key dramatic moment, and gradually reveal the back story later on. In fact, plots can unfold in any conceivable order. It is important, however, that a writer has a sense of what their story is. Audio drama can offer a genuine luxury of detail and depth, but it must have a story to tell, a story which the writer can develop into an effective plot. It is for this reason that, throughout its history, radio drama has always been one of the most important and exciting forums for the adaptation of cultural works. Earlier in this book we mentioned the hugely popular *Lux Radio Theater* (1934–55) which offered its listeners live, fully authorized adaptations of Hollywood movies. Similarly taking screen media as his source inspiration, in 2002 the producer Carl Amari launched *The Twilight Zone Radio Dramas* which adapts episodes from Rod Serling's television series *The Twilight Zone* (1959–64), using (and sometimes carefully updating) the original scripts held in the Serling archives. As well as these major, official projects, there are interesting examples of fan culture in relation to audio adaptation. For example, 2007 saw the launch of the unauthorized podcast drama series *Buffy Between the Lines*, a multiple-episode, fan-created audio drama that fleshes out and creates adventures to complement Joss Whedon's popular television series *Buffy the Vampire Slayer* (1997–2003).

However, the key source for radio adaptation is, unsurprisingly, narrative fiction. Radio drama has always turned to pre-existing works of fiction and their tried and tested stories as a source for new works of audio. For example, the first sustained series of horror plays on US radio – *The Witch's Tale* (1931–38) – had a special interest in adaptation. Alongside many original works, the show's writer–director Alonzo Deen Cole produced radio versions of classic horror literature, such as *Frankenstein* and *Dr Jekyll and Mr Hyde*; and more obscure works by less well-known writers of the uncanny, such as John William Polidori, Prosper Mérimée and Théophile Gautier. *The General Mills Radio Adventure Theater/CBS Radio Adventure Theater* (1977–78) also presented fine adaptations of literature ranging from the well-loved to the obscure. As well as discovering neglected works, radio drama can permit detailed and substantial dramatizations. For instance, Betty Rowlands's adaptation of Robert Louis Stevenson's *Dr Jekyll and Mr. Hyde* for Australian radio in 1942–43 comprises 52 episodes of 15 minutes each: that is an adaptation totalling over 13 hours in duration. The highly popular US radio series *The New Adventures of Sherlock Holmes* (1939–47) featured adaptations of Arthur Conan Doyle's stories and all-new works for the Victorian super sleuth. Between 1989 and 1998, BBC Radio succeeded in the unprecedented and not inconsiderable task of adapting Conan Doyle's entire Sherlock Holmes oeuvre. In a similar spirit, between 2009 and 2010, the BBC presented radio dramatizations of all eight of John le Carré's 'George Smiley' Cold War espionage novels (four adapted by Shaun McKenna and four by Robert Forrest), and in 2011, BBC radio embarked on dramatizing all of Raymond Chandler's Philip Marlowe novels. The confidence of these enterprises emerges out of the BBC's long-established tradition of the adaptation of fiction which commenced with its dramatization of Charles Kingsley's *Westward Ho!* in April 1925. As is evident, the BBC continues to give adaptation a prominent place in its radio drama output, including serialized interpretations of favorite or neglected works, which can be more ambitious than the more high-profile screen equivalents. Sometimes there can be radical experimentation, as in the BBC's radio adaptation of B. S. Johnson's *The Unfortunates*, discussed earlier, which really came into its own in its post-broadcast online presence.

As well as being a perennially important form of radio drama, adaptation can also present writers with an excellent 'way in' to radio writing. After all, a successful and engaging story is already there, and this can be used as raw material that can be shaped and crafted into a radio play. Children's literature and fairy tales can be a particularly exciting way into this: as we saw earlier, the 1950s radio adaptation of *The Chronicles of Narnia* was particularly effective and delighted its original author C. S. Lewis. In our own time, Marques W. Brown, Artistic Director of Chatterbox Audio Theater and scriptwriter, reveals:

> I personally enjoy adapting children's literature and folktales, because there is already inherent in this kind of writing a wonderful balance between story, character and sound that often translates well to audio theater. Perhaps it's because stories have always been meant to be told to children, and told WELL at that. (Brown, 2010)

Chatterbox's repertoire (available as free downloads via their website or iTunes) certainly explores the rich potential of this, as can be seen in Teresa Morrow's *Esmerelda the Ugly Princess* (2009), a delightful fairy tale for stage and radio specifically for children, as well as Kyle Hatley's ambitious and powerful adaptation of Carlo Collodi's *Pinocchio*, which is re-imagined into a three-part audio adventure (totalling approximately four hours in duration) very much aimed at a mature audience.

There are, however, risks with adaptation. Although it may give a budding audio writer a source to work with, it can present major difficulties. The worlds of fiction and audio drama are very different. Although radio can be richly textured and ambitious, the audience has to be able to follow what is happening. When we read a novel, we immerse ourselves in the fictional world and can hold what is constructed there through a relationship with the author's words. Our reading is measured and moderated by our own idiosyncratic pace and methods of reading. Radio is more immediate and has to take us with it or we are left behind, wondering what on earth it is that is disappearing into obscurity. Moreover, to place complete trust in the original work and flatly shift it into an audio script is treacherous. The danger is that an adaptation can come across as leaden or confusing: either way, the adaptation will rapidly become boring. Annie Caulfield provides helpful advice from the independent radio drama producer John Taylor with regard to adaptation:

- Distil the number of characters down to the bare minimum.
- Seek clarity of character and storytelling throughout.
- Make all encounters significant.
- Ensure each scene has its own tension. (Caulfield, 2009, p. 104)

Exercises

- Consider how you might adapt a story you know well into an audio version. You might like to take a fairy tale as an example to start with. Who are the indispensible characters? Are there essential locations? What is at the core of the story?
- Think of a story that you love or know well, take two characters from it and experiment with dialogue. How do they talk to each other? How can the theme and story be filtered through the dialogue?
- Repeat the previous exercises, but this time use a short news item (from a newspaper, the internet or even television). This could be a quirky or humorous incident (e.g. the 'cat and its owner stuck up a tree' kind of story) or a high rhetoric encounter from the political arena.
- Take two characters from different stories (this could again be from fairy tales or news items) and put them together. Where are they? What do they say to each other? Does a conflict, agenda or story begin to emerge?

As well as adaptation, audio drama has the potential to allow dramatists to develop experimental and innovative ideas that they might be hard-pushed to realize on screen or stage. Laurence Raw edits *Radio Drama Reviews Online* and is an audio drama reviewer who is passionate about the form and its potential, especially for new writing:

> In a mediatic world supposedly concerned with the idea of 'choice,' the world of radio and audio drama is perhaps the one place where

> plays of all cultures and types can get produced. And still it is the best way for new writers to experiment with different types of work, whether on the BBC or elsewhere. In addition, directors/producers are not faced with the same financial pressures as their colleagues in television, and hence have a greater freedom to produce. (Raw, 2010)

Audio writers are well aware of this: Kyle Hatley of Chatterbox Audio Theater celebrates the medium when he says, 'I feel wonderfully free writing for audio. There's an elasticity to it that allows me to play and challenge the rules' (Hatley, 2010). A similar sentiment comes from another contemporary scriptwriter, Marty Ross. Ross began his writing career in theatre, but unfortunately found the opportunities to be limited. When BBC Radio Scotland became interested in his writing, his career began to flourish and, in return, Ross was able to explore the limitlessness of audio drama. As the website of the UK-based on-line audio station Wireless Theatre Company explains,

> Audio drama remains (Marty Ross's) favourite form, for the liberty it offers a writer whose work sticks up two fingers at the dominant 'social-realist' aesthetic. In what other medium would a writer like him enjoy the imaginative freedom to range from the Arctic ice floes to the dream lives of expressionist poets, from alien invasions and demonic seductions in the Scottish highlands to a polythene bag washed up the beach of a seaside town, full to bursting with ancient terrors? (Wireless Theatre Company, 2011)

As this statement reveals, audio drama can liberate writers from the dominant mode of writing for the performance media which continues to be social-realism: in other words, contemporary screen and stage drama is typically dominated by works which endeavour to capture the surface reality of life in its plot lines, design and performance style. The closing phrase in the above quotation alludes to a play that Ross wrote specifically for the Wireless Theatre Company which proves the potential of the radio form for fantasy. In *Medusa on the Beach* (2009) Ross develops a simple but powerful idea: two policemen arrive at a beach in England and find a number of statues. What seems like an experimental art exhibition turns out to have a more fantastical and shocking source. A woman found a plastic bag containing the head of the Medusa, one of the terrifying Gorgons from Greek legend. The play is a comedy, but is built on a highly atmospheric and compelling idea. It could be filmed, but the acute dialogue and its contextual soundscape – the sound of the sea, the distinct voices and, of course, the petrifying of the Medusa's victims – makes this a highly evocative work. The recent films *Percy*

Jackson and the Lightning Thief (Chris Columbus, 2010) and *Clash of the Titans* (Louis Leterrier, 2010) both feature Medusa characters, but these are high-action, special-effects-driven adventure movies. Marty Ross can take the same abject monster, but remove her from a predictable genre and put her at the heart of a subtle and witty, yet nonetheless disturbing, comedy. Interestingly, in the same year the 19 Nocturne Boulevard audio drama podcast company produced Julie Hoverson's *For Art's Sake* (2009), a similarly unsettling comedy about a Gorgon producing statues for the New York art scene.

In addition to the reimagining of myth, audio drama can effortlessly push fantasy to the furthest degree. It can be as interiorized and intimate as a dream, but as Sam Boardman-Jacobs warns any would-be writer, radio has the potential to take listeners 'to their darkest nightmares' (Boardman-Jacobs, 2004, p. 12). Horror and science fiction have always had a special position in radio drama because of their ability to exploit the simultaneous scope and intimacy of the form. They have a prominent place in Old Time Radio: numerous examples are mentioned throughout this book to which we might add *The Hermit's Cave* (1935–44), *Inner Sanctum Mysteries* (1941–52), *The Mysterious Traveler* (1943–52), *Mystery in the Air* (1947), *X-Minus One* (1955–58) and British shows such as *Journey into Space* (1953–58) and *The Price of Fear* (1973–75; 1983). Radio creators still find audio a powerful form for exploring horror and science fiction: indeed, many contemporary examples in this book demonstrate how often podcast drama ventures – if not specializes – into the terrifying and the fantastic. For an example of a work that leads us into the uncanny, we might consider Julian Simpson's *Bad Memories* (BBC, 2011), an inexorably chilling work (recorded on location) about mysterious voices emerging on recordings. Kyle Hatley's three-part podcast drama 'The Dead Girl' (Chatterbox Audio Theater, 2007) is a complex exploration of issues such as Catholicism and loss of faith within the priesthood not dissimilar, in aspiration, to Graham Greene's *The Power and the Glory* (1940). However, towards the end of the first part of the play, there is a genuinely disturbing sequence in which we hear the recording of an autopsy during which a clearly dead corpse reawakens. This is a moment of 'zombie horror', of course, but Hatley's well-crafted and reflective narrative makes this arresting launch into the uncanny profoundly unsettling.

Rosemary Horstmann makes an important observation for anyone approaching audio drama when she states, '(Although) the characters in a radio play must use human language they don't have to be human beings. Animals, plants and inanimate objects can be brought to articulate life and pressed into service as part of the cast' (Horstmann, 1997, p. 36). As a case in point, she cites J. C. W. Brook's *Giving Up*

(BBC, 1978) a radio play about a man struggling to give up smoking in which we hear the various parts of his body in dialogic conflict. An older example we could add is 'Let the Lilies Consider', a 1948 episode of *Quiet, Please* in which flowers start to talk to the gardener who planted them. We hear their eerie, delicate voices, and while on screen the lilies might be ludicrously comic or outright science fiction, using audio drama Wyllis Cooper creates a haunting work that is dreamlike and disturbing in equal measure. An even more audacious flight of fancy is to be found in one of Norman Corwin's classic radio plays *The Undecided Molecule* (17 July 1945), an epic drama in which a molecule is put on trial for being unable to decide what element or entity it wants to belong to. As a more recent example, we might consider Annie McCartney's 'kitchen comedy' *Staring into the Fridge* (BBC, 2010). In this delicately written play, the central character, Maggie (played by Annie McCartney herself), is a woman experiencing a midlife crisis. Her children have grown up and no longer need her, and her boyfriend is completely unreliable. As a result, she finds herself increasingly isolated and unfulfilled. Suddenly, she strikes up a relationship with her refrigerator:

FRIDGE: (. . .) I'm not the adventurous type. I couldn't bear to end up in a landfill polluting the planet.
MAGGIE: How do you know about landfill?
FRIDGE: Your friend Dougal. He thinks I'm not eco-friendly enough.
MAGGIE: Does he?
FRIDGE: He thinks I'm oversized. I've heard him say that to others when you're out of the room. Says I'm destroying the coral reefs.
MAGGIE: That's awful.
FRIDGE: I think he's jealous of my ice-making facility.

The dialogue is witty and satirical and the listener accepts the playful conceit. At the same time, by literally giving the Fridge a voice (the role was played by the popular Northern Irish actor James Nesbitt), Annie McCartney has been able to create a play which is a 'serious' comedy – and ultimately a love story – exploring the pertinent contemporary issues of identity, society and alienation. As in the aforementioned *Quiet, Please* episode, it would be difficult to put this story in a visual medium in a way that 'works': of course, bringing inanimate objects to life does happen on screen, but it is something we might associate with genres such as horror or children shows, especially cartoons. McCartney's play is evidently in the tradition of other domestic comedies, such as Willy Russell's stage play *Shirley Valentine* (1986) in which the eponymous heroine, another middle-aged woman, finds solace and companionship by talking to the wall in her kitchen. Significantly, unlike Maggie's fridge, Shirley's wall can never answer back.

Exercises

- Jot down the details of a dream – or nightmare – you have had. How would you turn that into an audio scenario for sound effects and voices?
- Find the 'voice' of a non-human entity, an inanimate object or location. This could be the voice of a housefly, a derelict house, an ocean, and so on. How can this create a point of view for the listener? Can you use it to explore issues of identity or society? Can you make versions which are humorous and versions which are serious?

Engaging the audience

Hopefully, we have demonstrated how fantastically liberating radio drama is, but let us remember Shaun MacLoughlin's warning that 'the craft of writing a radio play is one of the hardest to master (MacLoughlin, 2008, p.14). This is partly because audio drama, despite its seeming 'simplicity', has to achieve a number of things in order to be effective. If we turn to Laurence Raw, we obtain an insight into how a radio reviewer approaches a work of drama, which in turn offers 'clues' to the creation of 'good' audio: 'Every radio work I approach with the same kind of expectations – does it make creative use of the medium, and how does it tell its story?' (Raw, 2010). As far as a reviewer is concerned, to make good audio drama we need to fully explore the potential of the form, but also tell a story lucidly. A fundamental challenge, by implication, is that we need to *engage* the listeners and *keep them engaged*. So how do we 'hook' our audience? First of all, let us not forget that a theatre spectator or a person who has gone to the movies is fulfilling their part of the deal: they have paid their money and they will give the performance a dedicated amount of attention. In fact, to walk out of a show you have paid for is quite a statement. TV is an admittedly 'freer' mode of spectatorship, with people frequently channel-hopping until they see something they want to watch or something that *makes* them watch. But even a TV viewer may have sat down deliberately to *watch*, especially in relation to drama. In contrast, it is perhaps unusual to have a radio listener who has deliberately sat down with no other intention than to *listen*. Although this can be a great pleasure for many people, it is perhaps something of a luxury and even a learned mode of experience: it is much more likely that listeners are driving, eating, doing household chores, text messaging or even half-reading a magazine or book. This takes us back to the concept of 'secondariness' that we discussed earlier in this book.

Listening to an audio broadcast in a group is a case in point: you will notice how people fidget, scribble and doodle, or gawk out the window, while with TV there is a literal focal point. As we have suggested, radio listening is perhaps a *learned* skill. This has always been one of the key challenges of audio drama: how to get your listener engaged and attentive when it is easy to be distracted. In the Foreword to Gordon Lea's pioneering book on radio drama, R. E. Jeffrey writes that, although it is clear that 'Radio Drama has a great future' (Lea, 1926, p. 11), it has to be acknowledged that it is the 'most difficult branch of radio art' (Lea, 1926, p. 12) not least as there is a key challenge for would-be radio drama listeners: they need to *learn* 'how to listen' (Lea, 1926, p. 12). If we return to Laurence Raw, we realize that the listeners have more of an *active* role than they might expect, but this is a learned status:

> I am interested in how voices and sounds paint a picture and work on the listener's mind; I believe that all listeners have to 'fill in the gaps' for themselves. Those 'gaps' are what you might call interpretive gaps – creating a mental picture, you might say. There may be no fixed rules for creating such conditions, but any good radio drama has to do it. I liken radio drama to a kaleidoscope – lots of sounds working simultaneously – voices, sounds and music. It creates a stimulus for the listener to create pictures for themselves. What I am trying to say is that radio drama places demands on listeners; they have to train themselves into playing an active role in the communicative process. Sound effects and music help stimulate this process. (Raw, 2010)

We cannot, however, put the entire burden onto the listener. Audio creators, not least the writers, have to face their own responsibility. Shaun MacLoughlin is unambiguous in his stark warning:

> The switch off button is never far off. As a writer you probably have about a minute, two at the outside, to engage your listener. However wonderful the rest of the play, if your beginning does not captivate the listeners, they will never stay to be enchanted. (MacLoughlin, 2008, p.19)

As MacLoughlin suggests, the beginning is everything. Although this has a particular urgency in audio drama, it is a key issue in creative writing as a whole. Let us consider, for a moment, narrative fiction. In a way that is apposite to consider in relation to audio drama, some of the greatest openings to novels have a sense of a living voice, talking directly to us. Here are some opening lines from classic works of fiction:

> Mother died today. Or maybe yesterday, I don't know.
>
> (Albert Camus, *The Outsider* (1942))
>
> This is the saddest story I have ever heard.
>
> (Ford Madox Ford, *The Good Soldier* (1915))
>
> 'Take my camel, dear,' said my Aunt Dot, as she climbed down from this animal on her return from High Mass.
>
> (Rose Macaulay, *The Towers of Trebizon* (1956))
>
> If you really want to hear about it, the first thing you'll probably want to know is where I was born, and what my lousy childhood was like, and how my parents were occupied and all before they had me, and all that *David Copperfield* kind of crap, but I don't feel like going into it, if you want to know the truth.
>
> (J. D. Salinger *The Catcher in the Rye* (1951))

In each case, we want to know more or, perhaps more exactly, we *need* to know more. In Camus, who is speaking? Why doesn't the speaker know when his or her mother died? What is the relationship between the child and the mother? Is the speaker in a state of shock or completely indifferent? With Ford, what is so sad? We all know sad stories – what will make this the saddest story ever? Who is speaking? Will I feel the same? The Macaulay has a very different tone: it is immediately quite humorous, with a sense of character. It feels instantaneously eccentric and somewhat incongruous. Where in the world is this happening? Who is this evidently bizarre 'Aunt Dot' who apparently rides a camel to church? Who is she speaking to? In Salinger, what is the 'it' the speaker is going to tell us about? Also the sense of character here is fascinating: the refusal to tell us all the 'crap' we might want or expect to know makes us all the more desperate to know what is going on. In all these cases, a handful of words has the potential to lure us in and keep us reading: we need to know more and get to the bottom of the case. In short, we are hooked.

Not all novels function like this. Take, for example, the opening two sentences of Joseph Conrad's *Nostromo* (1904):

> In the time of Spanish rule, and for many years afterwards, the town of Sulaco – the luxuriant beauty of the orange gardens bears witness to its antiquity – had never been commercially anything more important than a coasting port with a fairly large local trade in ox-hides and indigo. The clumsy deep-sea galleons of the conquerors that, needing a brisk gale to move at all, would lie becalmed, where your modern ship built on clipper lines forges ahead by the mere flapping

> of her sails, had been barred out of Sulaco by the prevailing calms of its vast gulf. (Conrad, 1925, p. 3)

The novel is no less a masterpiece of fiction than the other examples, but its opening relies on an omniscient narrator giving us a detailed overview of the world in question. *Nostromo* is Conrad's longest novel; he knew he was creating a 'broad canvas', and it is like a painting in words. Does it hook the reader? If it does, it probably does it in a different way than with the immediate sense of 'voice' that we saw in the other examples. The Conrad opening certainly provides an exotic and exciting location and a sense of history and timescale, and the subsequent novel abounds with action and intensity, but if it was to be adapted into drama (rather than a reading), it would need to be conveyed in a different way and through different means.

The opening

We have used narrative fiction as a way into the topic of 'hooking' the audience. Let us now consider the opening in audio drama. This can be done in a number of ways. An obvious one is through the use of music, which can create a mood and an atmosphere and, in the case of a theme tune, can be a key signal to the listener. The focus for us at this point, however, is the script and the voice. A classic series from US radio was a show called *Escape* (CBS, 1947–54), which specialized in highly dramatic adventure plays, frequently adapted from works of fiction. Although the opening to the program could vary, its standard format is usually along the lines deployed in this transcript of an episode called 'A Study in Wax' (1 February 1953):

> ANNOUNCER 1: Tired of the everyday grind? Ever dream of a life of romantic adventure? Want to get away from it all? We offer you . . . *Escape*!
>
> MUSIC: Mussorgsky's *Night on Bare Mountain* [the *Escape* theme tune]
>
> ANNOUNCER 2: *Escape*, designed to free you from the four walls of today for a half hour of high adventure.
>
> ANNOUNCER 1: You are trapped in a snowbound cabin in northern Canada, with the temperature slowly dropping, while across the table from you, his eyes staring at you, is your only companion: a madman waiting for his chance to kill you.
>
> ANNOUNCER 2: Listen now as *Escape* brings you Antony Ellis' terrifying story: 'A Study in Wax'.
>
> (MUSIC)

JACK: It was late October when the radio shack burned down. We never did decide whose fault it was. Maybe Kobel with his cigarettes. Or maybe me. Anyway I guess the whole thing began when we lost the phone transmitter and receiver. Kobel and I had been sent up to the Northwest Territory by the Canadian Geodetic Survey people. It was a long job. And the biggest part of it was the loneliness. I remember what Kobel said as we watched the government supply boat steaming off.

The opening speech springs out of silence, asking us three questions which tempt us with an invitation to enjoy a dose of escapism. After this the music begins dramatically. The show's theme tune is actually secondary to the opening voice. After this, the second announcer offers us a definition of the show and its duration. We return to the first announcer, who provides us with a description specific to this episode, establishing location and the critical, perilous situation. Perhaps most importantly, the announcer implicates *you* in the story: 'You are trapped . . .' After this, the story will bring to life the two characters, and the subsequent play is a magnificent example of economic characterization with the two characters going stir-crazy in their claustrophobic and snowbound cabin.

Other classic shows from the same era use a similar concept. *Quiet, Please* always used this format:

ERNEST CHAPPELL: Quiet, please. (SEVEN SECONDS SILENCE) Quiet, please.
MUSIC: Franck's *Symphony in D minor* [the *Quiet, Please* theme tune]

The voice comes out of the silence and then there is a gripping – not to say daring – seven-second silence. During the most famous era of *Lights Out* (1934–47), a popular horror radio show, the writer–director Arch Oboler always provided the opening speech:

ANNOUNCER: Arch Oboler's *Lights Out* . . . everybody.
SFX: GONG CHIMES FOUR TIMES
ARCH OBOLER:
It . . .
SFX: CHIME
Is . . .
SFX: CHIME
Later . . .
SFX: CHIME

Than . . .
SFX: CHIME
You . . .
SFX: CHIME
Think . . .
SFX: CHIME CHIME
This is Arch Oboler bringing you another in our series of stories of the unusual. And once again we caution you: these *Lights Out* stories are definitely not for the timid soul, so we tell you calmly and very sincerely, if you frighten easily, turn off your radio now.
SFX: LOUD AND PROLONGED GONG CRASH

The openings to *Escape*, *Quiet, Please* and *Lights Out* are all very arresting, whetting our appetite, perhaps even defying us to listen. In our time, the podcast drama series 19 Nocturne Boulevard has developed a trademark opening very much in the tradition of the golden-age shows:

MUSIC: THEME TUNE UP AND CONTINUES UNDER:
MALE ANNOUNCER: 19 Nocturne Boulevard.
MAN'S VOICE: 19 Nocturne Boulevard? Not far. When you hit Howard, hang a right. Howard meets Philip at a weird kind of angle. Then you cross James and Poe. You can't miss Nocturne. It's just past the automat.
SFX: CAR DRIVES AWAY
MALE ANNOUNCER: 19 Nocturne Boulevard. Your address for suspenseful stories of the speculative, strange and supernatural. Tonight's story is . . . [TITLE OF EPISODE INSERTED HERE]
SFX: KNOCK ON DOOR. DOOR OPENS.
FEMALE HOST: Yes? This is 19 Nocturne Boulevard. Won't you step inside?
SFX: FOOTSTEPS. DOOR CLOSES.
FEMALE HOST: Did you have any trouble finding it? What do you mean what kind of a place is it? Why it's . . . [LOCATION OF THE PLAY INSERTED HERE] Can't you tell?

As well as having a familiar and alluring opening, radio drama can also draw us in with other techniques, such as the lyrical. As a case in point, let us look at the opening to a play we mentioned earlier, Dylan Thomas's *Under Milk Wood*:

FIRST VOICE (*Very softly*):

To begin at the beginning:

It is spring, moonless night in the small town, starless and bible-black, the cobblestreets silent and the hunched, courters'-and-rabbits' wood

> limping invisible down to the sloeblack, slow, black, crowblack, fishingboatbobbing sea. The houses are blind as moles (though moles see fine to-night in the snouting, velvet dingles) or blind as Captain Cat there in the muffled middle by the pump and the town clock, the shops in mourning, the Welfare Hall in widows' weeds. And all the people of the lulled and dumbfound town are sleeping now. (Dylan Thomas *Under Milk Wood: A Play for Voices* (BBC, 1954))

At first glance, this may seem convoluted and obtuse: long sentences; complicatedly structured; unfamiliar, ambiguous and invented words. This looks like something you could only read on the page in silence. However, take a moment now to take it *off the page*: give it a living voice and read it out aloud. Although it does not lose its complex structure and detail, it can be completely compelling when read aloud: poetic and rich and almost dreamlike, we want to hear more. The two narrative voices are of instrumental importance to *Under Milk Wood*, and yet Thomas is careful to ensure that they offer more than mere exposition: the narrators introduce us to the characters in the village and enlighten us as to location and action, but they also provide us with a transcendent understanding of the texture, mood and soul of Llareggub.

As, first and foremost, a poet, Dylan Thomas demonstrates his sense of rhythm and intonation. This was particularly well realized in the first production of the play, which starred Richard Burton as the First Voice. The choice of language and syntax is especially important in audio drama, in which homonymic or ambiguous words can cause confusion. Annie Caulfield emphasizes the importance of reading your own writing aloud, as this is the best first test. It can alert us to overlong sentences as well as inadvertent tongue twisters, as Caulfield demonstrates: 'Too many similar sounds in a sentence will sound silly when spoken; sometimes sentences descend into simple sequences of hissing' (Caulfield, 2009, p. 79).

Exercises

- Think of an opening line that will engage and intrigue a listener. Does it make sense? Does it puzzle us enough to want to hear more? Does it shock or scare us? Does it make us laugh?

'Spelling it out'

As well as the actual 'sound' of the words and the structure of the sentences, a fatal trap for the audio writer is putting too much information into narration. Although the temptation can be strong when wanting to make the audience 'see', over-detailed narration can quickly become unwieldy, patronizing and eventually tedious: the more we are forced to envision, the more superfluous and non-engaging this can become. This principle extends beyond narration. Marques W. Brown of Chatterbox Audio Theater explains,

> You have to keep your listener engaged, and good writers know how to do that. There is a fine line between great descriptive writing and boring exposition, though, and we have to describe more to our audience than your average play, film, or television show. The balance between exposition, dialogue, music, and sound effects is crucial, and if you don't stand back and listen to the piece as a whole, and edit yourself as you go, you can end up with a big, loud mess. (Brown, 2010)

The challenge for any audio writer is to strike a balance between, as the saying goes, a rock and hard place. On the one hand, the writer has got to make sure that the listener 'gets' what is being said and what the situation is. On the other hand, the writer must ensure that the sequence is not 'overdone'. For instance, the temptation to 'spell out' is very perilous, as it can be patronizing, annoying and even inadvertently ridiculous. As Shane Salk, co-creator of the *We're Alive* serial warns, some audio dramas 'spell out everything as if the audience is full of morons' having lone characters talking to themselves simply to spell out physical actions and pointless detail ('I think I'll just pick up these purple scissors . . .'). Salk continues,

> 'Spelling it out' can be a real instinct for people when they're beginning to work in audio. *It's radio – they can't see anything!* But, of course, you don't *need* to see everything. You need to give the audience an idea of what's around. You need to let them know where they are, what's around, but in a subtle way. It is a challenge to learn that when you're beginning. (Salk, 2010)

It might be tempting to write a line like 'Phew, it is so hot out here on the beach! Let me put on my sunhat and my shades. I need a drink of water, too.' This line is essentially putting physical actions into dialogue – spelling out the actions – and it is unnecessary. The same thing could be achieved much more effectively by using the sound of a beach and have the character say 'Phew, it's hot . . .' Timothy West's comedy *This Gun That I Have in My Right Hand is Loaded* (1972) deliberately ridicules the dangers of overstating in radio drama, as this extract demonstrates:

> LAURA: What's that you've got under your arm, Clive?
> CLIVE: It's an evening paper, Laura.

(PAPER NOISE) I've just been reading about the Oppenheimer smuggling case. (EFFORT NOISE) Good gracious, it's nice to sit down after that long train journey from the insurance office in the City.

LAURA: Let me get you a drink, Clive darling.

(LENGTHY POURING, CLINK)

CLIVE: Thank you, Laura, my dear.

(CLINK, SIP, GULP)

Aah! Amontillado, eh? Good stuff. What are you having?

LAURA: I think I'll have a whisky, if it's all the same to you.

(CLINK, POURING, SYPHON)

CLIVE: Whisky, eh? That's a strange drink for an attractive auburn-haired girl of twenty-nine. Is there anything wrong?

LAURA: No, it's nothing, Clive, I . . .

CLIVE: Yes?

LAURA: No, really, I –

CLIVE: You're my wife, Laura. Whatever it is, you can tell me. I'm your husband. Why, we've been married – let me see – eight years, isn't it?

LAURA: Yes, I'm sorry Clive, I . . . I'm being stupid.

The humor of this play depends on the lavish overstating and redundant detail. The play pretends to have been written for a person who cannot see the action or the characters. The 'writer' overcompensates to a preposterous degree. Presumably, a person would recognize that it is a newspaper tucked under someone's arm; a husband would not describe what his wife looks like to the woman herself; and the sound effects may strive to be helpful, but are more than is needed. The sequence masquerades as an attempt to make the listener 'see' everything clearly and becomes an enjoyable spoof in the process. The actor Samuel West uses the play to provide a stark warning to any would-be radio writer:

> (*This Gun That I Have in My Right Hand is Loaded*) is still used in good drama schools to illustrate the pitfalls of the genre, but listening to the odd *Afternoon Play*, it's possible to conclude that writers have taken it as a blueprint rather than a cautionary tale. Good radio writing is a real art. I think a good radio play is better than any other sort of play, but by the same token, a bad one is so much worse. Radio is the most unforgiving medium, more revealing of untruth than any other. Nothing distracts you from whether you believe the reality of what you are hearing. (West, 2007)

Samuel West suggests that some radio drama still suffers from overwriting. It perhaps reflects a tendency to 'spoon feed' or even the desire to *impose* a vision on the audience. However, as Shane Salk emphasizes, this should be resisted:

> Just because you've imagined it looking a certain way doesn't mean that everyone has to see it the same way. It's like an inkblot test. The radio drama's job is not to tell everybody what everything looks like. A radio drama's job is to give a framework of 'what's going on' and what the environment is like and let people do their own thing. (Salk, 2010)

This takes us back, yet again, to the active role of the listener in the creation of meaning.

Rather than constructing a play with a great deal of depth and detail, the writer should employ what Donald McWhinnie calls 'concentrated and intuitive short-cuts' (McWhinnie, 1959, p. 51). An excellent example of this is the BBC Radio 4 series *Old Harry's Game* (2009), a comedy series set in hell, written and directed by, and starring, Andy Hamilton as Satan. The series' effectiveness lies in its simplicity. There is music, a macabre and dramatic theme, but it is used sparingly only at the beginning, end and in-between scenes. There are very few sound effects and very little in the dialogue that describes 'hell'. The action seems to be taking place in a void from which we form our own picture, drawing on our own stock of images of how hell should be: is hell Dante's *Inferno*, a William Blake etching, or is it, as Jean-Paul Sartre suggested, other people? The comic narrative and the images evoked in *Old Harry's Game* are stronger because of the lack of 'visual' distraction:

> THOMAS: I've got a hobby; tap dancing. Watch!
> SFX: TAP DANCING
> PROFESSOR: Now, that's impressive. Especially with cloven feet!
> THOMAS: Fred Astaire says I'm a natural. My feet just glide across the floor.
> SATAN: Your feet will be nailed to the floor in a second.
> THOMAS: Sorry, My Prince.
> SATAN: Don't do it again.

Old Harry's Game demonstrates the quality of 'less is more' very well. The writing summons up a tremendous series of images: a cloven-footed devil tap dancing with Fred Astaire in hell? Impossible on screen. Perfect on radio!

Over all, although the final product can be the 'kaleidoscope' of components reviewer Laurence Raw mentions, we must not forget the benefits of essential simplicity. Just as we need a coherent story, we should consider Salk's concept of the 'framework'. This is also why David Accampo emphasizes the benefits of keeping the script simple:

> Personally, I like really stripped-down scripts when writing. Because so much of our show was driven by dialogue, it helped me in the scripting process to remove all non-essential elements and really just focus on the two people in the room, what they're saying, as well as what they're refusing to say. (Accampo, 2010)

Some of the best radio drama succeeds in constructing a simple situation. 'The Thing on the Ice' (Icebox Radio Theater, 2009), written and directed by Jeffrey Adams, is a simple but gripping story of a fisherman who encounters the supernatural while trapped in his hut during a storm: the play's economy enhances the suspense and impact of the piece. The British playwright Edward Bond's first play for radio, *The Chair* (BBC, 2000), is set in the future of 2077, but presents the simplest of situations. In the play, a woman sees a soldier on a street with a prisoner, waiting to be collected. She takes down a chair from her apartment and the soldier sits on it. This simple act has profound consequences. The play is set in the future, but it is not the elaborate science fiction that radio drama can create so brilliantly: on the contrary, Bond creates a play that has a compelling impact on the imagination with its simplicity – a small group of people and one chair that can rock society to its foundations.

The aforementioned David Accampo is co-creator of *Wormwood* (2007–10), a podcast drama in which mystery and adventure is combined with elements of the supernatural and horror. It is a long-running and ambitious drama, but despite its scale, each scene and sequence within the drama reveals the simplicity that Accampo swears by. A central character in *Wormwood* is Doctor Xander Crowe (Arthur Russell), who was a leading psychologist until a disturbing case led him into exploring the occult. As the series begins, it transpires that Crowe was recruited by Don Marino, a gangster, whose daughter seemed to be possessed. The daughter committed suicide, and Marino has a vendetta against Crowe. Very early in the first episode ('The Coming Storm'), two of Marino's henchmen catch up with Crowe. After menacing him they declare:

> VINCENT: Say, Doc, is it true what they say? That you always wear that glove on your hand because you don't want anyone to see how *disgusting* it is?
>
> JOHNNY: That is what I heard.

XANDER CROWE: Gentlemen, listen to me. Now I admit I've had a few cocktails. There are two of you, aren't there?
SFX: CROWE IS PUNCHED
JOHNNY: Say, uh Vincent . . . What say we take a look at the Doc's hand?
VINCENT: Why, Johnny, I think that is an excellent idea.
SFX: PUNCHING SOUNDS UNDERNEATH
JOHNNY: Hold him.
XANDER CROWE: Please! You don't want to do that!
VINCENT: Oh my God! What is that! Holy Christ! It's withered and dead!
SFX: UNCANNY SCREAM

The terror that grips the henchmen means that Crowe is able to escape. It is a straightforward scene and simply written. Crowe's sardonic humor – joking about seeing double – does not detract, but in fact adds power to the menace of the scene. The sequence is made compelling not just by the clear focus of the scene that the listener can visualize, but by Todd Hodges's eerie chamber music, which builds in volume beneath the action. It is an effective way to introduce Crowe's uncanny hand. It is up to each of us to imagine how his hand looks (it is certainly shocking enough to stop the hoodlums in their tracks) and the scream at the end of the sequence as Crowe escapes is effective, as it is hard to pinpoint: is it from the monstrous hand itself? Crowe's hand becomes an important 'character' in *Wormwood* and it seems to have a mind of its own – moving and gesturing independently of Crowe – and in episode 8 ('By Small Hands') his hand is able to unlock a cell door without a key and point Crowe and a sheriff towards crucial evidence. The characters are strong, the situation is clear and the dialogue is easy to follow. The elements of thriller (violent gangsters and a daring escape) and fantasy (the uncanny hand) combine to keep the listener engaged and intrigued enough to listen on . . . and on.

Mariele Runacre Temple is the artistic director of the Wireless Theatre Company, and her insight as a person who commissions audio drama is illuminating:

> A radio play allows the listener to visualize the character in their head (something people don't do enough of) so the characters *must* be strong and the dialogue must be rich and believable, the words written form a much greater part of the finished product; bad lines cannot be obscured with stage business. It is such an intimate medium, just the listener and the words, so a script needs to be as strong as possible. (Runacre Temple, 2010)

The point that your characters must be strong is immensely important. While in the more visually based performance media there are various possibilities and skills related to physical presence and proxemics, in audio this has to be mediated through the voice. In addition, it is essential that you work on the distinctiveness of your characters: to have, for example, five women of the same age and same social class might prove confusing for a listener. In a visual version, the audience could see the one who has red hair, always wears jeans or jewellery, and this will help differentiate the characters. In an audio drama, what they say will be the key to this. For that reason, you might want to consider exploring the use of accents, different vocal register and, of course, using fewer characters.

Exercises

- Write short sections of dialogue which present a first meeting or an argument and subsequent reconciliation.
- Taking the short sections of dialogue you have written, experiment by putting them in a variety of situations: during a power cut; a snowstorm; on a crowded train; and so forth. Also, experiment with giving the characters something to do as they talk: running for a bus; pulling their bag out of a puddle; eating a sandwich. Do these changes in environment and action have an impact on the trajectory of the narrative and characterization?
- Introduce some other characters into your dialogue. How can you ensure their voices are distinct? What advantages emerge by having differences between the characters' voices?

Approaches to writing

We have seen the advantages and the pitfalls of audio drama with a good range of examples along the way. When it comes to writing an audio play yourself, it is important to realize that there are many ways to write a play. Writing guidelines located on the websites of the BBC and other audio theatre companies can all be immensely beneficial, especially regarding core principles, copyright, technical and formatting issues: they can ensure that we are not wasting the time and energy of ourselves and others. The BBC website is particularly helpful when it spells out the type of slots it has for different genres of drama and the significance of these in relation to duration (15-minute, 30-minute or much longer pieces) and audience. As well as guidelines, there are a number of books entirely devoted to radio writing, some of which are cited in our bibliography. These can be constructive and encouraging. For instance, Vincent McInerney provides a helpful acronym: ODARE. As he explains,

> All classically constructed writing works in the same fashion: Opening, Development, Argument, Resolution, Ending (ODARE). That is, the basic well-made story should contain these elements in sequence. We should have a firm, interesting
>
> OPENING which draws in the listener by an intriguing and positive beginning that captures the attention and introduces the main character(s) who
>
> DEVELOP the story by elaborating the plot, and set up the
>
> ARGUMENT which will usually mean pitching the main characters and their points of view/beliefs against each other until the
>
> RESOLUTION occurs, at which point the Argument or conflict is resolved, for good or bad, and the story moves into its
>
> ENDING where all the threads are finally pulled together and the listener is presented with a complete and rounded work where all queries have been met and all questions answered. (McInerney, 2001, pp. 59–60)

After this, McInerney builds on this essential structure at length, demonstrating the stepwise process of expansion and development that the writing of a radio script entails.

Plays are not the only type of dramatic writing in radio. Earlier in this book we used the example of a Red Cross advertisement to demonstrate how even a work a few seconds in duration can be arresting and moving. Radio commercials are a long-established form from the earliest days of sponsorship. The extreme economy demanded of the contemporary radio advertisement means that the form can be a challenge to write, but also a fruitful exercise for any writer interested in writing for audio. Writing a 15-second commercial can be an excellent springboard from which you learn skills that will inform the writing of your multi-episode epic! To this end, we are pleased to include Rik Ferrell's useful guide to writing radio commercials (*Writing Effective Radio Ad Copy: Six Steps to Successful Radio Commercials*) as an appendix to this book.

However, we must remember that when it comes to essential creativity, it cannot be pinned down so easily. After all, as Tim Crook writes, 'I do not believe you can discover and produce great radio drama through formulas' (Crook, 1999, p. 160). Never forgot that writers are human! Each person may find a different way of working. In writing this book, the authors conducted numerous interviews, and the degree of idiosyncrasy is fascinating – and it should also be encouraging. For instance, here is Kyle Hatley's account of his writing process:

> I have the worst attention span on Earth. So I know that if I'm bored – even for a second – I'm gonna start cutting. Or I'm gonna start rewriting or throw it out all together. I use my gut almost entirely. And the guts of my collaborators in the room. I lean very heavily on my ensemble: my actors, musicians, technicians, sfx team, etc. I watch them listen and if they look bored, I know something's wrong. In addition to keeping myself from being bored in the listening to it, I'm also hyper-sensitive to whether or not it actually creeps ME out. It has to interest ME. It has to move ME. It has to scare ME. If it doesn't, I'm doing something wrong. (Hatley, 2010)

We see the balance here between the personal and the social. Hatley is acutely aware of his own instinct as a writer, trusting his own sense of engagement and boredom. At the same time, he shows how important it is to *share* the work with others and to trust the feedback that you receive (or detect). Audio drama can be a very intimate form, but like all the performing arts, it is a collaborative process. Hatley sums up how important it is to learn to be objective:

> I'm always hoping to maintain a sense of good storytelling while also being as objective as possible so that I can 'play' the part of the listener while writing and directing and hopefully learning how to bring the audience and the story as close together without ever getting in the way. (Hatley, 2010)

Another member of Chatterbox Audio Theater, Robert Arnold, explains how he learned the craft of audio writing:

> I for one have learned an enormous amount by just sitting down and *writing*. I've also learned a ton by *listening* to other shows, both classic and contemporary. You learn what NOT to do by listening to a bunch of terrible shows. I've had listening experiences that I'd never wish on anyone. At the same time, I've been enormously affected by shows, sometimes when I least expect it. You try to recreate that experience in other people. You write what moves you, and you hope it moves others. (Arnold, 2010)

As this suggests, it is important to keep experimenting and keep writing. It is also helpful to continue listening to audio drama. By listening to audio drama, you will gain a critical mass to work with. You will find work that you like and dislike, and this will enable you to develop a sense of the potential of the form and discover your own tastes and, hopefully, your own aspirations.

Exercises

- Listen to some examples of audio drama and assess what has been done well and what has been done poorly. If something works well, can you determine why? If something is disappointing, can you understand why it didn't work? What was supposed to be achieved? How could it be improved? How would you rewrite it to make it work?
- Using the guidelines in the appendix, experiment with writing a variety of radio commercials.

Some key points

1. Keep things simple, at least at first.
2. Think in terms of audio. Take heed of producer Mariele Runacre Temple's experience of receiving scripts:

    > For us, it is very important that the writer has written a radio play. This may sound rather obvious, but (despite our guidelines) we receive a large number of scripts that start along the lines of 'We see the sun setting through the window of Jenny's room, she sits staring into space, a longing look on her face – we can tell by the sun it is afternoon. She is tall, with long dark hair . . .' etc. – which shows to us that not only does the writer not understand the medium, but that they haven't even taken the time to actually adapt their play (which isn't always as easy as just removing the stage directions!). (Runacre Temple, 2010).

3. Enjoy the wonderful freedom audio offers you. As Shane Salk says: 'You're not tied down by location or props or anything. Everything is possible. Go crazy!' (Salk, 2010).
4. Remember that writing is just one component in a thrilling and symbiotic mixture of writer, producer, performer and listener. However, a good story can be the beating heart that brings an audio drama to life.

5
Production

The craft of producing drama for radio

If radio drama is about painting sound pictures, then the radio drama producer is a consummate and multi-skilled artist. This chapter is concerned with the creative and technical aspects of production: the craft of capturing the drama for radio, for which the radio drama producer has overall responsibility. The BBC radio drama producer coordinates a team of actors and technicians who have expertise in various aspects of production. However, an effective producer will have an excellent understanding of the work of all members of the team, in order to make informed decisions on the technical and creative possibilities available. In the non-professional world, which most of us inhabit, the role of the radio drama producer is far less defined. In a community radio station, the drama producer could potentially write the script, find the actors, record and post-produce alone. Whichever way you look at it, the producer needs to know all aspects of the craft. This chapter attempts to unravel the multiple layers of responsibility attributed to radio drama producers. It offers insights and exercises to allow the reader the opportunity to develop knowledge of and experience with the different aspects of production. The ultimate aim is for an understanding of the professional processes of radio drama production to be developed and applied to the circumstances available. This will ensure that successful radio drama can be produced, whatever resources are available. The technical terminology of radio drama production will be new to some readers, and a glossary has been included at the end of this chapter.

Equipment

The miracle of radio drama is how cheap it can be to produce. There is no need to fly your cast and production team to the Amazon to successfully create a drama based in that location. It is perfectly possible to create a convincing drama based in seventeenth-century England without spending a fortune on historical costumes and sets. Furthermore, radio drama can be produced with absolutely minimal technical resources. If you have use of a studio of any kind, there will be more production options, but it is far from essential to record in a studio. This section offers audio drama recording options to suit all budgets, grouped into three general categories: *No studio*; *DJ studio*; *Specialist Sound Studio.*

No studio

This option is the most basic, but is perfectly adequate for recording radio drama on location, rather than in a studio. The location recordings can be enhanced by adding pre-recorded sfx and music at the post-production stage, if editing facilities are available.

Essential

- Mono microphone, audio recorder (or recorder with built – in microphone), microphone stand and headphones
- Selection of spot sfx (Note: further information on spot sfx can be found in the Sound Effects section later in this chapter.)
- Water supply nearby (Drama often requires characters to make, pour or consume drinks.)

Desirable

- A selection of stereo and mono microphones
- A digital hard disk recorder, capable of recording stereo at 128 Kb/s (Mp3 quality or better). XLR microphone inputs. USB interface
- Commercial online or CD database of pre-recorded sfx
- Computer with USB interface and digital audio editing/mixing software

DJ studio

A typical 'on air' radio studio of the kind used in a small commercial, community or student radio station, can be adapted for radio drama use. The more space there is available around the mixing desk, the better, since successful radio drama requires performers to stand and move around.

Essential

- Mono microphone
- Flexible microphone stand, which can be angled to accommodate standing performers
- Recording device (mixing desk connected to audio recorder or computer capable of recording one or more microphone inputs)

- Headphones
- Selection of 'spot' sfx
- Water supply nearby

Desirable

- A selection of stereo and mono microphones
- Ability to connect one or more free-standing microphones to the recording device
- Computer with multiple sound cards to enable simultaneous recording and replay
- Special effects, such as EQ and reverb
- Commercial online or CD database of pre-recorded sfx
- Loud speakers
- Two or more sound-absorbing acoustic screens

Specialist sound studio

These studios are normally used for recording music, but do adapt very well to radio drama. Typically, they consist of a reasonably large sound-proofed room (the studio) and a linked control room, where the sound is actually recorded. There is normally line of sight between the two areas via sound-proofed glass.

Essential – In Studio

- Mono microphone
- Selection of spot sfx
- Two or more sound-absorbing acoustic screens
- Headphones for spot sfx technician

Essential – In Control Room

- Recording device (mixing desk connected to audio recorder or computer capable of recording one or more microphone inputs)
- Loud speakers
- Talkback system to studio
- Water supply nearby

Desirable – In Studio

- A selection of stereo and mono microphones

- A spot sfx collection
- Ability to vary acoustic properties of the studio – screens with contrasting absorbing and hard surfaces, curtains, hard and soft areas of flooring
- Loud speakers or headphones for performers

Desirable – In Control Room

- Commercial online or CD database of pre-recorded sfx
- Computer with multiple sound cards to enable simultaneous recording and replay
- Special effects, such as EQ and reverb

Microphones for radio drama

In theatre and on screen, we see actors move, we see when they enter or leave the scene, we see their position in relation to one another; this gives us a sense of perspective. The tool for conveying the presence of a character, a sense of movement and perspective in radio drama is the microphone.

There are many types of microphone, offering all levels of recording quality. Microphones can be connected via cable to the mixing desk or recording device. Sometimes, perfectly acceptable microphones are built into the recorders themselves. Most recording devices will enable you to control the sound level of the microphone, which should be set before any recording. The highest sound level 'peak' should be at –3 decibels (dB). Peaks above 0 dB will cause a distorted sound. Though some microphone properties are particularly useful for radio drama, it is possible to achieve a good radio drama recording with the simplest and cheapest of microphones. The most important thing is to understand the properties of the microphone available to you and to appreciate how these properties can help you to record radio drama effectively. Broadly speaking, microphones are either mono, with one audio sensor, or stereo, with two audio sensors. In the case of stereo microphones, the audio sensors can be within one single microphone casing or two separate microphones positioned at right angles to each other; called a 'stereo pair'.

A mono recording sounds two dimensional: The listener hears how close or far away characters are from each other. If all the listening circumstances are correct, then a stereo microphone provides the listener with a three dimensional sound picture. In addition to distance, the listener can hear the characters to the left, right and centre, as well as moving from left to right, in semicircular pattern. Please see the Listener Experience section below for further information on listening to stereo.

All microphones have a 'live' area, where the sound being recorded is clear and distinct, and a 'dead' area, where the sound is distant and unclear. In addition, stereo microphones have an 'in phase' area, where the positioning of characters in the stereo field sounds distinct, and an 'out of phase' area, where the positioning sounds indistinct and woolly.

Mono microphone

Stereo microphones are usually used for recording professional radio drama. However, in the early days of radio drama, mono microphones were perfectly adequate, as they are today. A mono microphone of the kind often found in a DJ-style radio studio or a simple reporter microphone can produce very acceptable results. Interestingly, radio drama is the only radio genre in which the 'dead' area of the mono microphone is just as important as the 'live' area. It is the use of the 'dead' area and the point of transition between the 'live' and 'dead' areas that enable actors to portray distance and movement. An exploration of the working area of the microphone (sometimes called the 'field') is a useful exercise. The best way to do this is by means of an experiment.

Exercise

After checking the sound levels of the microphone, assign one or more members of the group to listen and make notes. The remaining members should speak into the microphone at different positions around, above and below the microphone. Make notes on where the voice sounds distinct and clear and where it sounds distant.

Your findings will depend on the type of microphone you have. A clear sound at all points of the microphone indicates that you have an omnidirectional microphone: one which picks up sound all around it. Imagine a spherical lollipop that represents the microphone field, with the microphone at its centre. You may find that your microphone sounds 'live' at some points and 'dead' at others. This pattern suggests that you have a 'directional' microphone. If so, ask one member of the team to walk around the microphone, speaking into it at all times. You should now be able to determine the transitional point on the microphone

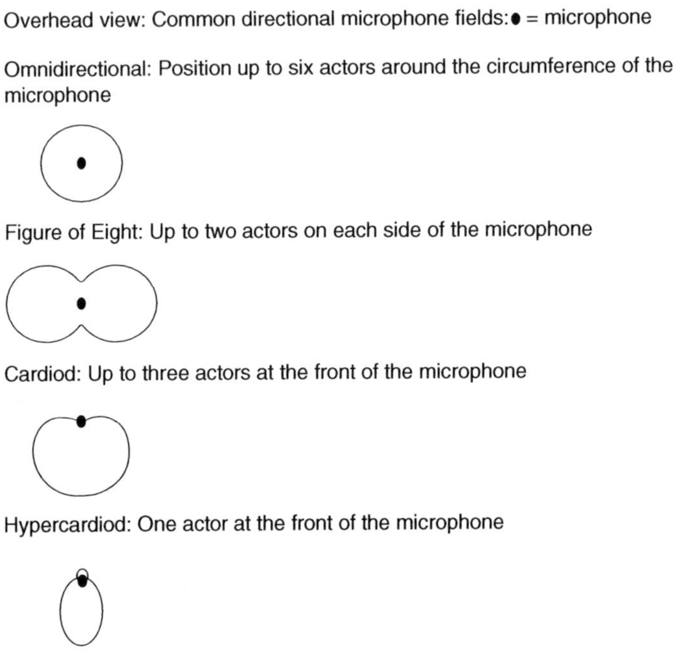

Overhead view: Common directional microphone fields:● = microphone

Omnidirectional: Position up to six actors around the circumference of the microphone

Figure of Eight: Up to two actors on each side of the microphone

Cardiod: Up to three actors at the front of the microphone

Hypercardiod: One actor at the front of the microphone

Figure 5.1 Overhead view: Common directional microphone fields

between the 'live' and 'dead' areas. Various fields are possible and multi-directional microphones have switchable fields.

Stereo microphone

Using a stereo microphone requires some additional attention to technical detail at this stage. A stereo microphone is essentially two mono microphones – one for the left side (A) and one for the right (B). It is important that A and B are set to the same sound level (balanced), otherwise sounds recorded through A will sound louder or quieter than those recorded through B (unbalanced). Some recorders and microphones have a single stereo input, requiring just one cable to be connected; the sound levels are automatically balanced. Others have two mono inputs, requiring separate connections for A and B. In this case, it will be necessary to 'pan' A fully to the left and B to the right on the mixing desk or recorder and manually adjust the sound levels of each. The 'live' and 'dead' properties that are so important in mono microphones for radio drama are irrelevant when using a stereo microphone. Only the 'in phase' area is useful

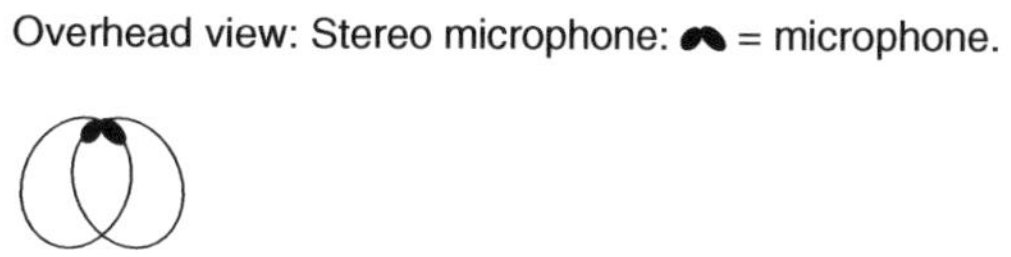

Overhead view: Stereo microphone: ● = microphone.

Figure 5.2 Overhead view: Stereo microphone

as sounds in the 'out of phase' area lose their distinct stereo imagery and sound very odd.

Exercise

This exercise will enable you to establish the 'in phase' and 'out of phase' areas of the stereo microphone.

Assign group members to listen and make notes, and actors to position themselves at different locations around the microphone, and at different distances from it, and to speak into the microphone one at a time. From this, it should be possible to determine the centre and extent of the 'in phase' area, roughly the shape of a semicircle.

The listener experience

Before making any decisions on what microphone to use, it is important to consider how the listener will actually hear the radio drama. Although mono, stereo and surround sound recording are infinitely possible, other important considerations are the circumstances of the broadcast and the equipment available to the listener. FM stereo radio is currently the most listened to form of radio, though many listeners do not actually listen in stereo, either because they do not have a stereo radio or because they are not positioned correctly or listening on headphones. The best stereo listening occurs when the listener and the two sound sources form an equilateral triangle. Stereo is only really effective when the listener sits motionless between the two sources of sound or wears headphones. As we have discussed in the 'Theories of Radio Drama' chapter, radio listening is normally a secondary activity, so this form of intense listening to radio is relatively uncommon. Digital and satellite technologies mean that surround sound radio drama can be considered as a recording option. However, similar to stereo, the listener is required to be in a fixed position for the full effect. Whatever microphone you decide to select, it is important that the drama is still effective for the listener in the most basic circumstances: the small, mono radio on the kitchen shelf.

A note about binaural and surround sound

Stereo is very effective in conveying the relative positions of characters and a range of movement from left to right, but the picture it paints is not entirely accurate. Think of the microphone as an ear, so when we are recording in stereo the left microphone = left ear and the right microphone = right ear. The problem is that the microphones in the stereo pair are normally locked together, whereas our ears are not; they are on either side of the head. This means that the stereo pair is not picking up sound precisely as we would hear it for real. The resulting sound is unnaturally close; some producers describe it as 'inside the head'. For most producers, this is not a significant issue. After all, radio drama does not set out to give the listener a photographic image of the 'real' world; instead, it provides audio clues to trigger the imagination to fill in the detail. However, other producers are particularly interested in conveying the most accurate picture possible, and for them, recording techniques such as binaural and surround sound are useful. In binaural stereo, a dummy head is used. The head is 18cm across, roughly the same as the human head, and the stereo pair is separated, one microphone on each side. The sound is therefore picked up by the microphones in the same way as our ears would hear it. The resulting recording is much more accurate. Instead of being 'inside the head', the sound is as it would be in real life; outside the head and around us. The effect of binaural stereo can only be heard on stereo headphones, but the positioning of the characters to the left, right and even behind is much more realistic than simple stereo. Surround sound for radio works on the same principal as surround sound for cinema or home theatre. Similar to stereo and binaural stereo, it assumes that the listener remains in a fixed position between the sources of sound – five or more loudspeakers or surround sound headphones. Producing a surround sound recording is much more complex and requires surround sound software. Mono microphones are positioned at intervals around the sound source to be recorded. These are then mixed with any other sounds required in the drama, such as music and sfx, and a surround sound pan control is used to create a full 360-degree spectrum. While it is technically possible to broadcast radio in binaural and surround sound, it is rare. However, an increasing number of radio drama downloads and DVDs make use of this technology to great effect, such as the audio drama horror downloads available at *3DHorrorfi* (2011).

Creating movement and perspective – mono and stereo

Now that you have explored the properties of microphones available to you, it is time to consider how they can be used effectively for radio drama. In most speech-based radio, the voices we hear are static. In the radio studio, the presenters and contributors rarely move. The DJ sits at the mixing desk, the discussion panel sits around a table; even the radio journalist on location normally presents the report from a fixed, standing position. In radio drama, the opposite is true. We are attempting to create an impression of reality and, for most of us, real life involves a lot of movement. This section considers the use of microphones to convey movement and perspective, which will be useful for producers and performers alike. The 'Performing' chapter discusses this issue in more detail from the perspective of an actor.

'*Let me tell you a secret . . .*': Creating perspective

In mono, the positions of the characters in relation to each other – the perspective – can be conveyed to some extent by the actors' positions relative to the microphone. If a scene involves an intimate conversation between two characters, you would expect the characters to sound as if they were close to each other. Place the actors equidistant from the microphone. A conversation in which one character is at a distance can be achieved by placing the actor in the 'dead' area or at a distance from the microphone.

In stereo, further subtlety is possible. Characters can be placed in different positions within the stereo field. Again, using an example of a conversation between two characters, this can be achieved by placing characters to the left and right of a stereo microphone. The conversation can be made to appear more intimate by moving the actors towards the centre of the microphone, or more separation between the characters can be achieved by positioning them far left and right.

'Now . . . where did I put my purse . . .': Creating movement

Though stereo perhaps offers more options for creating a sense of movement, mono provides perfectly acceptable options. If your microphone is 'directional', the actor can move from the 'live' to the 'dead' areas to seek that purse. The character can sound as if she is in a different room simply by speaking into the 'dead' area of the microphone. If you are working with an omnidirectional microphone, a similar effect can be achieved by moving away from the microphone or turning your back to it.

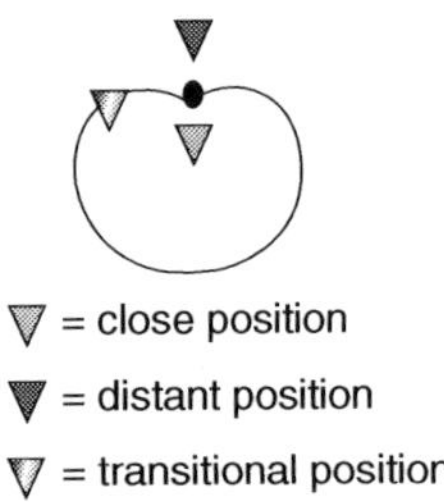

Figure 5.3 Overhead view: Movement and perspective; mono, cardioid microphone

In stereo, actors can move around the stereo field, creating movement from left to right. They can also move back, or turn away, from the microphone, to create a sense of moving away. Remember to only use the 'in phase area', as described earlier.

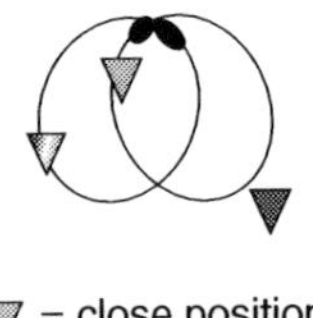

Figure 5.4 Overhead view: Movement and perspective; stereo microphone

Exercise – movement and perspective

This exercise, for a group of 5 students, introduces techniques for creating a sense of movement, distance and perspective in radio drama. The technical requirements are flexible. The exercise can take place in a sound studio, if one is available, but can also be achieved in an ordinary room, using portable recording equipment.

You will need the following:

- Copies of the script for each member of the group
- A microphone mounted on a stand

- Recording equipment (a sound studio with mixing desk, if you have one. Otherwise, a portable recording device is fine.)
- Spot sfx
- A group of 5 students (taking the roles of 2 actors, a spot sfx operator, a technician, a producer)
- Pen and paper

Script – movement and perspective exercise

INTERIOR KITCHEN
SFX: STEWART IS WASHING UP

1. LOUISA: Hiya, I'm home.
2. STEWART: Hi, I'm here. In the kitchen.
3. LOUISA: What's for tea?
4. STEWART: Oh – I'm not sure. I'll just need to check what we've got in the fridge. OK – onions, mushrooms, a green pepper, half a tin of tomatoes. I could make a pasta sauce out of that lot.
5. LOUISA: Sounds lovely, but needs garlic, doesn't it?
6. STEWART: Yep – can you check in the cupboard? Have we got any?
7. LOUISA: No, looks like we've run out.
8. STEWART: Maybe not – check the vegetable rack.
9. LOUISA: No, can't see any there either. I'll go round the shop and get some.
10. STEWART: OK – bye . . . Hey – hang on – can you get some spaghetti at the same time?
11. LOUISA: No probs. See you in a minute. (SHE LEAVES)

Instructions

1. After reading through the script, draw a map of the kitchen, as you see it in your mind's eye, showing the location of the fridge, cupboard, door, and so forth.
2. Consider the properties of the microphone available to you. As a group, discuss how the actors and spot sfx operator could use the microphone's properties to convey a sense of movement.
3. Plot the position of the microphone and the 'journey' of the actors throughout the scene on your map, using arrows and the line numbers as indicated in the script. It may help to think of this in visual terms. If this was a film, who is the camera focused on at the opening of the scene? With Stuart and his washing up or with Louisa as she comes through the door?

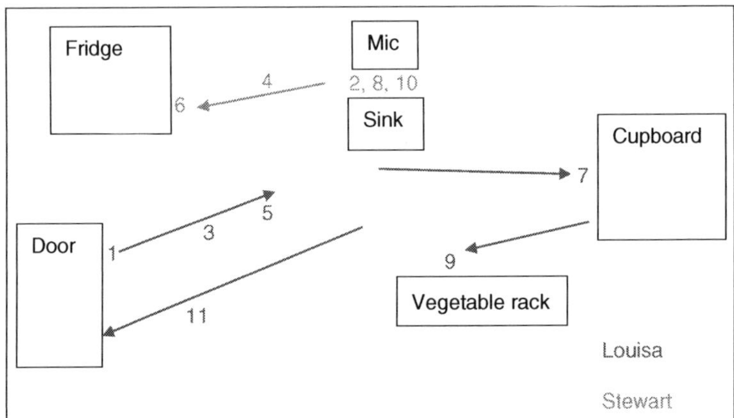

Figure 5.5 This is an example of how you might plot the scene.

4. Remember that the positioning of the spot sfx in relation to the actors is important. They must sound like they are taking place in the same location as the related dialogue.
5. Think about performance techniques! It is one thing to use microphone technique to make the voice sound distant, as if the character is in the next room. The effect won't work overall, though, unless the actor can actually project the line as if she is calling from another room.
6. Rehearse and record the scene.
7. Listen to the recording. Consider the extent to which you were able to convey a sense of movement, distance and perspective in the scene.
8. If you have more than one kind of microphone available, you can record different versions and consider the relative merits of each.

The subtle microphone

Now that the technical details of microphone use for radio drama are established, it is time to apply your knowledge to producing radio drama. Each scene in radio drama has what Alan Beck (1998) describes as a 'point of listening'. This represents the physical position of the characters in relation to each other and the significance of each character within the scene. The 'point of listening' determines which characters and events in the scene are prioritized. When we are presented with a radio drama script, it is tempting to think that we have to dramatize every single nuance of that script for the audience. Not only would this be technically difficult to achieve, but it would also be very confusing for the listener. Consider this script:

SARA IS IN THE KITCHEN. PETER IS IN THE LOUNGE.

1. PETER: Sara – get a move on. It's nearly 9. The footy's starting any minute now.
2. SARA: OK – just coming. I'm getting a beer. You want one?
3. PETER: No, but grab that bar of chocolate for me – it's behind the cheese in the fridge.
4. SARA: (ENTERS LOUNGE) Come on – you haven't even switched the TV on.
5. SARA: (IN AN OFFHAND MANNER) Can't find the chocolate, by the way.
6. PETER: Typical. You're always saying you can't watch football without beer. And you know it's the same with me and chocolate. I suppose I'll have to find it.
7. PETER: And I'm blaming you if I miss the beginning.

If we attempted to give equal attention to every location and movement, the listener would quickly become confused as we cut between the kitchen and the lounge. The production team must agree on the 'point of listening' in the scene. In order to do this, it is necessary to establish the motivations and important events in the scene. Does the scene demonstrate Peter's frustration with Sara? Does it demonstrate that Sara is selfish? This will, in turn, inform the technicalities of how the scene is produced. A good way of thinking of this is to imagine that you have a single surveillance camera. Where will you point the camera

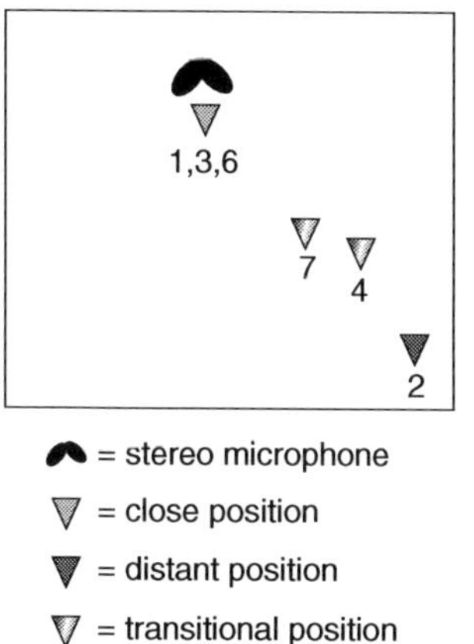

Figure 5.6 Studio plan showing actor positions at each line

to capture the scene? Which character will it focus on? In radio drama, the microphone takes the place of that surveillance camera; the microphone is positioned to draw the listener's attention to the main character or event. Radio producers often call this position the 'sound centre'. In Figure 5.6, the production team has determined that the scene conveys Peter's frustration with Sara, which in turn has confirmed the 'point of listening' and the 'sound centre'. The character we are 'with' is Peter, and the location is the living room.

Exercise

Apply an alternative interpretation to the scene and plan how this will affect the 'point of listening' and the 'sound centre'. How does it alter things if Sara's selfishness becomes the main event? Or what if it is important to convey that the TV is broken or that there is no chocolate in the fridge? Where will you position the surveillance camera/microphone? Using Figure 5.6 as an example, draw a plan to plot the relative positions of the actors to the microphone for each line.

Setting the scene

Good radio drama producers understand how to provide the right clues: the audio stimuli that will combine with the power of the imagination to produce the desired images. Often, it is a combination of different audio stimuli which will produce the desired effect. To understand the different kinds of stimuli, we will use the example of the stage in theatre and consider its audio equivalences.

Creating location and ambience – the audio backdrop

The painted backdrop in theatre suggests the overall location. In Richard Rodgers and Oscar Hammerstein's *Oklahoma!* (1943), the backdrop is typically a sweeping plain, with a distant, picturesque farmhouse. In Claude-Michel Schönberg and Alain Boublil's *Les Misérables* (1980), it is a nineteenth-century Parisian street. The backdrop does not normally convey a precise location, but a general impression of a location. On screen, the equivalent of a backdrop might be an image to establish the location, such as a shot of a busy emergency room at the beginning of a hospital drama. It is not the role of the backdrop to tell the story, but rather to give a suggestion of the location which will be enhanced with the addition of actors, lighting, props and music. Similarly, in radio drama there is an audio backdrop, usually called 'atmos' (short for atmosphere). The atmos suggests the location of the drama. It is tempting to try to compensate for the lack of visual backdrop by trying to establish every aspect of the location through the atmos. It is important to think of the atmos as just the background layer of sound, to which you will add others. The atmos should be subtle and non-intrusive. It can be helpful to record it in advance of the rest of the production so it can be played to actors to help them gain an understanding of the location you are trying to convey. Good atmos usually consists of several different sounds. The sources of the sound will depend on the atmos you are trying to create. In many cases, the most successful atmos will be recorded on location. For example, if an atmos of a small, intimate restaurant is required, this can easily be successfully recorded by visiting an appropriate venue with a portable recorder (with the owner's permission, of course!). It is not always possible or desirable to visit a particular location in person. In this case, a bank of recorded atmos sound effects is available through websites, sometimes as free downloads and sometimes for a fee. CD sound effect libraries can also be purchased. These pre-recorded sounds are most useful for difficult-to-visit locations – depending on where you live, it might be a bit tricky to get to a South American rainforest, a Himalayan mountain or a market place in Mumbai, for example! Lateral thinking is sometimes an advantage when it comes to creating sound effects of all kinds, including atmos. Remember: it is perfectly possible to create convincing atmos from several different sources. There are many excellent websites devoted to creating atmos, which will give you inspiration. This example describes an inventive way to create a wind effect:

> Try turning a bicycle upside down (a touring model rather than a mountain bike . . . the tires are smoother). Spin the tire and press a piece of stretched silk/parachute-pants/winter-parka against it. Out comes wind in the form of a modulating white/pink noise. (Watson, 2010)

Exercise

How would you create the atmos of a volcano? Or rush hour on a city transit system? Or a bar getting gradually busier? You'll need to think creatively about all the different sounds you are likely to hear in those environments. What layers of sound will you need, and how will you go about creating or finding them?

Sound effects

If atmos helps set the general audio environment, then sound effects (sfx) make it specific. They are often linked directly to the dialogue and are integral to the drama. Good examples are the sounds of pouring a drink, a telephone ringing, a door knock. If atmos is the equivalent of the stage backdrop, then sound effects are the props. There are two main sources of sound effects: *pre-recorded sfx*, available on CD or online and *'spot' sfx*, which are created 'live' at the time of recording the drama. The job of the sfx team is infinitely complex and creative in searching for the most perfect sound achievable in a given situation. Usually, a few sfx are specified within the script, but it is the job of the sfx team to identify where additional sfx may be needed to clarify events or to enhance the drama.

Exercise

Read the following lines of dialogue.

STEVE: John – what's happened? What's wrong? You are shaking all over.
JOHN: I can't . . . I can't . . . talk . . . right now . . . Just let me in – quick.
STEVE: Yes, of course – sorry. What can I do to help you – I don't understand what's happened. Are you hurt?
JOHN: No . . . not hurt exactly. I . . . don't know how . . . how to tell you.
STEVE: Sit down there and try to calm down. I'll get you a drink.
JOHN: No – no time to sit down. But give me that drink, and you're gonna need one too, when you hear this.

No sfx have been specified in the script, but without them the scene is lifeless, and the listener will have difficulty building up a mental image of the scene. Discuss what spot sfx you could include to bring the dialogue to life.

Now consider different interpretations of the script. You may have made an assumption about the location of the characters. How will the sfx change by moving that location? For example, if you imagined the characters in a house, try changing the location to a tent. How does this alter the sfx used?

Now consider the historical era. You may have assumed the drama is taking place in the present day. Try locating it 100 years in the future, or 100 years in the past, or in a different country, and consider how the sfx will change.

Record different versions of the script.

Spot sfx

There is no doubt that creating spot sfx represents one of the most enjoyable endeavours in radio production. It provides an opportunity to be infinitely creative; sfx technicians are pursuing an honorable craft which dates back to the beginning of sound design for silent film.

The craft of the spot sfx technican

From the very earliest days of radio drama, sfx were crucial to the process of creating radio drama. Richard Hughes, the writer of *A Comedy of Danger*, acknowledged that the inspiration for the sfx came from the tradition of cinema. Even though early film had no recorded soundtrack, sfx and music were added 'live' in the cinema, and it was film sfx technicians who created the first sfx for radio drama (Crook, 1999, p. 90). The ingenuity of these pioneers of sound really cannot be overestimated. The creation of spot sfx was clearly a matter of much ingenuity and pride, as evidenced by the detailed documentation from the 1930s to the 1950s. Sound 'men', as they usually were, employed all manner of creativity and panache, and clearly took their jobs very seriously. An early pioneer of radio in the United States, Waldo Abbott (1941), provides some helpful hints on creating sound effects. To convey the sound of a cow being milked, he suggests squeezing two ear syringes alternately into a bucket, adding helpfully 'It is advisable to have an additional supply of syringes if the effect must last for a length of time' (Abbott, 1941, p. 166). In his account of sfx technicians in radio, Robert L. Mott cites one of the pioneers, Ora Nichols, who rose to the challenge of the sfx that the flourishing form of radio was demanding. Mott describes how Nichols would search junk shops, car wrecking yards and even people's garbage looking for objects that would make an interesting or useful noise. The result of her efforts meant that

> Soon the shelves of the CBS sound-effects department began to spill over with mechanic's tools, household items, children's toys, medical instruments, business machines, garden tools, luggage, motors, carpenter's tools, and just about anything else that was capable of making a sound. (Mott, 1993, p. 73)

In addition, those redoubtable pioneers of sfx made the discovery that objects do not always sound like they should: in other words, real ice being thrown into a glass does not sound as real as two metal bolts being dropped into glass. Similarly, gunshots were sometimes less effective (or reliable) when fired from a stage gun than when they were created by smacking a metal rod against a leather seat. You might like to try these or other examples, such as twisting bubble-wrap to create the sound of a crackling fire, or rubbing a wet cork against an empty glass bottle to create the sound of a squeaking rat.

In the radio industry, innovative approaches persist to this day. *The Crazy Dog Audio Theatre* produces both studio-based and live radio drama for RTE Radio 1 (the National Broadcasting Company of Ireland). Their website provides a lot of detail on the wonderful sfx that are created for their productions:

> CRASHES/COMMOTION: We use a variety of CRASH BOXES. The CRASH BOX is a metal biscuit tin filled with glass, a cup, a couple marbles, a small wooden block or two and a few coins. The different size boxes with varied contents produce different crash and commotion sounds. Using a small wooden or cardboard box again produces a different sound as sometimes the metallic sound of the biscuit tin is sometimes inappropriate. For other commotion sounds we bash together 3 or 4 cardboard shoe boxes. We collect empty boxes of various sizes and materials: metal, cardboard, plastic and wooden just for commotion sounds. (Crazy Dog Audio Theatre, 2011)

The long-running BBC soap opera *The Archers* also has creative approaches to spot sfx, such as this example of the birth of a lamb: 'Farty yoghurt squidged through clasped hands . . . then a heavy wet towel being dropped onto recording tape . . . Always makes me laugh, without fail!' (Greig, 2010).

Spot sfx collection

It is really useful to build up a collection of spot sfx. Here are some suggestions for forming the basis of a good collection.

> *Essential*:
>
> Crockery, cutlery, kitchen utensils, glass bottle, old audio or video tape (which can be used for various undergrowth sounds), sticks, various kinds of plastic bag.
>
> *Desirable*:
>
> Purpose-built spot sfx, such as a door box with different kinds of door fittings, hinges and knockers, gravel 'pits' (shallow wooden boxes with different floor surfaces, such as paving stones or gravel), a staircase, a sink with running water.

Exercise

Using only spot sfx and the infinite power of your imagination, create the following sounds:

- A building on fire and toppling down
- Footsteps on ice
- Sawing off a limb
- A large bird in flight

Pre-recorded sfx

Spot sfx were the mainstay of early radio drama, but as recording technologies improved, so did the possibility for including pre-recorded sfx in radio drama. By the 1940s, well-resourced radio stations had access to a bank of recorded sounds. These added new levels of sophistication to what might be achieved in radio drama. Abbott cites the example of a particularly conscientious producer who, in the pursuit of accuracy, was keen to set up sound recording equipment in a local hospital 'in order to record the shrieks of a person injured in an automobile accident' (Abbott, 1941, p. 160). Such devotion to detail is rarely called for today, but it still remains the case that it is not always practical, or desirable, to use spot sfx. Consider this dialogue:

EXTERIOR: NEVADA DESERT
SFX RATTLE SNAKE
STEVE: Just keep really still.
SOROYA: Yes –really still.
STEVE: Now slowly – move back. No sudden movements.
SOROYA: Ok – yes – very slowly.
STEVE: I'm going to whack it with this big stick.
SOROYA: What – are you mad?
SFX RATTLE SNAKE STRIKES
SOROYA: Aaargh! Quick – do something!
SFX HITS SNAKE WITH STICK
STEVE: (PANTING) Did it get you?

Clearly, recording a scene with a live rattlesnake is not a good idea! Although it could be an exciting challenge to create the sound of a rattlesnake in the desert, it might prove more efficacious to use a recording. Similarly, a skid of tyres, a battlefront, a charging elephant, or a TV being thrown out of a hotel room are difficult to create in a studio. This is where pre-recorded sfx come into their own. In the early days of radio drama, pre-recorded sfx were mixed in from 'gram' (vinyl record) at the time of recording the drama. The sophistication of digital editing and mixing means that most pre-recorded sfx are now mixed with the dialogue and spot sfx after the main recording: 'post-production', to use a term borrowed from the film world.

An example of podcast drama that uses extensive post-production is Christof Laputka's science fiction drama series *The Leviathan Chronicles* (2008 onwards). In Chapter 3 of the first season, a central character, Macallan Orsel (Liz Craynon), meets a psychiatrist who she hopes might provide information on the mystery she is beginning to unravel. Their initial dialogue takes place in a coffee shop, and we hear the other customers and ambient music. They leave the coffee shop and we hear street sounds before they depart in the psychiatrist's car. Stopping at traffic lights, Macallan asks him what 'Leviathan' is. We hear encroaching traffic noise and a beeping horn as he begins to explain, when suddenly a vehicle crashes into their car. After the prolonged sound of smashing metal and shattering glass, we hear blasting car horns and alarms, and the narrator's voiceover:

> As the Taurus crossed 79th Street, a black Range Rover barrelled across the red light at high speed smashing into the driver's side of the car. The Rover continued to push the Taurus down the intersection until it was pinned against a traffic light on Macallan's side. The sudden stop caused Macallan's head to smash against the side window, opening a two-inch gash on her forehead. All of the airbags deployed, and for a split second Macallan had thought she saw the doctor's nose explode in a violent gush of red. She struggled to remain conscious as she felt every bone in her body shift.

The description may seem long, but it is deliberately precise (almost like a detailed police account), which is in startling contrast to the violence of the sequence and the cacophony in the background. Post-production has constructed an elaborate soundscape which captures the horror of the accident juxtaposed with the calm exactitude of the narrator.

Using pre-recorded sound is generally much more complex than spot. The main difficulty is precisely matching the sound with the script, in terms of the accuracy of sound and its duration. In most situations, sfx that you pre-record yourself are going to sound better than any you will find online or on CD. For example, if you need the sound of a contemporary train pulling into a station, then the most authentic sound you can get will be at your local railway station. However, if you are looking for the sound of the train which transports Harry Potter to Hogwarts, you will probably get the most authentic sound from a CD or online. The advantage of pre-recording sfx yourself is that it is more likely to fit with the dialogue. Consider the following script:

EXTERIOR: NEVADA DESERT
SOROYA: My leg – it's . . . it's going numb. Wait – what are you doing?
SFX CAR DOOR OPENS. STEVE GETS IN.
SOROYA: No – don't leave me.
STEVE: (THROUGH CAR WINDOW). Look – you can't move OK? It'll just make the poison spread further. Just keep that tourniquet tight. I'm going to get help. Be back straight away – promise.
SFX CAR DOOR SHUTS. CAR DRIVES OFF
SOROYA: Steve . . . No . . . Don't leave me.. . . STEVE!
STEVE (CALLING FROM CAR WINDOW) I'll be back. Just keep still.
SOROYA: STEVE . . . Steve!

As a member of the sfx team, you will know how fast you want the car to pull away and how long the sound must last to fit the script. If you depend on an online or CD sound, it will be much more difficult to match with the dialogue at post-production.

Exercise

Write a short scene, involving two characters preparing and eating food. Record two versions of the scene. Record the first version using spot sfx only. For the second version, record just the voices. Afterwards, mix in online or CD sfx. Which version is the most successful and why? Consider your answer from the perspective of the listener, the sfx team, the producer and the actors.

In the search for the best possible sfx solution, the team must find a compromise between what is desirable and what is actually achievable, striving to make the best possible decision to suit the circumstances. Wherever it is possible, the number one choice for the perfect sfx is probably 'spot'. Number two is sfx pre-recorded by the sfx team and, bringing up the rear, online and CD sfx, which provide a solution for otherwise unattainable sounds – like that angry rattlesnake or a high-speed car crash and aftermath!

sfx signals

Sit quietly: no talking, no moving. What can you hear? Chances are you are aware of far more sounds than you are normally. This is because our ears and brains 'tune in' to sounds that are relevant to us – almost like a camera zooming in and out. We would go mad if our brains forced us to attach equal significance to every sound that we can technically hear, so we are selective. It's just the same for radio listeners. The radio listener does not need to hear every sound that may theoretically be possible. She does not need to hear every footstep to understand that a character is walking. It is up to production team to select the most appropriate sound – the sfx signals – on behalf of the listener. Sometimes less is more. A cow mooing at the beginning of a farmyard scene is enough to indicate that location for the listener. We do not need to hear the cow continually mooing throughout the scene. It would distract the listener from the main point of the scene. In a scene in which a cop is chasing a robber, the listener does not need to hear pounding footsteps for five minutes, followed by a scuffle, to understand that the cop has chased and caught the robber. In this sense, radio drama is not showing reality. It is conveying an *impression* of reality. It is the listener who converts that impression of reality, the sfx signals, into *reality*.

Exercise

Select an action scene from a film of your choice: a chase or a fight. Consider how you would construct that scene for radio. What sfx signals would you use to indicate the event for the listener?

Acoustics – the science of sound

According to the Chambers English Dictionary (Chambers, 1992, p. 11), acoustics is 'the science of sound'. In radio drama, it means so much more. 'Acoustics' is the nature of sound in different locations. A producer will refer to an 'outside acoustic' and, with the addition of the atmos track, discussed earlier, that outside acoustic can be located anywhere in the world, at any time. An 'interior acoustic' usually requires more detail on the size and shape of that interior; for example, a cathedral sounds very different from the interior of a car.

While this book is not particularly concerned with 'the science of sound', it is important for the radio drama producer to have a basic grasp of how sound behaves in certain environments. The following section is, undoubtedly, 'technical', but stick with it, and you'll see how you can apply some basic technical knowledge to producing convincing radio drama locations.

Chain reaction

To begin, a little background on sound waves: Sound is produced when an object vibrates, so when our vocal cords vibrate, *sound waves* are produced. We can hear these vibrations when the sound waves cause our ear drums to vibrate. This sets off a chain of vibrations in the ear, which are sent as electrical impulses to the brain, which interprets the impulses as sounds. A microphone behaves in a similar way to our ears; it senses the vibrations from the sound waves and converts them into electrical impulses. However, the microphone is not selective. It does not interpret the sound waves as the listener's brain does; it just captures them. Sound waves consist of a whole range of audio frequencies, measured in Hertz or KiloHertz. I like to think of Hz/KHz as the notes on a piano; the low notes represent low frequencies and the high notes represent high frequencies.

How do sound waves behave in different environments?

What happens when sound waves hit obstacles should be a primary concern of the radio drama producer, as this is the main reason one location sounds different from another. When sound waves come into contact with an obstacle, some of the sound is absorbed into the obstacle (*absorption*), some bounces off it (*reflection*) and some passes through it (*transmission*). How much sound is absorbed, reflected and transmitted depends on the obstacle and the audio frequency of the sound waves.

In an open outside space, like a field, there are no obstacles, which means there is no reflection, so the sound wave simply dies away.

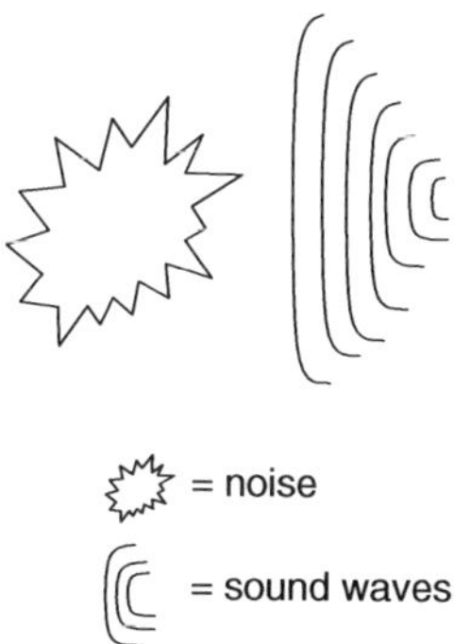

Figure 5.7 Sound waves; outside

When a sound wave hits a hard, flat surface, like a double-glazed window, most of the sound will reflect. Basically, the sound will bounce off the surface, creating an additional sound – an echo or reverberation. This is why a kitchen, where there are usually lots of hard, reflective surfaces, sounds slightly echoey.

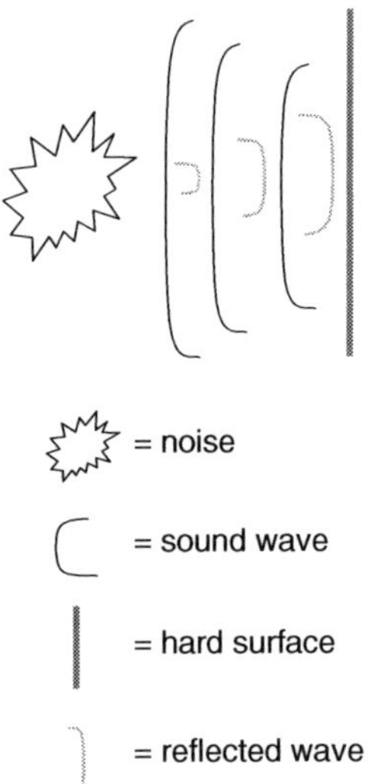

Figure 5.8 Sound waves; reflection

If sound hits a soft surface, more of the sound will be absorbed into that surface and less of it will be reflected. There will be fewer echoes. In a living room, for example, you might expect there to be a carpet, soft furnishings, curtains, all of which will partly absorb sound and minimize the reverberation.

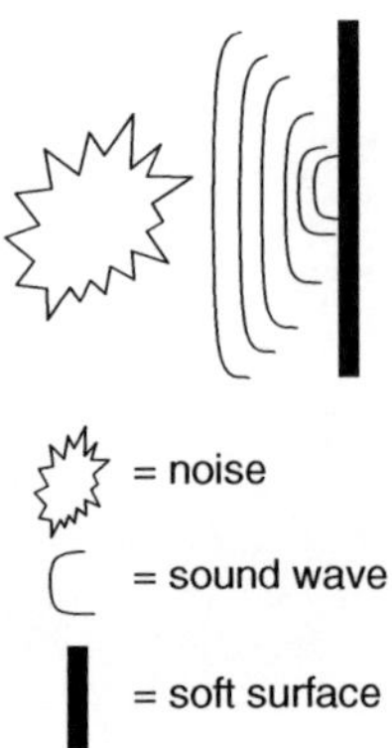

Figure 5.9 Sound waves; absorption

Unless a surface is completely soundproof, part of the sound passes through the surface – transmission. When your neighbour has music playing loudly, you will probably hear the thump, thump of the bass through your wall, more than you will hear the high frequency sounds. This is because the bass frequencies are more easily transmitted through the wall, and the high frequencies are more easily absorbed or reflected.

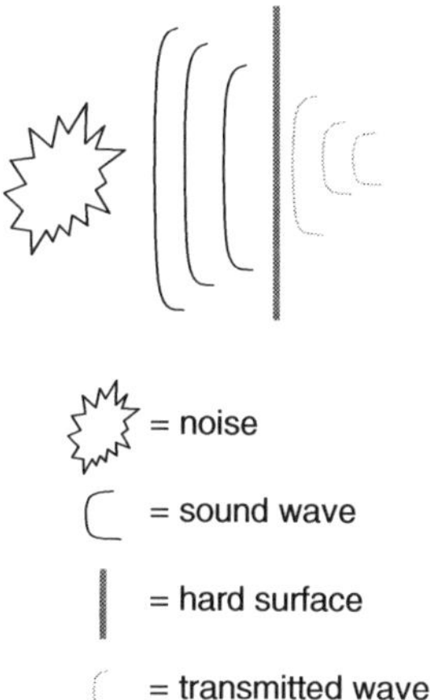

Figure 5.10 Sound waves; transmission

Exercise

Using a portable recorder, take an 'acoustic walk'. Select three or four locations that you expect to have different acoustic properties, including an outside location. Walk from one location to the next, describing the location and recording your observations. Listen to your recording and note how your voice sounds in each location. Draw diagrams to explain why your voice sounds different in each location.

Acoustics for radio drama

Ok – science lecture over. So what does all this mean for radio drama? As described earlier, a professional radio drama studio will have pre-determined areas to mimic different acoustics: A 'live' area, with some hard surfaces and a 'dead' area with absorbent surfaces, such as acoustic screens or curtains. How you tackle creating your own acoustic variation depends very much on what facilities you have available to you. Let's take the example of creating an outside acoustic in a studio. As we have discussed, outside there is no reflection – so no reverberation. When you speak outside, your voice sounds thin and weak, because the sound waves are not being reflected. To mimic this, you'll need to minimize the reflective properties of the studio. In a professional studio, the 'dead' area is the best place to do this. The sound waves are absorbed by the surfaces in the dead area. There is minimal reflection, so the voice will sound weak, similar to how it sounds outside. In a less-than-perfect studio situation, you can try using acoustic screens, a mattress or thick curtains – anything that will absorb the sound. This effect can be enhanced by removing some of the bass frequencies from the voice – either at the time of recording through the EQ on the mixing desk, if you have one, or later at the post-production stage (see Post-production section).

If you do not have a professional quality studio available to you, then the best solution may well be to record outside with a portable recorder. The recording location does not need to be precisely that indicated in the script. A rural location can be successfully recorded in a quiet urban area and an atmos track of bird song added during post-production to complete the countryside idyll.

Exercise

Consider how, using the facilities available to you and no post-production, you would create the acoustics of the following locations:

- Inside a car
- Bathroom
- Bedroom

Post-production

Post-production is perhaps one of the most rewarding and creative parts of the radio drama production process. At its most basic, it is an opportunity to 'tidy up' the recordings made during the production process; to smooth out sound levels, to remove mistakes and get the scenes in the right order. However, this is only the beginning. The most unpromising of recordings can be given new layers of meaning and sophistication by the simple addition of different special effects, sfx, atmos and music. The extent of post-production possible or desirable is really determined by what you have managed to achieve during the production stage. This section simply opens up to the reader what might be *possible*. It begins with a discussion of specific post-production techniques and effects, before moving on to some advice on how to tackle the post-production process as a whole.

The basics

Post-production used to be much more difficult. In the days before digital recording and editing, professional drama was recorded on quarter-inch tape, and editing consisted of physically cutting out mistakes with a razor blade and sticking the pieces back together with sticky tape. Any mixing or other effects had to be done through a mixing desk. Computer-based audio editing software has revolutionized this process, and ever more sophisticated software, some of it available as free downloads, has replaced the razor blade and mixing desk. During the post-production process, it is essential to listen very closely. It is useful (but not essential) to have different quality stereo and mono loudspeakers available. Remember that the listener will not necessarily hear your drama on stereo headphones or good quality loudspeakers. To be sure that your drama is acceptable whatever the listening conditions, you should check it on headphones as well as loudspeakers. Make sure the volume on the headphones or loudspeaker is loud enough to hear the recording very clearly.

Effects for radio drama

The majority of audio editing software comes with a bewildering library of *effects* (sometimes called *special effects*). In most cases, the library will have been devised with music production in mind. Titles such as 'flanger' and 'chorus' are more usually associated with electric guitars than radio drama. Having said that, many of these effects can be very useful for the radio drama producer and can be used to recreate different acoustics. It is a useful exercise to explore the effects available on your software, but here are a few commonly found examples:

Reverb

As discussed earlier, when sound waves hit hard surfaces, they bounce off, causing audible reflections of that sound. Reverberation can be simulated in audio editing software using a tool normally called 'reverb', 'delay' or 'echo'. The type of reverberation produced depends on the nature and size of the space in which the original sound occurs. A large room with reflective surfaces, such as a church, will have a lot of reverberated sound. The interior of a car will not. Most audio editing software can simulate these different kinds of reverberation, which means that you can use them to recreate quite precise locations. Most software has preset reverb programmes, which allow you to apply effects such as 'concert hall' or 'small room' to sounds. It is also normally possible to vary the settings of the reverb to create exactly the desired acoustic.

Reverb – Common Adjustable Settings

In most audio editing software, it is possible to adjust the following settings, to achieve the desired effect.

- Delay Time – determines how soon after the original the echo will begin
- Feedback – how many echoes of the original sound you hear
- Wet/Dry Mix – determines how much of the echo you want to mix with the original sound
- Diffusion – how quickly the echoes build up
- Decay Time – how long it takes the echo to die away

Some Typical Reverb Settings

- Large room – short Delay Time, low Diffusion, long Decay Time
- Canyon or a large open area, enclosed by walls – long Delay Time, low Diffusion, medium Feedback, long Decay Time
- Tannoy announcement – long Delay Time, low Diffusion, low Feedback, low Decay Time

Filters

Filters are also extremely helpful in refining the replication of certain acoustics. Variously described as 'eq', 'filter' or 'shelf', this feature allows you to isolate certain frequencies and add or reduce level at the point. As we discussed earlier, a good way of thinking about frequency is to compare it to the notes on a piano; low notes = Hz, high notes = KHz. Now imagine that every note on the piano has its own volume control, so you can add or remove level at that frequency. EQ can be used very effectively to remove unwanted frequencies or to add depth to sound by adding level to certain frequencies. One particular application of EQ in radio drama is to simulate how voices sound in different environments.

Some Typical EQ Settings

Sound to be replicated	EQ solution
Outside: There is no reflected s ound, so voice frequencies are not amplified in the way they are inside and tend to sound 'thin'.	Remove low frequencies. The precise frequency will vary, but you are likely to hear the most impact between 100 Hz and 1 KHz.

Lounge: High frequencies tend to be absorbed by soft furnishings.	Remove high frequencies. Play with the 5 to 6 KHz range.
Kitchen: Middle and high frequencies are amplified when they reflect off the hard surfaces of a kitchen. Bass frequencies tend to transmit (remember the bass music thumping through the wall we discussed earlier?).	Boost middle and high frequencies – between 2 and 3 KHz.
Telephone/transistor radio: Telephone lines restrict the frequency range and transistor radios have small, tinny speakers.	Remove everything below 300 Hz and above 3.5 KHz.

Exercise

Write a short play which takes place in three contrasting locations (such as a beach, bedroom and restaurant), with no more than three characters and just a couple of lines in each location. Record the dialogue in a studio or quiet area. Use special effects and mix with atmos to create the locations.

Music

The supreme importance of music in radio drama cannot be overemphasized. Crook draws on the observations of BBC Director of Talks Hilda Matheson, who stressed as early as 1933 that music plays a crucial role, equally as important as the actors' performance, and should be given consideration in the planning stages of radio drama equal to that of the plot, theme and characters (Crook, 1999, p. 92). In contemporary radio drama, music has many functions. It can be an indicator of mood; it can locate the drama at a particular point in history, even in a particular place; lyrics can add additional meaning to text. The theme tune for the world's longest-running soap opera, *The Archers*, is so strongly embedded in the British psyche that comedian Billy Connolly suggested, to great applause, that it should become Britain's new national anthem (An Audience with the Big Yin, 2002).

A word about copyright

Educational establishments usually have agreements under which commercial music can be played and used in projects for educational purposes. If you intend to broadcast commercial music, on radio or via the internet, a fee is payable to the performer and the copyright owner. However, a large amount of copyright-free 'mood' music is available to download from the internet. There are usually regulations associated with using this for broadcast, so read the small print very carefully. Though the music is rarely attributed to a particular artist, it is usually categorized according to ambience or era, so can be very useful in radio drama.

Exercise

Record the following two scenes. Mix your recordings with different kinds of music to create alternative versions: one set in the 1960s and one contemporary. In the second scene, use music to create different moods, such as comedy, foreboding and fear, or happy anticipation.

SCENE 1
JANINE'S BEDROOM. JANINE AND SUSIE ARE LISTENING TO MUSIC AND GETTING READY TO GO OUT.
SUSIE: Ow – you just burnt my ear.
JANINE: Oops – you should have paid to go to the hairdresser's if you wanted a professional job.
SUSIE: I know. I'm such a cheapskate. Aren't you ready yet? It's nearly ten. We'll miss the bus.
JANINE: Give me a chance. You'll have to do my hair now. I can't go out with it looking like this.

SCENE 2
OUTSIDE. SUSIE AND JANINE HAVE BEEN RUNNING.
SUSIE: Too late. It's gone.
JANINE: Your fault. All that fussing about which shoes to wear.
SUSIE: Oh, come off it. I wouldn't be seen dead in those red ones.
JANINE: Well, those stilettos better be comfortable. We've got a long walk, thanks to you.
THEY WALK ON.
SUSIE: Did you hear that?
JANINE: What?
SUSIE: Footsteps. I think someone's following us.
JANINE: (TURNS ROUND) What, where, I can't see anyone.
SUSIE: (CROSSLY) That's right. Make it obvious. No chance of making a quick getaway now, is there.
JANINE: Yeah, right. Like you could get away quickly anywhere in those shoes.
SUSIE: Stop a minute. There he is. Behind that tree.

Scene changes

In a theatre, a new backdrop falls; on screen, we cut to a new location. On radio, a series of conventions have developed to indicate how we move from one location or time to another.

- The Fade Down, Fade Up

This is the most common form of scene change. Fade down the atmosphere of one scene over roughly five seconds. After a second or two of silence, fade up, over roughly five seconds, on the atmos of the next scene. This is used to signify either a change in location or the passing of time.

- The Cross Fade

This method is used for a swift scene change, such as when characters move from one room to another in real time. The 'fade down' and 'fade up' are overlayered, so there is no silence in the middle, but a smooth mix from one atmos to the next.

- The Segue

This is a much sharper cut between scenes. It usually signals an immediate shift in perspective. This device is used frequently in *Number 10* on BBC Radio 4. The production draws heavily on filmic techniques, one of which is the use of sudden segues, similar to a 'cross cut' in film (BBC, 2009).

- Music

The use of music as a bridge between scenes often signals a change of mood or the passing of time.

Exercise

Record this short drama extract following the directions, to experiment with some different techniques for changing scene. You can also apply effects and sfx to create the different locations, if you wish.

SCENE 1
FROM A RADIO . . .
REPORTER: You can almost feel the tension here outside the Moonlight Cocktail Bar, as the fans await the arrival of tonight's guest of honour, the world famous film star Penelope Stewart.

SEGUE TO

SCENE 2
OUTSIDE THE MOONLIGHT COCKTAIL BAR
REPORTER: And at last the waiting is over. Here she is – it's a white limo, the door opens and Penelope steps gracefully from the car. She's a vision in pink lace and gold sequins. (FADE OUT TO SILENCE DURING THE NEXT LINE). I can confirm that only a handful of guests have actually . . .
FADE DOWN

SCENE 3
FADE UP ON THE LOBBY OF MOONLIGHT COCKTAIL BAR
SUSIE: I never thought we'd get though that crowd. Good job I got tickets last week.
JANINE: I know. Let's go up in the lift. I can't walk another step.
SFX LIFT DOOR OPENS
CROSSFADE TO

SCENE 4
INTERIOR LIFT
JANINE: Ok – here we go. Floor 3, Moonlight Cocktail Bar.
SUSIE: Oh boy, am I ready for that cocktail.
FADE DOWN

SCENE 5
FADE UP ON INTERIOR BAR
SUSIE: Singapore Sling, please. What you having, Janine?
JANINE: Bottle of beer.
FADE DOWN

SCENE 6
FADE UP ON SINISTER MUSIC (HOLD UNDER NEXT SCENE)
EXTERIOR STREET

SUSIE: Ouch – I've got terrible blisters. I'm taking my shoes off.
JANINE: Susie – don't turn round, don't make it obvious – I think that guy is following us again.
FADE OUT MUSIC

Putting it all together: Planning the recording and post-production process

Current approaches to producing radio drama are the result of nearly 100 years of experimentation and refinement, as producers constantly strive for the best method possible with the resources available. The technological enhancements which have taken place over this period have perhaps had the most impact on the nature of radio drama production. The increasing capacity for radio drama to be pre-recorded from the 1940s onwards distanced the genre from the 'live' tradition of the theatre. The use of quarter-inch tape for recording from the 1950s meant that editing became easily achievable. The net effect of these developments was that radio drama no longer needs to be produced live. It can be recorded in sections; performers can be recorded separately and mixed with other elements, such as sfx and music, at a later stage. This technique has been common practice in since the 1970s, but the development of digital editing and mixing technologies have streamlined and enhanced the production process further. The separation of production into different stages can produce sophisticated results, but it is more complex and time consuming. When planning the production, there are many variables to consider, such as the budget, actor availability, and technical possibilities. Producers do a great deal of preparation before actually recording the play. The script must be written, the characters cast and decisions made on the recording locations and technical requirements. Detailed schedules have to be prepared so that the play can be produced within the budget and with the resources available. In a professional drama situation, such as *The Archers* on BBC Radio 4, there is an overall editor who leads a team of writers and producers, and programmes are planned months in advance. The time allocated to the studio production is very limited, because studios, actors and technicians are expensive. A 13-minute episode is rehearsed and recorded in just two hours (*The Archers*, 2011). Clearly, meticulous planning makes the best use of expensive studio time, and one of the most important decisions the producer makes is the extent to which post-production is to be used. Another important factor is whether or not to record scenes chronologically. While chronological recording will help the actor to realize his character's 'journey' throughout the play, it may create production difficulties. Consider this radio drama outline:

SCENE 1
NEVADA DESERT: STEVE AND SOROYA
Soroya is attacked by a rattlesnake.

SCENE 2
JOHN'S HOUSE IN A SMALL TOWN IN NEVADA: JOHN AND ELLA
John and Ella discuss their plans for the evening, Ella leaves.

SCENE 3
NEVADA DESERT: STEVE AND SOROYA
Steve leaves Soroya to get help.

SCENE 4
JOHN'S HOUSE IN A SMALL TOWN IN NEVADA: JOHN AND STEVE.
Steve arrives and breaks the news of Soroya's plight.

If the drama is recorded in sequence, the process will not be straightforward. The team will need to create the Nevada desert and lounge scenes twice and keep the actors waiting around during scenes in which they are not required. Time = Money! A compromise must be reached; one that enables the actors to perform to the best of their ability, but also enables the production team to do its job efficiently. Generally speaking, it is best to plan the recording schedule to minimize the time with the actors and the equipment. As discussed earlier in the Sound Effects section, spot sfx should be added at the time of recording, as this will help the actors to pace their performance to match. Wherever possible, atmos should also be added at the time of recording, as this will help the actors with a sense of the location of the scene.

At the post-production stage, an organized approach is also required. The following list suggests how you should approach this:

- Subdivide the recording into separate scenes and save each as a separate file.
  Then working on one scene at a time:
- Correct any overall problems with levels. Edit the original recording, so you have only the audio you need.
- Add atmos track and any additional sfx needed.
- Effects – add reverb and filters.
- Mix – listen very carefully to set the level of the atmos and sfx, relative to the speech.
- Internal Fades – excluding the beginning and end of the scene, add fades to atmos and sfx.
- Mix Down – select all the tracks and mix them down to one track.
- Final fades – add a fade to the beginning and end of the mixed-down scene.
- Name and Save the mixed-down track.
- Compile – when you have mixed down all the scenes in the drama.
- Scene Changes – add pauses, fades, cross-fades and music as necessary.
- Final Mix Down – select all the scenes and mix down to a final, single track.
- Name and Save the mixed-down track.

Conclusion

This chapter has provided the reader with an overview of how radio drama is produced today. The level of detail may seem daunting to the novice, but in reality, radio drama is very achievable, with a minimum of expertise and equipment; and it is tremendous fun. Dip in and out of the different sections and try the exercises. Experiment with sfx, as the pioneers did in the 1920s and 1930s and find your own way of creating radio drama. For them, there were no rules, no fixed ways of doing things. Use the information in this chapter as the starting point, but remember that the future of audio drama production is for you to discover.

Glossary of technical terms

Atmos – an abbreviation of 'atmosphere'; the background sound of a location.

Clip – a selected section of track.

Cross-fade – when two or more sounds mix together. Unlike 'fades', there is no overall loss in level, as one sound gradually replaces the other.

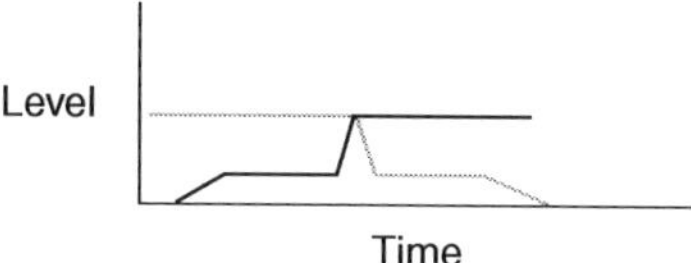

Figure 5.11 Cross-fade

Edit – the process by which mistakes are removed. In audio software packages, this is achieved by selecting the audio, following which it can be deleted, moved, copied, cut or pasted.

Effects/Special Effects – can be used to replicate the acoustic properties of different rooms/environments.

- Reverb, echo and delay – simulations of sound reflections.
- Filters/EQ/Shelf – isolate and boost or reduce sound at different frequencies.

Fade – A gradual increase or decrease in level. A quick fade 'in' or 'out' will make the entry and exit of that sound smooth, rather than sudden. A slower fade will allow the sound to be introduced more gradually (such as a car approaching from a distance).

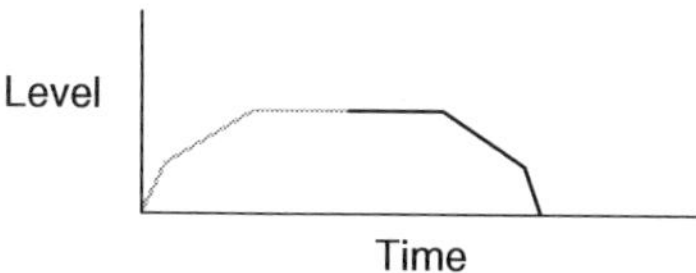

Figure 5.12 Fade up and fade down

File – a single piece of audio, which can be mono or stereo.

Levels – a visual representation of how loud sound is. Normally measured in decibels (dB). Aim for the highest level (peak) to be –3dB.

Mix Down/Bounce to New/Quick Mix/Export – A completed scene is likely to consist of multiple clips and tracks. 'Mix Down' combines all (or selected) clips and tracks into a single stereo or mono track.

Multitrack – several tracks layered over each other.

Pan – to adjust the balance of sound between two sources. To create accurate stereo, the A signal should be panned fully left and the B fully right.

Segue (pronounced 'seg-way') – an almost instantaneous cut from one sound or scene to the next.

Sfx – an abbreviation of 'sound effects'; 'live' or pre-recorded sound which is not speech-based.

Spot sfx – 'live' sound effects created during the performance.

Track – a piece of audio.

6 Performing

The art of radio performance

The art of acting has been defined and refined since the beginning of civilization. Over the centuries, each culture developed its own particular form of performative expression – Noh and Kabuki in Japan and Commedia dell'Arte in Italy, to name but a few – and these traditions continue to inform and enrich performance to this day. Radio performance is less than 100 years old, but has its roots in the same fertile soil as all modern day theatre. As early as 1926, radio professionals were beginning to identify the unique qualities of radio drama performance:

> Their acting, as a means of interpretation of the play, must be moulded to a new technique. They have none of the aids of gesture or facial expression to give point to the spoken word. All that on the stage is seen as part of the actor's art has to be conveyed by voice alone. This sounds impossible and at first would appear not to be a breaking through of limitations into a freer sphere, but a multiplication of limitations. We must of course admit that radio drama has its own conditions and certain limitations, but they are of such sort that they only hamper the development of the inessential. (Lea, 1926, p. 36)

In writing this chapter, the challenge has been deciding where to begin. Where does 'acting' end and 'radio acting' begin? The answer, of course, is that the two are inseparable. The radio actor cannot see her function as distinct to that of the stage actor; it draws on the same set of attributes and skills. Constantin Stanivslaski, perhaps the most influential Russian actor of the twentieth century, attempted to define the necessary attributes of the theatrical performer: 'You must have, in addition to the help of nature, a well worked-out psychological technique, an enormous talent and great physical nervous responses' (Stanislavski, 1967, p. 17). The great radio actor will also have these attributes, but has the additional challenge of conveying them to the audience using just the microphone. Clearly, it would be beyond the scope of this book to give the art of acting the true attention it deserves, so this chapter concentrates on applying performance techniques to the medium of radio. For this reason, an experienced stage actor will have the opportunity to focus her skills on the particulars of radio performance. That does not mean to say that the reader needs an in-depth knowledge of acting. Every newcomer to the wonders of theatre needs a 'way in' to appreciating its rich traditions. For one beginner, it is seeing a pantomime for the first time, while for another, it could be taking part in a school play. Why not choose radio as a 'way in' to appreciating the theatre? In many ways, it is less daunting: it does not matter what you look like, there's no visible audience to make you nervous and you don't have to learn your lines! This chapter begins by discussing the techniques of radio drama performance, moving on to the more artistic considerations and finally encourages the reader to bring all the knowledge together to prepare and perform.

Technical matters

Here, a basic understanding of the technical requirements of radio drama performance can be developed, beginning with the intricacies of working with a microphone. The discussion then moves on to performative techniques. The reader is strongly encouraged to read the paragraphs on microphones in the Production chapter before commencing this section.

Loving the microphone

> Many actors, when new to radio, are inhibited by the microphone. Try and learn as quickly as possible to overcome any fear. It won't bite. As an actor you need to learn to master it. The best way to do this is to treat it as the ear of your best friend or lover. Learn to caress the microphone with your voice. (MacLoughlin, 2008, p. 150)

The knowledge that such a small electrical device is the only means of capturing your dramatic performance can be quite intimidating for the radio actor. For sure, the actor has a relationship with the technical team, the producer, and the other actors, but nothing is as important as the actor's rapport with the microphone. The microphone is the means by which the radio actor connects with the invisible audience, as well as with other aspects of the drama; the fellow actors, sounds, music. The microphone is at the centre of the performance. Nothing must block the actor from the microphone, and everything the actor says and does must include the microphone. So this has to be love!

Establishing the relationship

Before we move on to more detailed aspects of microphone performance, let's begin with some basics. It is important to understand what kind of microphone you are working with. Is it stereo or mono? Is it multi-directional? If you are not sure, check before you begin using the microphone.

Some golden rules:

- Do not touch the microphone, and take care not to touch the stand or cable.
- Never blow or shout directly into a microphone from close range.
- Never put a script between your mouth and the microphone. Putting the script behind and slightly to one side of the microphone can work well.
- Do not look down (move your script higher as you reach the bottom of the page).
- Remember that your primary relationship is with the microphone. Your performance should be directed towards the microphone, rather than fellow performers.

Common problems and how to avoid them

'Popping' is an electronic thud or pop caused by hard sounds close to the microphone, such as saying the letter 'p' or making a sudden exhalation. 'Blasting' is caused by a loud noise made directly into the microphone, which results in a harsh, distorted sound. Both can be avoided by moving slightly further away or to one side of the microphone. Some experimentation with the microphone will allow you to establish under what circumstances your voice is likely to pop and blast and therefore to make the necessary temporary adjustments to your position at the microphone.

How close to the microphone?

Most speech-based radio tends to be static. The presenter establishes where her voice sounds clear and, from then on, remains in this position. In radio drama, there is a lot to be gained by adopting different positions in relation to the microphone. This way you can convey movement, depth and perspective. The distance between the sound source (in this case, the mouth) and the microphone is known as the 'working distance'. The most common working distances are:

1. Narrator – half an arm's length from the microphone
2. Close – a hand's length
3. Dialogue – arm's length
4. Leaving/arriving – turn away from the microphone or move slightly into the dead side
5. Distant – turn back to microphone or use the dead side

The microphone should be positioned roughly at chin level. When actors are of very different heights, a compromise will be necessary, such as using separate microphones for each actor.

Understanding working distance

The following exercises offer an opportunity to experiment with particular working distances and to understand the effect they have on performance.

Position 1 – narrator

For the novice radio actor, position 1 is the easiest to master. It involves little movement and no interaction with other characters, so offers a good opportunity to work on building a relationship with the microphone. The microphone represents the audience, but it can feel odd at first to be communicating with it alone. The following exercise is a useful first step towards that process of communication.

Exercise

Use any text available to you: a short story or a newspaper article, for example. Ask a partner to stand directly behind the microphone, on a level with your eyes. Standing half an arm's length from the microphone, practice holding the script correctly, as described earlier, and direct your speech towards your partner. Practice this a few times, gradually directing your speech towards the microphone instead of your partner. Finally, ask your partner to move out of your line of sight. Read again, speaking into the microphone, but this time, simply imagine that your partner is still behind the microphone.

A note about reading fluently

Many of us are not comfortable reading out loud. However, being at ease with your own voice is an essential prerequisite for the radio drama performer. Reading to young children is a very rewarding way of improving your reading skills. If you have no children of your own, read to younger brothers and sisters or cousins. They will not judge your reading ability, but simply immerse themselves in the story, giving you the opportunity to practise without fear of criticism. You need to get used to hearing your own voice, too, so record yourself reading stories. Listen to the recordings and make notes on how you could improve your reading the next time. When you get more confident, practise varying the pace of your reading. Professional radio presenters 'read ahead'; as they speak the first line, they are already reading the next. As you get more comfortable reading aloud, try to read ahead.

Position 2 – close

One of the characteristics that distinguishes radio from other forms of media is its ability to communicate with an audience on a very intimate and personal level. If you have spent any time alone with your radio, you will understand this. Freddy Mercury, the extrovert lead singer of Queen, captured that very personal experience in 'Radio Gaga', his nostalgic homage to radio. Radio drama is second to none in its ability to exploit this characteristic. One of the established conventions of radio drama is that characters can step outside their external persona to reveal their inner thoughts and feelings to the audience alone. This technique is known variously as 'internal voice' or 'inner monologue'. We'll call it 'internal voice'.

Read the following script extract:

BUSY CAFÉ: CONNIE AND MAX ARE DRINKING COFFEE TOGETHER
MAX: . . . So I said to her, you've got to be kidding. Over my dead body. I'm not lending you my essay. Cheeky cow. Can you believe it?
CONNIE: (INTERNAL VOICE) He's so boring, boring. SHUT UP.
MAX: Connie – are you even listening to me at all?
CONNIE: (DIALOGUE VOICE, DISTRACTED) Um, yes. Max, I really need to go now. (INTERNAL VOICE) shower, 5 minutes; dry hair, 10; make up, 10; bus at 7 . . .
MAX: (INTERRUPTS) Ok, let me walk you home.

CONNIE: (INTERNAL VOICE) I'll never make it. Need more time. OK. Shower, 2; hair, 5 . . .
MAX: Connie?
CONNIE: (DIALOGUE VOICE) Great – let's go. (INTERNAL VOICE) Marvellous. That's all I need.

Achieving the perfect internal voice is a matter of performance and technical knowledge. Connie's internal voice quality must be different to her voice within the dialogue. In the case of the example above, Connie's internal voice is angry and frustrated. Her voice within the dialogue is distant and distracted. The microphone itself can be a significant help in distinguishing between internal and dialogue voice. One reason a close microphone technique is recommended for internal voice is that it produces an effect called 'bass tip up', in which the bass frequencies in the voice are exaggerated. This means that the voice quality can sound very different when it is close to the microphone, which can be very helpful to the performer. The sounds the mouth makes, such as lip smacks, tongue sounds, breaths and so on can also enhance the feeling of intimacy. The perfect 'close microphone' position is going to be different for each performer. All microphones are slightly different, and so are our voices. The important thing is to achieve a technical voice quality and performance that is distinct from the main dialogue. The performance of internal voice can also be enhanced by production techniques, discussed in the Production chapter, such as altering the acoustic or adding special effects like reverb.

Exercise

Write a short monologue, beginning 'Come here, I want to tell you a secret!' Try to write as if you are telling a secret to a friend and use conversational, simple language and short sentences. Start at a hand's distance from the microphone, but experiment with your working distance to achieve an internal voice quality. Remember to avoid popping and blasting and try to attempt different emotional voice qualities, such as frustration, humour and intimacy.

Position 3 – dialogue

Let's consider a scene involving a conversation between two characters which takes place in a living room. When working in stereo, the actors usually stand side by side at the microphone, so the eye contact which would occur in real life is restricted. The interaction and relationship between the characters must be made apparent to the audience through the voice only. The Radio Drama Performance section later in this chapter offers some guidance on the performative aspects of working with dialogue, but here we will consider the technical requirements. The voice levels must be roughly equal, and if working in stereo, the positioning of the characters within the stereo field must be logical. For example, typically where two characters are conversing, one character would be to the left of the stereo field and the other, to the right. The characters can be positioned close together towards the centre of the microphone, or to the left and right of it to create more of a feeling of distance between the characters. The Production chapter offers further insights into working within the stereo field, which readers will find useful.

Exercise

Rehearse this scene first without a microphone, with the benefit of eye contact. Then stand side by side at the microphone, at arm's length from it, and imagine that the microphone is the other character.

URBAN PARK: MAX AND CONNIE ARE SITTING ON A BENCH
MAX: I don't understand. I thought you liked me.
CONNIE: I did. I do. But this is just too much. You won't leave me alone for a single second and I can't stand it.
MAX: It's only because I love you, Connie. Just give me another chance.
CONNIE: No. I've had enough. I don't want to see you anymore.
MAX: I just don't believe you. There must be something I can do. Why don't we . . .
CONNIE: There is no 'we'. I'm going out with Joe now.

Position 4 – leaving/arriving and position 5 – distant

Similar to internal voice, the perfect sound will be achieved by a combination of appropriate performance and distance from the microphone. Positions 4 and 5 have much in common. It is largely a matter of how distant the character needs to sound. It may be helpful to think of characters in position 4 as being in the same room and characters in position 5 as being outside the room, the main difference being that a character in position 5 will sound much further way than the character in position

4. Consider these lines:

> KITCHEN AT BREAKFAST TIME.
> KATE: (POSITION 3 – CALLING OUT) Stewart! Can you hear me? Just get out of bed right now. You'll miss the bus.
> STEWART: (POSITION 5 – FROM UPSTAIRS) Stop going on, mum. There's loads of time.

Make a mental picture of the scene. The setting is the kitchen, and Kate is making breakfast. Stewart is away from the kitchen – upstairs in bed. The audience will need to hear that the characters are separated. First, Kate is calling from the kitchen upstairs to Stewart: as we have discussed earlier, speaking loudly into the microphone will cause distortion, so Kate must move slightly back from the microphone or direct her voice across, rather than into, the microphone. She'll need to project her voice to give the impression that she is calling upstairs, but avoid distortion by holding back more than she would if there were no microphone. Stewart, too, needs to speak loudly, or even shout, but his voice should also sound distant – as if he is upstairs. If a mono microphone is being used, he should position himself on the 'dead' side, which creates a distant sound. With a stereo microphone, move back as far from the microphone as the room size permits and turn away from the microphone (or even leave the room and close the door). Similar to Kate, he must project his voice. Distortion is likely to be less of a problem because of his distance from the microphone.

> STEWART: (AT THE DOOR) What's for breakfast? I'm starving.
> KATE: No time for that now. Pack your books. You can take a banana with you.

A little distance between the characters is still required. Kate is in position 3; Stewart is in position 4. The precise position will vary, depending on the microphone. In stereo, roughly 2 metres away is a good place to start. If the effect is not quite correct, turn slightly away or further back. In mono, the 'dead' side of the microphone can be useful; experiment with the area within which the microphone field shifts from 'live' to 'dead' (as explained in the Production chapter).

Moving between positions; avoiding the 'crouching tiger' effect

A silent character is an invisible character. Movement too is invisible in radio, unless you are making a sound when you move. If you say one line in position 5, then move to position 3 for the next, it will sound as if you have flown across the room – like a martial arts stunt artist, complete with wires. We call this the 'crouching tiger effect', after the famous Ang Lee film *Crouching Tiger, Hidden Dragon* (2000), which uses this technique fantastically well. Sadly, there's rarely a need for crouching tigers in radio drama, so if the character needs to move from one position to another, plan how to make that transition while speaking. You may even need to ad lib extra lines, or sounds, to achieve this. If you are working in stereo, it is important to remember the character's position in relation to the stereo field. For example, if the character is leaving the scene, ensure that the departure is on axis, otherwise a zigzag between left and right will be evident.

Exercise

Work through this script line by line and make notes on actor positions 1 through 4. How will you convey the movement? Remember that you can add lines if necessary to avoid the 'crouching tiger' effect.

CROWDED BAR

KAYLA: (INTERNAL VOICE) And again. 3 . . . 4. Yes. That's four times he's looked at me now. What's so wrong with a woman being alone in a bar anyway? He thinks I'm on the pull. Come on. Just look away. Don't worry, love. You're definitely not my type. Ten past nine. Where IS she?

KAYLA: (SEES STEPHANIE ENTER THE BAR: CALLS OUT) Steph, hey. Over here. Steph!

STEPH: I couldn't see you from over there. Everything ok?

KAYLA: Yeah – fine now, no thanks to you. Why are you so late? It's horrible sitting on your own, all sorts checking you out.

STEPH: Chill, Kayla. I'm going to the bar. What you drinking?

KAYLA: Stick another coke in there, hun.

STEPH: OK, give us your glass (SHE GOES TO THE BAR).

STEPH: (CALLING FROM THE BAR) Kayla – Oi Kayla. You want a vodka in there?

KAYLA: (INTERNAL VOICE) Hmm, it's going to be an interesting night . . .

Radio drama performance

Having mastered some of the more technical issues of radio drama acting, it is time to move on to matters more related to artistic performance. This section focuses on radio drama performance as a mode of communication, beginning with a detailed examination of the voice. As in everyday life, communication is not just verbal. Facial expressions, body language and movement all contribute to the communication process, as actor Elisa Eliot observes:

> It is not just your voice. It has to be really *acting*. It's just the same as acting with your full body, your emotions, your mind and all your tools, it just so happens that all your audience will hear is your voice. You must remember that even in voiceover, you can hear a smile, a wink and all of that even if your audience can't see it. (Eliot, 2010)

There's no doubt that radio acting is challenging in this respect. While there is no 'quick fix', the exercises and observations which follow are intended to help the reader to recognize and devise strategies to respond to these challenges.

Understanding the voice

The range of tools available to the radio actor to create performance is limited. In theatre, costume, set and props provide additional visual support for the actor. For the radio actor, the voice is of paramount importance. While sound effects and atmos can provide some additional support to performance, the voice will always be the primary means of creating performance. For this reason, it is essential that the radio actor has an in-depth understanding of how voices work in everyday life. This knowledge can then be used to identify some key voice traits, which become a basis for the radio drama performance. In this section, we'll attempt to identify those key traits and how they are commonly used in radio drama performance. This will provide an insight into professional radio voice work and some techniques which you can apply to your own performance.

The best way to understand how we use our voice in everyday life is to become an expert eavesdropper. Listen to conversation in an analytical way whenever you can, making notes on your observations. We have already touched on the importance of distinct voices in the writing chapter, and it is equally important in the performance area. Of course, no two voices are exactly alike, but there are some common characteristics. Male voices are deeper than female voices, which are, in turn, usually deeper than children's voices. With age, voices become deeper and mellower. They get louder, faster and higher when we are excited; quieter, slower and lower when we are tired. Physical exertion and emotion affect our breathing, with a knock-on impact on the voice. Our intonation (voice pitch) changes according to what we are saying. A question ends with an upward inflection; a statement of fact ends with a downward inflection. Despite these common characteristics, every voice is unique. Anatomy is partly the culprit – we are all built slightly differently – but add accent and individual characteristics, such as lip smacking or a lisp, and the variations are endless. For the purposes of radio drama, we can summarize the speech qualities that affect performance as follows:

- Volume
- Pitch
- Pace
- Accent
- Individual characteristics

The successful radio actor understands the impact of each of these qualities on performance. While *accent* and *individual characteristics* can only be developed through close observation and practice, strategies to control *volume*, *pitch* and *pace* can be developed and are the subject of further discussion below. It is easier to manipulate some aspects of speech than others. For example, if you are an adult, you have to be incredibly talented to perform the voice of a child successfully (one thinks of exceptionally gifted voice artists such as Nancy Cartwright, who creates the voice of Bart Simpson in *The Simpsons*). However, it is certainly possible to manipulate speech to improve performance by combining aspects of volume, pitch and pace. We will begin by considering the individual impact of each speech quality on performance.

Volume is one of the key ways we convey emotion in everyday life. We whisper a confidence, or shout in anger. The ability to reproduce a range of volumes is important for the radio drama performer. On stage, a full vocal range can be used without any problems. Even a difficulty with low volume can be overcome by forcing a whisper. However, radio drama performance requires a more subtle approach. Over-projected shouting or whispering can sound 'hammy' and create technical difficulties with the microphone. Creating an appropriate range of volumes is largely a matter of practice and experimentation. Generally speaking, when projecting your voice, move back slightly from the microphone (from position 3 to position 4) or turn sideways to the microphone, so you are not projecting directly into it. Whispering requires you to be closer to the microphone, but breathing and talking directly into the microphone will cause popping or blasting (see position 1), so try speaking sideways, rather than directly into the microphone.

The term *pitch* is used to describe the frequency range of the voice. Pitch, too, can be used to suggest emotion. Each voice has its own standard pitch range, roughly four or five different tones. As we have explained, gender and age have an impact on pitch. We must remember that emotion causes our pitch range to alter. For example, when we are upset or nervous, our voices tend to rise in pitch. Our pitch lowers if we are speaking intimately or we feel emotionally drained. Understanding this will enable the performer to vary pitch when conveying these emotions.

Listen to a live sports commentary on the radio and you will notice how the *pace* of the commentary builds with the excitement of the game. Excitement makes us speak faster. Controlled anger is slow. Hysteria is fast. One of the most common problems with radio drama dialogue is a lack of variety in pace. Real life conversation rarely sounds like a tennis match, so why should alternate lines of dialogue sound as if they are being batted back and forth? Conversations have peaks and troughs. There is also silence. Building pace variation into performance is an important skill to develop. As always with radio drama, the secret is close observation of real life. When working from a script, plan, with your fellow actors and director, where the peaks and troughs lie in each scene and mark them on the script.

Here are some script excerpts you can use to experiment with volume, pitch and pace.

SCHOOL PLAYGROUND AT BREAK TIME
ALICE: Can you believe what she's wearing?
HAYLEY: I know; talk about a yard sale reject. Look at her saggy skirt. Why does she dress like that? She's got loads of money to buy clothes.
ALICE: Yes, but some people just have no taste, no matter how much they spend. It would help if the colours didn't clash. Blue and purple together? I don't think so.
HAYLEY: Look out, she's coming.
ALICE: Hi, Sarah. Your hair looks nice today.
HAYLEY: Yes – have you had it straightened?

KITCHEN
STEWART: Sit down, dad. There's something I need to tell you.
DAVID: What is it? Are you OK?
STEWART: Yes – well, yes, I think so. You see, I borrowed your car.
DAVID: OK . . . so what happened?
STEWART: Well, I was just parking the car when I hit this tree. It's not too bad, I . . .
DAVID: What do you mean you hit a tree? How much damage is there?
STEWART: I knew you'd be angry. I just needed to get some bread, and I didn't have time to walk and . . .
DAVID: Yes, yes, but what about the car? How much damage is there?

STEWART: Just a tiny scratch. Well, maybe a tiny dent, too.
DAVID: I've only just got it fixed after the last time you borrowed it, and I told you then that I never want you to drive my car again. Where is it? Let me see it.
STEWART: I couldn't get it started. It's being towed to the garage.
DAVID: What? Towed? You said it was a 'tiny dent'.
STEWART: Sorry, Dad.

Reading versus communication

While communication is the primary function of radio, there are several distinct ways in which this is achieved. For example, news bulletins tend to be formal and declamatory in style, whereas a typical breakfast programme adopts an informal and conversational tone. Radio drama too is very often dependent on conversational modes of communication but this conversation is constructed; the verbal exchanges which would emerge naturally in everyday life are predetermined within the script. Nevertheless, it is important that the listener recognizes what is heard as 'natural'. In order to achieve this, the performer must develop a means of converting words on a page to spontaneous communication.

Exercise

This exercise will help you to think about how we communicate with each other in everyday life and to use the same techniques to communicate in radio drama. Work in pairs. If you have a camera available, it would be helpful to film this exercise.

1. Think about a great day out you have had recently and write four or five bullet point notes covering the most interesting events.
2. Stand in 'narrator' position 1 and ask your partner to stand opposite you, behind the microphone, where you can catch her eye. Tell your partner the story of your day out, remembering to focus your speech into the microphone, but using your partner to represent the listener.
3. Record and listen to your story. This technique should enable you to achieve a very natural, chatty style of communication. The challenge is to achieve a similar natural style when reading from a script.
4. Transcribe your recording, writing out word for word exactly what you have recorded, including any ums, pauses, etc. Now record the same story, but this time reading from the script, again using your partner to

represent the listener. Try to achieve the same natural style you achieved in the previous recording. Tricky, isn't it?

5. To improve your performance, you'll need to think about how you achieved that spontaneous, natural sound in the first version and try to apply it to the second. Concentrate on the non-verbal elements of storytelling. Consider the following:

   How did you use eye contact, facial expression, movement.

   How did you breathe; did it change through the piece?

   How did the pace vary?

6. Can you apply any of these techniques to the scripted version, to help you achieve that natural, spontaneous sound?

Lifting the words from the page

In theatre and screen performance, at some point during the rehearsal process, actors must cast aside the script and depend on memory. In radio, that moment never comes. One could be forgiven for thinking that being able to work from a script liberates the radio actor from the chore of learning lines and thus makes the job easier. While some actors may consider it an advantage not to have to memorize lines, working from a script presents different challenges. In many ways, the script is a barrier. As we have discussed earlier, physically holding the script is a delicate matter. It mustn't touch the microphone or be positioned between the actor and the microphone. It also creates a psychological barrier – an extra link in the chain from performer to audience. Shane Salk, who plays Angel in *We're Alive*, describes how he deals with the script:

> It really is physically demanding. You can see images from old time radio with people standing upright and holding scripts. But if you came into any of our sessions, it's exhausting. Absolutely exhausting. We never hold the script – we always have it on a stand because of the amount we move. You have to move, you have to be 'into this' when you're acting. (Salk, 2010)

To make a successful performance, the radio actor must convince the listener that there is no script, that the character is responding spontaneously. It's an easy thing to say, but the actual skills required to lift the words from the page can be difficult to achieve. Starting from basics, the ability to communicate the written word swiftly and effectively is an essential skill. It's not unique to radio drama; not even unique to radio. Professional presenters communicate very effectively with their audience. They manipulate their voices so that they are telling the audience the story in a way that holds the audience's attention. The symbols in Figure 6.1 represent some typical speech patterns.

- Emphasizing certain words, or syllables
- Pause
- Rising pitch ↗
- Lowering pitch ↘

Figure 6.1 Speech patterns

Exercise

This exercise will help you to understand how professional presenters manipulate speech patterns to communicate with their audience. You can then apply this technique to your own voice work.

1. Record a news reporter or news reader – from TV or Radio. Transcribe roughly one minute's worth of the presentation, so that you have a word for word script.
2. Mark the speech patterns on your script, using the symbols in Figure 6.1 (you'll probably need to play your recording several times to achieve this). What speech patterns occur regularly? Can you identify any regularly occurring patterns? You'll probably notice a regular pattern to the intonation. What are the advantages and disadvantages of the intonation pattern you observed – from the perspective of the presenter and the listener?
3. Record your own news or sport bulletin, marking the script with the same intonation patterns you observed earlier.
4. Try recording different versions, using different intonation patterns.

Making it sound 'real'

In the theatre, the biggest applause always goes to the actors, and often it is only when something goes wrong that the audience becomes aware of the nuts and bolts of the production: the scenery, lighting and the music. In radio drama, the relationship that the listener has with the actors is even more pointed, because radio drama is such a personal and intimate medium. However, the more one listens to radio drama and analyses all its component parts, the easier it is to appreciate that the performers are just one link in the chain. Behind the scenes, the production team provides the audio 'scenery' in the form of sound effects, wild track and music. The performer's responsibility is to work with that team to complete the 'picture' with speech and movement which connects the audio scenery to events in the narrative. For the casual listener, there should be no distinction between sound effects, actors and music; the team is working together to paint the whole picture. The responsibilities of the performer, then, are great. Not only is she the main focus of the listener's attention, she is also at the heart of all the elements of production, drawing them in to make the picture complete. The skill lies in making this complicated process invisible. The following paragraphs offer some observations and suggestions on maintaining the mystery; hiding the nuts and bolts of the radio drama production process under a cloak of invisibility.

Speech

In everyday conversation, we are very imperfect communicators. We speak in fragments, interrupt each other; finish each other's sentences. Radio drama writers suggest these nuances in the dialogue they script, but more often than not, performers have a role to play in portraying these speech patterns. Another reality of everyday life is that we never know what's around the corner. If radio drama is to be convincing, then the audience cannot know what will unfold. Of course, the actor is in the privileged position of knowing what will happen next, but it is her job to convince the audience that she, too, is ignorant and is on the same journey of discovery. Her words, actions and reactions must display no awareness of what is to come. There is an obvious conflict for the actor. Familiarity with the script is important in order to speak fluently, but that familiarity can be a barrier to a natural and spontaneous performance. There is no magic wand, no quick fix solution to this. Understanding how we react to each other in everyday life provides some insights that can be applied to radio performance. Here are some exercises to aid the observation process.

Exercises

Eavesdropping

When you are out with friends, don't say anything yourself; just sit back and listen to the conversation around you. Observe the flow of speech. You could even record it, making sure you get permission. Transcribe a few lines of the conversation you heard and perform it.

Play a game of Word Association

Choose a partner. The first person starts by saying a single word. The second player responds with a word that is related to the first word. And so on, until one player gets stuck, or makes a mistake. No proper nouns or multiple words, and no repetition.

It is perhaps even more informative to observe a game of Word Association. How do the players interact with each other? How long does it take them to respond? How does the pace build and fall?

Storytelling

Choose a paragraph or two from a story. In pairs or groups, experiment with joint readings of the story. Begin by reading a line in turn, trying to maintain the pace and tone of the previous reader. Now try swopping readers in the middle of a sentence. Finally, interrupt each other, so that the phrases overlap a little.

Movement

Most of us move a lot, without even noticing it. Try sitting absolutely still and see how unnatural it feels. Movement, however slight, is an integral part of radio drama. For the radio actor, the extent of any movement is limited to a small physical space within the range of the microphone. Shane Salk reflects on the physical demands of creating a sense of movement:

> Voice acting is a full body experience, meaning that you have to move your whole body because it shows in your voice – but do not move your feet! After any recording we are exhausted. Of course there are roles in stage drama that are completely exhausting, but in audio drama you very much need to be in shape. (Salk, 2010)

The question of whether or not to move your feet is really a matter of preference. Certainly, the performer needs to be within range of the microphone, and some prefer to use as much movement as possible, including moving the feet, as Elisa Eliot remarks: 'In order to create realistic sounds, especially in something like *We're Alive* where we're running and we're fighting and we're jumping, doing all kinds of exertions, we actually have to do them in order for them to sound real' (Eliot, 2010). Even in normal conversation, most of us move our hands and even our bodies. Next time you go out, watch your friends talking. Apart from talking, what *else* are they doing? Remembering to move is, for the novice actor, partly a matter of confidence. It is almost as if the microphone is providing a form of hypnosis from which the performer can't break free. The realization that you *can* move at the microphone is very liberating and has an immense impact on the quality of the performance.

Working with spot sfx

While the sound of movement is always required, it is not always possible or desirable for the actor to achieve this alone. Let's look at a scene which requires the character to make a slice of toast. We want to hear the character slicing the bread, turning the toaster on, buttering the toast, and so on, but imagine how difficult it would be for the actor to create those sounds while juggling with a script. A spot sfx technician will work alongside the actor to help create the overall performance. The technician can create the sound of bread being sliced, but the effect will be incomplete unless the actor vigorously moves his arm back and forth, creating the sound of movement in his voice. The position of the technician will vary depending on how the drama is being produced. When working in stereo, the position of the sfx in relation to the actor is important. You wouldn't want the slicing to sound as if it was happening to the left of the room if the character is to right. For this reason, when working in stereo, the spot technician often has to operate very close to the actor, on the same axis. In mono, the problem of location of the sound is easier to address, since there is no distinction between left and right. The only issue is to make sure that the slicing sfx sounds as if it is close to the actor. This can be achieved on a separate microphone, if necessary, though line of sight between the technician and actor is desirable so that they can coordinate their activities.

Putting it all together

Since the earliest days of radio drama, actors have worked in pressurized circumstances. In the 'golden age', radio drama was big business. There was a high demand for entertainment from advertisers and listeners, and radio plays were 'turned around' from script to air very quickly. A couple of hours of rehearsal, followed by a 'live' broadcast was a common situation. This put a lot of pressure on the radio drama performers of the time. Reminiscing on his experiences as an actor during the 'golden age', radio veteran Harry Bartell playfully compares the experience of a stage actor diligently developing his Stanislavskian performance over several months, with his own experiences of preparing for a radio play:

> (A) radio actor . . . was given 25 to 50 mimeographed pages of script. Four or five hours later he was expected to give a finished performance of a role timed to the second and coordinated with music and sound effects. The only information that he had about his role (or roles because he frequently had two) was the name of the character on the front page.

He colourfully concludes: 'Stanislavsky would have bombed' (Bartell, 1998).

BBC radio drama was not subject to advertiser demand, but it was, and still is, produced relatively quickly, compared to stage drama. Two days of rehearsal for a 45-minute play is usual, whereas a professional stage production is developed over weeks or even months. In such fraught conditions, the actor has a responsibility to be prepared. Imagine the shame of keeping the production team waiting because you have not taken the trouble to read and understand the script. Jim Gleason, who plays one of the principal characters in *We're Alive*, describes his preparation methods:

> When I am going to do a recording I approach it exactly as I would if I was going to be acting in a television or feature film – with two major differences. Firstly, I can wear what I like and don't need to worry about makeup! Secondly, I don't have to learn the lines, as the script is going to be in front of me. But I still break down the scene the same way I would if I was going to be acting in film or on stage or on camera. (Gleason, 2010)

Though the financial implications of delay are important in professional radio drama, it is equally important to behave in a professional manner in all circumstances. This section gives guidance on how an actor should prepare for a radio drama recording.

Constructing the character

Having a detailed understanding of the character you are portraying is fundamental to any performance, and the starting point is the script. You'll need to understand who your character is and his/her role in the narrative overall. This process is greatly helped if you have access to the writer. In talking about working as one character in a long-running serialized drama, Jim Gleason reveals that there is a symbiotic relationship between actor and the writer. The writer may have a founding concept and plans for the trajectory of the plot and its characters, but 'it works both ways', with 'the writer getting to know the psychology of the characters as embodied by their actors' (Gleason, 2010). Thanks to the visual dimension to radio drama provided by the internet, listeners can, if they so wish, become aware of the physical embodiment of the performer (although, rather like when your favorite novel is adapted into a movie, seeing the person behind the voice can be disillusioning!). *The Archers* website includes photographs of the actors who play each character. This brings into sharp focus a need for continuity, which draws on the combined skills of the writer and performer.

Clearly, detailed preparation is of the essence for the performer. How does the character develop throughout the story and what relationship does he or she have with others in the play? Some of the detail you require will be apparent in the script. Much of it, however, is down to personal interpretation. After a first read-through of the script, you should have some general ideas, and at this stage, you should discuss these with the production team, other actors and the writer (if possible). Once you have established that your ideas are broadly compatible, you will need to work your character through in detail.

Character preparation checklist

- Age
- Gender
- Sexual orientation
- Ethnicity
- Upbringing (location, social class, education, home life, parental occupation)
- Political affiliation
- Personality traits
- Appearance – how do I dress? (Some actors find that it helps to wear clothing and shoes that the character would wear.)
- Occupation
- Lifestyle (hobbies, disposable income, which shops does the character use)

Describe what happens to your character during the play and how he or she changes as a result. What is the significance of this to the narrative? Describe how your character relates to others throughout the play. Does it change? What is the 'journey' your character makes and how does it change him or her? Scenes are often not recorded chronologically, so it is important to be able to identify at what stage your character is in the narrative. Look at the play scene by scene.

Narrative checklist

- What is my purpose in this scene?
- What happens to me during this scene?
- What has happened in previous scenes that has had an impact on my behaviour at this point?
- What was I doing in the moments leading up to this scene?
- What is my relationship with the other characters at this point?

Exercise

Apply the Character and Narrative Checklists above to the script extract below and make notes for each character. Remember, you'll get one or two clues from the script, but you'll need to create much of the detail yourself. If you are working with others on this exercise, it will be interesting to compare notes and see how many different interpretations there are.

KITCHEN: LATE EVENING
STEVE: Coffee? That'll warm you up.
SARAH: Umm, yes – actually, I'd prefer a hot chocolate.
STEVE: Coming up. I wonder what's keeping them?

MOOR: LATE EVENING
LOUISA: Where's the map. We must be lost. This is the third time we've crossed this stream.
SEAN: In my backpack – front pocket – can you reach it?
LOUISA: Yes – here we are. Which way up does it go?
SEAN: Oh, typical. Didn't you do geography at school?

KITCHEN: LATE EVENING
SARAH: Still no answer from the mobile – must be out of juice.
STEVE: Here you go – one hot chocolate. Do you want more sugar in it?
SARAH: No ta, but pass me one of those biscuits to dunk. I think we should give it another 10 minutes, then go and look for them.

MOOR: LATE EVENING
SEAN: I'm cold, my feet are soggy and my nose is dripping. This is the last time I ever go out walking with you.
LOUISA: Oh cheer up, for goodness sake. Look – there's a pub just over there.

Applying the technical knowledge

In preparing for the recording, it's also important to remember the technical issues discussed earlier in this chapter. In addition to your notes on the character and narrative, it is important also to plan how you will use microphone positions 1 through 5. Don't forget to specify where you will move from one position to another.

Exercise

Read through the script below and make notes as follows:

1. Looking at one line at a time, jot down the emotional state of the characters through the scene. Consider how the changing emotions can be performed.
2. Plot the actor positions throughout the scene (choosing from position 1 through 5 as outlined above).
3. Consider how Kate will move from the kitchen to the front door and back again, avoiding the crouching tiger effect. Remember, you may need to 'ad lib' a line or two to make it work.
4. Consider what Stewart is doing while Kate is at the front door. How can this be conveyed? Remember: silent = invisible.
5. Rehearse, record and listen to the recording. Do the emotions of the characters change? Does the movement sound logical and believable, or are there crouching tigers?

KITCHEN: KATE IS WASHING UP. STEWART IS PACKING BOOKS INTO A BAG.

KATE: For goodness sake, Stewart. It's ten to nine. You're going to miss it.

STEWART: Alright, mum. Just stop going on about it. I'll be able . . .

SFX: DISTANT FRONT DOOR BELL RINGS

KATE: I'll get it. You need to pack your stuff. Don't forget the banana.

SFX: KATE ANSWERS THE FRONT DOOR

POLICE OFFICER: Mrs. Jones? I'm Sergeant John Fowler from Cardiff Central Police.

SFX: KATE AND POLICE OFFICER ENTER KITCHEN

KATE: Yes, what is it, What's wrong?

STEWART: Look – if this is about that trouble down at the park, I can . . .

POLICE OFFICER: (INTERRUPTS) It's about your daughter, Hannah.

KATE: Yes – she left for school about an . . . Oh no. What's happened?

The recording process

When one considers all the effort that has gone into preparing for this moment, the recording process can be strangely anticlimactic. Typically, the voices and spot sfx will be recorded first. If you are lucky, you may hear a little atmos too, through loudspeakers. Everything else happens in post-production. The scenes probably won't be recorded chronologically, and you will have very little idea of how the finished play will sound at the time of recording. This makes the preparation you have done all the more crucial, as this is probably the only way that you will be able to give a convincing performance. The producer or director has a big role to play here, discussing your preparation with you and helping you understand how each scene will sound at the end of the production process. This takes us back to Elisa Eliot's explanation of the *We're Alive* director Kc Wayland's good practice in 'bringing the "other" audio, the audio we *don't* hear, to life in the studio for us so that we can bring that into the acting' (Eliot, 2010).

Active directing

At this point, it is worth mentioning the importance of a good working relationship between the director and actor. Not only should directors help to put the drama in context and, when necessary, assist the actors in preparation and interpretation; they can also have an active role during performance. In the early days of radio a whole system of directing hand cues and symbols developed. This is especially important in all-live broadcasting in which the director needs to coordinate the play (not dissimilar to an orchestra conductor), but has to do so in absolute silence. Even in pre-recording it has its place. Various handbooks and online guides provide details of hand cues, but here are some key symbols that might be useful:

- Stand By: director keeps hand above head with palm facing outwards
- Cue to start: director points at performer
- Softer or quieter: hand, palm down with fingers outstretched, repeatedly moving downwards
- Louder: hand, palm up with fingers outstretched, repeatedly moving upwards

- Move away from microphone: raised hand, palm outwards, gestures pushing performer away
- Move closer to the microphone: director pulls raised hand towards self
- Slow down: smooth sideways motion with the hand as though stretching something elastic
- Faster: rapidly draw circles with finger
- Cut: slicing gesture across neck

Remember, the director should get the attention of the performer who needs the cue. This might be direct eye contact, but is more likely to be learning the skill of 'being aware' of contact so that the performers do not need to take their eyes off the script.

Exercise

Take a script and experiment with various hand cues. How can this determine, moderate and control the flow and 'sound' of the performance?

Studio Etiquette

The professional attitude we have discussed throughout this chapter should also be continued during the recording. Here are some pointers:

- Don't wear noisy clothes or jewelry: leather jackets, fussy clothes, heavy shoes or bangles risk making distracting noises.
- When asked to 'give level', *don't* mumble '1, 2, 1, 2, 2', into the microphone like a roadie in a band. Read a little of the script in character and at the volume and distance from the microphone you intend to use during the recording.
- Make sure you check what signal the producer will give to you to start your line. In a professional studio, it's usually a green 'cue' light. In less formal circumstances, it could be a nod, thumbs up or wave.
- If there are several actors or a spot sfx technician using the same microphone, step away from the microphone when you are not speaking to give them room.
- If you 'fluff' (make a mistake), don't make a big fuss. Simply go back a couple of lines and repeat. Your mistakes can usually be edited out later.
- Be careful with your script. Gently place used pages on the floor.
- At the end of the recording, stay silent until you have the 'all clear' from the producer.

Conclusion

Acting for radio is very pure, in the sense that the voice is the only means of performance. There's no makeup or costume to help build the illusion, no set or props. In this sense, the actor's skill is pared down to the bare essential: an ability to enthral, enthuse and stir the emotion with the voice alone. While there's no doubt that this is exposing and challenging, many actors enjoy the immediacy of radio. The physical clutter of stage performance is gone, allowing the actor to build a particularly intimate relationship with the audience and speak from the mind. The presence of the script during recording is similarly liberating. Though detailed preparation is still necessary, lines do not have to be memorized. This chapter has attempted to introduce the techniques of radio drama performance and provided some stimulation to develop basic knowledge. For readers who wish to improve, Alan Beck's book *Radio Acting* (1997) is rich with personal anecdotes and expertise and is the definitive text on professional-level radio drama performance.

Case study: *The Terrifying Tale of Sweeney Todd!*: An experiment in the re-creation of live radio drama

Introduction

In 2008, staff and students at the University of Glamorgan decided to conduct a teaching and research experiment into live radio drama. The experiment was focused on the creation of a new script modelled on the classic 30-minute formula of the 'golden age' horror show. Sound effects were designed to be created entirely live. Original music was composed for the production following conventions appropriate for the music of the chosen era. All voice acting, sound effects and music were performed live in the studio by students and faculty staff with an invited audience in attendance. In addition, the play was broadcast live on air via GTFM, a local radio station. The play was also webcast live via the GTFM and university websites. The recording of the play was subsequently rebroadcast several times and was then lodged as a free download on iTunesU.

Choice of Script

Sweeney Todd presents a fascinating and probably unique story in terms of its origin, legacy and cultural reinvention. Almost certainly an urban legend, it still has advocates, most notably Peter Haining, who insist it is a true story. A popular 'Penny Dreadful' in the 1840s, *The String of Pearls* was inevitably dramatized, and George Dibden Pitt's play became a favourite melodrama on the stage. In the twentieth century and beyond it transferred to the screen with Sweeney Todd interpreted by a surprisingly diverse range of actors including: Moore Marriott (1928); Tod Slaughter (1936); Freddie Jones (1970); John Miranda (1970); Ben Kingsley (1998); Ray Winstone (2006); and Johnny Depp (2007). And that *not* exhaustive list only features those who have played the demonic Mr. Todd in film adaptations of the tale. Sweeney Todd has become an icon of horror: not like Transylvanian icons, the fantasy horrors of Frankenstein, Dracula and the Wolfman made so popular in Universal movies; Sweeney Todd is a horror icon of the 'possible', and as such has joined the sepulchral pantheon inhabited by Jack the Ripper or Norman Bates. Interestingly, while the fortunes of Frankenstein and Dracula in their incarnation as popular culture icons may have waned somewhat, Sweeney Todd becomes a very apt monster for our time. *Van Helsing* (Stephen Sommers, 2004), with its eclectic mix of Dracula, Frankenstein and Jekyll and Hyde, may have flopped at the box office, but contemporary horror has triumphed with the *Hostel* films, the *Saw* films and numerous other examples of *feasible* horror in which the serial killer Mr. Todd and the cannibalistic cook Mrs. Lovett would fit comfortably.

Sweeney Todd is also a story that continues to survive as a fine template for adaptation. There are countless allusions, accretions, echoes and exploitations of the story. This probably explains why for someone like Peter Haining the story has become true: a myth so rich that it must have a basis in fact, a legend that seems belittled if it is merely fantasy. At the heart of the Sweeney Todd legend is a barber working on, or near, Fleet Street in the City of London. He kills his victims when they come for a shave with or without his cutthroat razor in combination with his lethal chair-cum-trapdoor which throws each victim into the cellar below. Mrs. Lovett is Todd's partner in crime who helps to loot the bodies and disposes of the corpses by using the flesh as meat for her pies. Robert L. Mack's *The Wonderful and Surprising History of Sweeney Todd* (2007) demonstrates how the story's flexibility rests on two key components: the serial killer and cannibalism. The barbershop, the cutthroat razor, the pie shop, the London setting, and so on are all essential ingredients, but at its heart the serial killer and cannibalism are the key 'anxieties' that underpin the ghastly appeal of the text.

It is clear that the Sweeney Todd legend emerges out of contemporary concerns which, if anything, become more pertinent as time goes on: to start with, what has become known as the serial killer. The flaunting of the Sixth Commandment – Thou Shalt Not Kill – is a long-term anxiety for Judaeo-Christian civilization. But it's one thing to be Cain killing Abel and another to commit murder again and again . . . The modern city in the nineteenth century was a place of danger as well as wonder: a place like London had grown beyond what one person could ever know, and murderers exploit this. The greatest emblem of this is a real figure who comes after the legend of Sweeney Todd: Jack the Ripper. Whoever he was and wherever he was from, he continues to be popularly described as 'London's most notorious son' in tourist guides. He abides, as he remained uncaptured fuelling perennial speculation and conspiracy theories. Certainly one important factor in the Jack the Ripper case is the fact that he was not an axe-wielding maniac, but a *skilled* killer, thought to have anatomical knowledge – maybe a butcher, but quite possibly a *surgeon*. Likewise with Sweeney Todd, there is the *audacious* terror inherent in this skilled man's trail of murder. Barbers have a proud heritage as pioneering surgeons with an important role in the history of medical science, working alongside physicians to preserve lives and cure the afflicted. It is in some ways the beginning of modern horror. If Jack the Ripper is a very modern monster, so is Sweeney Todd. But there is another audacity to the Sweeney Todd story: we may be able to deal with the concept of the lone killer, the isolated maniac. But in comes Mrs. Lovett – the partner in crime. This problematizes the notion of the killer even further. It's much easier to cope with the isolated criminal, or even the double life, than partners in crime.

The terrifying world of Sweeney Todd makes for a fantastic visual setting on stage and screen, but it also has the potential to make even more tremendous radio. The barbershop, the pie shop, the conjoining cellar and the gruesome acts of murder and cannibalism could dwell happily in the dark terrors of horror radio. We decided that an all-new adaptation of this classic and familiar tale would present all members of the creative team and the audience with a delightful thrill ride into audio drama.

Producing *The Terrifying Tale of Sweeney Todd!*

The 'golden age' of radio drama was a unique period in the history of radio: a time of unprecedented development during which the radio drama techniques we use today were born. While there are plenty of opportunities to read about this exciting era, *The Terrifying Tale of Sweeney Todd!* allowed students and staff to step back in time and experience the 'golden age' for themselves. The equipment used to make radio drama developed quickly between the 1920s and 1950s, so for the purposes of our production, it was important to focus on one particular time. We selected a point when the technology was relatively advanced: 1940. By this time, radio drama was immensely popular, and the high demand from listeners and sponsors produced a frenetic, inventive, adrenalin-fuelled industry. A typical production was 'turned around' from script to broadcast in an incredible four or five hours, and the atmosphere in the studio must have been electric as actors, technicians, musicians, producer and director frantically prepared for the 'live' show. Recreating this exciting environment with a group of students and staff was challenging, but extremely gratifying.

The high demand for radio drama meant that radio acting was an excellent career choice in the 1940s, but it required particular dedication and versatility, as the experiences of this actor demonstrate:

> I did the show on CBS [from the Wrigley Building], ran across the street to the Tribune Tower [the home of WGN] . . . and I had about three minutes plus the commercials to make the show [at The Merchandise Mart, then-home of WMAQ]. (Darnall, 1998)

Such demands are rarely placed on radio actors today, but the cast of *Sweeney Todd* was keen to try out this way of working. In order to produce a similarly intense experience, the actors were not allowed to see the final script until a couple of days before the production. Performers in the 1940s could only dream of such a luxurious rehearsal period, but for our relatively inexperienced cast, the tight timescale presented a significant challenge and a healthy dose of adrenalin. The build-up to the production began about a week before the broadcast date. Only two of the five actors had previous experience with radio drama, so the starting point was to familiarize the cast with radio drama performing techniques. In the 1940s, there was very little training in performance for radio specifically, and directors often fulfilled this role. However, text books of the era clearly recognized that acting for radio was a subject that deserved some attention. *Handbook of Broadcasting* (Abbott 1941) and *Radio Drama Acting and Production* (Kingson, 1950) give a flavor of the skills required of radio actors and provide excellent short script exercises to help actors develop technique. Interestingly, the exercises are as relevant today as they were at the time of publication and were invaluable in helping the cast to understand the requirements of radio performance. While these exercises were of a technical nature, other sessions introduced sample scripts from the golden age, many of which are available on the internet from excellent websites such as the *Generic Radio Old Time Radio Script Library*. The sessions began with readings, but quickly developed into studio-based performances, which allowed the cast to apply the techniques they had learnt to a complete script.

In the studio, the actors were able to experiment with microphone technique for the first time. Ribbon microphones, with 'live' and 'dead' areas were in use during the 1940s and, while we didn't have access to working antique microphones, it was possible to simulate their directional properties using contemporary microphones. The technicians had an opportunity to work alongside the performers to experiment with sound effects. During the 1940s, the majority of sound effects were 'live', and a tremendous amount of ingenuity was involved in creating appropriate sounds from objects which, often, bore no relation to the object being conveyed. For example, scrunching cotton wool between the hands was used to simulate footsteps in snow, and the sound of an army marching was created by shaking dried beans in a shoe box.

While the actors and technicians were in the dark about the final script at this point, the musicians (composer, keyboard and violin) were privileged with an early reading. This enabled them to compose and rehearse an overall theme, as well as some shorter melodies and chords, which would be used at key moments during the production to indicate the passing of time or to create a particular mood.

The moment when the cast was finally introduced to the script was marvellously exciting. The exercises and studio sessions had equipped the actors, musicians and technicians with the skills to perform 'live' radio drama, and now came the opportunity to put it all into practice. We began with a couple of straight 'run-throughs' to familiarize the cast with the play, and then undertook a more detailed rehearsal of each scene. Similar to a theatrical rehearsal, the initial emphasis was on characterization and motivation. However, the technical demands of radio meant that a significant amount of time was also spent 'blocking' the actors and sound effects technicians in relation to the microphones and resolving differing voice levels. The role of the director was significant in 'live' radio drama in the 1940s and was similarly crucial in our production. The director managed the performance from start to finish, cueing performers, musicians, sound effects and technicians in the manner of a conductor with an orchestra. John Carlile's *Production and Direction of Radio Programmes* (1942) illustrates the elaborate series of hand signals which was devised to facilitate silent communication during broadcast (we have covered some of these already in the Performance chapter). Our director used these hand signals during rehearsals and, later, during the 'live' broadcast to communicate messages from the control room and stage directions such as 'slow down' or 'move closer to the microphone'. The sound effects technicians and musicians were equally important members of the 'orchestra' and were controlled by the director in our production in a similar way. The technicians created some extraordinary sound effects for the production. The gruesome sounds of Todd slashing the throats of his victims was achieved by ripping a piece of cloth and gargling with yoghurt. The sound of the bodies being dismembered to be made into pies was achieved by hacking and sawing at cabbage and celery, accompanied by squelching wallpaper paste. Interestingly, the sfx team could not improve on the sound of a real cutthroat razor on a strop for Todd sharpening his razor, and therefore used this in the broadcast. The musicians worked closely with the performers and technicians to integrate evocative musical phrases and chords at key moments.

The scale of the production was such that it was impractical to produce *Sweeney Todd* in the radio studio available to us, and so the performance took place in a small theatre. The microphones were linked to a mixing desk within the theatre control room and fed, via internet stream, to the radio studio. The theatre space was large and more reverberant than a radio studio, which compromised the sound quality somewhat, but ensured that there was plenty of room for the large cast and a studio audience. The role of the studio audience in *Sweeney Todd* was rather contradictory. In the 1940s, studio audiences were normally only present when they had a particular role to play, such as providing audible audience interaction during a radio comedy show. The studio audience of *Sweeney Todd* had no particular role, other than to observe the production. For inexperienced radio actors, the notion of consciously ignoring the studio audience to focus on the radio listener alone presented a challenge. During the rehearsal period, the performers were reminded to keep their performances 'small' and not to attempt to engage the studio audience. Nevertheless, the melodramatic nature of the play, with its gory sound effects, did draw a reaction from the studio audience, which was difficult for the actors to ignore.

Sweeney Todd was produced 'live' on GTFM radio, a community station in Wales, and was simultaneously streamed. The play was very different from the typical output of GTFM, which consists of contemporary music, chat, news and sport. For this reason, it was necessary to ease the listeners into the play. This was achieved by 'wrapping' the play within a longer programme, during which the presenter set the scene by talking about the 'golden age' of radio and playing music from the era. It was important to create the right atmosphere in the theatre, too. Photographs of radio drama productions from the 1940s show actors dressed smartly. Our actors dressed in a similar way, which helped them to stay focused on the era, but also to understand how the mode of dress affects performance. The choice of shoes, for example, makes a big difference to the sound of movement in the drama.

As the time of broadcast approached, the tension in the theatre was palpable. GTFM radio was patched through so that the cast and studio audience could hear the presenter's build up. The director explained a little background to the play and counselled the studio audience to observe only and remain quiet. Thirty seconds before the play was scheduled to start, the theatre was silenced and the cast waited nervously for the red light which signalled that they were 'on air': *The Terrifying Tale of Sweeney Todd!* was 'live' on radio!

We encourage you to listen to the recording, but we have also included the full script. Why not use the script as a way into your own practical experiments? Perform and record the script with your own music and sound effects and actors.

"The Terrifying Tale of Sweeney Todd!"
by
Richard J. Hand

NARRATOR
JOHN CLARK
MRS. LOVETT
SWEENEY TODD
JOANNA
STEPHEN

1. MUSIC: INTRODUCTORY, UP BEAT BUT TURNS SINISTER AT END

2. NARRATOR: Good evening, my friends . . . Tonight we have a classic story for you: one of the most notorious, gruesome, horrific, strangest tales that ever heard tell. A tale set in London in the days of the late Queen. Picture to yourselves the Victorian fog; London, city of money and industry, city of wonder, city of danger. London, the great wen, spreading like a canker, deadly as a creeping smog. A city all too real for this fantasy. Yes, rest assured this tale is just a flight of fancy. Or is it? Who could dream up a tale of such depravity, of such cutthroat cruelty and murderous meat-mongering by a barbaric barber and a pernicious pie-maker. For tonight our story can only be The Terrifying Tale of Sweeney Todd!

3. MUSIC: DRAMATIC

4. NARRATOR: Just a final word of warning before we begin. I know sometimes during our early evening broadcasts you, my loyal friends, like to sup on dinner while we sup on horrors. But tonight maybe it's a night for bread and water. Unless you can swear, swear on a grave, swear in a court of law, that you know where every ingredient that you consume came from, then maybe you should push that plate aside . . . And so, my friends, let us go to London . . . It is in the glory days of Queen Victoria, and we find ourselves in a small pie shop in a courtyard off Fleet Street . . .

1. MUSIC: MYSTERY
2. SFX: PLATE AND CUTLERY
3. CLARK: To be honest, madam, it was the smell that brought me here . . . Walking down Fleet Street, half lost and perishing with hunger, I caught a whiff and followed my nose! And there it was: Mrs. Lovett's Pie Shop!
4. LOVETT: Ha, ha, ha! Good news for me, eh? And a batch of pies straight out the oven.
5. CLARK: Delicious! Wondrously delicious! Meat and gravy, flaming hot, with a golden crust. [EATS] Exquisite! Delectable! A Lovett pie, eh? And Mrs. Lovett, I *do* "love it"! Er . . . What meat do you use?
6. LOVETT: What meat, sir? Veal. The finest quality veal, fed on the creamiest milk and slaughtered by the hand of a master butcher. A drop more wine, sir?
7. CLARK: Oh yes, blood-red claret in the glass.
8. SFX: WINE POURED
9. CLARK: [DRINKS] It's great to be back in London after all this time. Twenty years I have been away. Voyaging in the tropics and in Africa. The dark places of the earth, avoiding the spears of savages and the cannibal's pot. Ha! There are places in the world untouched by the light of the civilization, Mrs. Lovett, of such depravity . . . Oh, it is good to be back in London!
10. LOVETT: Welcome back, sir!
11. CLARK: In all those years abroad I cannot tell you how much I missed this old city. And most of all – the food. For years I have craved a good British pie. On the ship to London I was slavering for one. This is the first English pie I have had in twenty years, Mrs. Lovett, and it doesn't disappoint. But tell me, how goes business for you? You are in the buzz of the city, but hidden away down this courtyard. And the lane to here is, forgive me, inauspicious.
12. LOVETT: But I can always trust a discerning customer's nose, sir.
13. CLARK: Very good! Very good!
14. LOVETT: And I have my regulars – men from the Fleet Street dailies.
15. CLARK: Newspaper men?
16. LOVETT: Yes. They'd sell their grandmothers for a story such is their appetite for a yarn and lucky for me, they have an equal appetite –

1. CLARK: For Mrs. Lovett's pies!
2. LOVETT: Quite so.
3. CLARK: Well, I will be your regular, too. I mean to stay a while. Back, at last, from the corners of the Empire I have made my fortune and intend to enjoy my profits in the greatest city in the world.
4. LOVETT: First stop was the Bank of England, sir?
5. CLARK: No. I'll tell you a secret – my fortune is about my person. And behold . . .
6. MUSIC: DRAMATIC CHORD
7. LOVETT: A string of pearls!
8. CLARK: All real! All perfect!
9. LOVETT: Ooh, they're lush!
10. CLARK: Touch them, Mrs. Lovett, please, touch them.
11. SFX: PEARLS RATTLE
12. LOVETT: Oh, beautiful. They must be worth hundreds!
13. CLARK: Thousands, Mrs. Lovett, *thousands*!
14. LOVETT: I can tell!
15. CLARK: I'll take them back now, thank you. Where might there be a jewellers? Someone who would give me a fair price for these beauties?
16. LOVETT: Now let me think . . . Yes, I believe can help. But it all depends on the impression you can cut, sir. A full belly will help – it gives an air of comfort and plenty. You're worth thousands already!
17. CLARK: I see . . . But what can give me a cut above the rest? A fair lady upon my arm, Mrs. Lovett?
18. LOVETT: Ha, ha! That will come later, sir!
19. CLARK: What of Mr. Lovett . . . ?
20. LOVETT: Deceased, sir.
21. CLARK: Ah. Now that our friendship is taking leaps and bounds, my name is John Clark. You may call me John.
22. LOVETT: You need a shave.
23. CLARK: I see your reason.
24. LOVETT: You will profit on a *smooth chin*.
25. CLARK: I know that I am somewhat rough about the jowls. I have missed the cutthroat razors of London – the sharpest in the world! I noticed a barbershop next door.
26. LOVETT: Yes, Sweeney Todd's. I recommend him most highly. There's never been a single complaint about him. The sharpest blade of any barber in London. Like an artist he is. He is to the chin and the neck what Michael Angelo was to marble.
27. CLARK: He'll make a work of art of me, will he?

1. LOVETT: Yes, sir. Quite rejuvenating too! Keep your appointments with Mr. Todd and you'll never age a day.
2. CLARK: Very well! So a fellow like me desires a full stomach, a smooth chin and *then* a fair lady upon my arm?
3. LOVETT: Ha ha ha! We'll meet again after Mr. Todd has given you his special treatment. That I promise.
4. CLARK: There's no time to waste.
5. LOVETT: Indeed not! Just tell Mr. Todd that I sent you and just say that Mrs. Lovett said you could *do with a serious polish*. He'll understand.
6. CLARK: 'I could do with a serious polish.' How very true! Er, what do I owe for you the pie and claret, Mrs. Lovett?
7. LOVETT: Let's not worry about that now . . . I'll see you after Mr. Todd has worked his magic on you and we'll settle up then.
8. CLARK: And poor Mr. Lovett deceased you say!? Ha ha!
9. LOVETT: Ha ha, yes, God rest his soul!
10. MUSIC
11. SFX: SHOP DOOR AND BELL
12. CLARK: Mr. Todd?
13. TODD: Yes, it is I.
14. CLARK: How do you do.
15. TODD: A shave is it? I was going to close up the shop soon.
16. CLARK: I must say this is not quite what I expected. Are your blades clean? Rather malodorous: no aroma of soap.
17. TODD: There are plenty other barbers in London, you know.
18. CLARK: I'm sure there are. But I was advised to come here.
19. TODD: Oh yeah? Who was that then?
20. CLARK: Mrs. Lovett, next door. Told me to inform you that I could benefit from a *serious polish*.
21. TODD: Did she now? I see! Please take a seat. Comfortable, sir?
22. CLARK: Yes, but what a most extraordinary chair. Never seen such a strange chair.
23. TODD: My own design.
24. CLARK: (sarcastic) You should take out a patent.
25. TODD: Just might do that, sir.
26. CLARK: It's large, like a throne!

1. TODD: My customer is king, sir.
2. CLARK: Quite.
3. TODD: Just sit back in the chair, sir.
4. CLARK: Very well.
5. TODD: New to London, are we?
6. CLARK: You are in error, Mr. Todd. London and I are very old friends. But I haven't been here for twenty years. That is a long time.
7. TODD: Looking for friends in the big city, eh?
8. CLARK: I have family, thank you very much. A niece whom I haven't seen since she was a mere child. She's the daughter of my late sister.
9. TODD: So now you've made your fortune in lands far afield, back you come to retrace those blood ties.
10. CLARK: I don't think that –
11. TODD: Sit back in the chair, sir.
12. CLARK: Please, Mr. Todd, I must insist that you hurry up and shave me so that I may take my leave.
13. TODD: Very well. Let's lather you up.
14. SFX: LATHER BOWL
15. TODD: Keep still, sir.
16. SFX: LATHER BRUSH
17. TODD: That's it, on your chin and your cheeks. My own recipe of soap this is.
18. CLARK: And most unpleasant it is, too!
19. TODD: Ssh, don't talk. Just sit back in the chair and keep still. Now where's my blessed strop? Here it is. You can only get a close shave with a razor sharp blade that can slice a human hair down the middle.
20. CLARK: Get on with it!
21. TODD: Of course, sir.
22. SFX: STROPPING RAZOR
23. TODD: There we go. Sharp enough. I shall begin.
24. SFX: RAZOR ON ROUGH SKIN
25. TODD: And now the delicate touch, sir. The last time I'll say it: just sit back in the chair and keep nice and still. Rest your head back so that I can trim your neck. That's it, that's it, that's right!
26. SFX: RIPPING SKIN! A SHRIEK CUT SHORT!
    WINDPIPE RASPING! THROAT GURGLING!
27. TODD: Ha, ha! And now, down you go, down you go: to hell with ya!
28. SFX: MECHANICAL LEVER
    TRAP DOOR OPENS
    HEAVY WEIGHT OF BODY CRASHES AT DISTANCE
    TRAP DOOR CLOSES

1. MUSIC: DOOM-LADEN
2. SFX: FOOTSTEPS DESCENDING ON STONE STEPS
ATMSOPHERE OF ECHOES
RATS SQUEAK
3. TODD: Cursed rats infesting my cellar! Cha!
4. SFX: RATS PANIC AND DISAPPEAR
5. LOVETT: You should clean this place up. Rats love a charnel house. It stinks down here.
6. TODD: Mrs. Lovett – here already . . .
7. LOVETT: Yes, your good neighbour. About her business.
8. SFX: COINS
9. TODD: Huh, I see you waste no time about that.
10. LOVETT: Those in our business have no time to waste! Ah, here they are! These are what I was looking for! Look, Mr. Todd, a string of pearls.
11. MUSIC: DRAMATIC CHORD
12. TODD: I see why he needed a serious polish now. They must be worth hundreds.
13. LOVETT: Thousands according to him. Let me wear them. Just for a moment.
14. SFX: PEARLS RATTLE
15. TODD: They suit ya.
16. LOVETT: Just think. Sell these and we could retire from our trade.
17. TODD: Yes. Or I could make a better chair.
18. LOVETT: And I could buy a bigger oven. No time to waste. Off with his clothes.
19. SFX: BOOTS AND THICK CLOTH ETC.
20. TODD: Onto the slab.
21. SFX: HEAVY WEIGHT ON SLAB
22. TODD: Pass the hatchet and the saw.
23. SFX: WET SAWING AND CHOPPING INTO . . .
24. MUSIC
25. NARRATOR: So now you know the work of our dastardly partners in crime. Addicted to crime and cruelty. A perfect mechanism for execution, a perfect method for disposal. Every time the perfect crime. Or was it? Poor John Clark – did you say you had a niece?
26. MUSIC
27. JOANNA: But what can have happened to my uncle? You see, here is his letter saying when he would arrive. And the shipping office sent a message confirming that he disembarked.
28. STEPHEN: Do not worry so, my dear Joanna, there must be rational explanation.

1. JOANNA: His ship arrived days ago. He should be here by now.
2. STEPHEN: Perhaps he's been renewing his acquaintances? Many years since he's been in London after all!
3. JOANNA: He would have been here by now – or have sent a message. I simply know it. Look at the letters he sent me up to now. Brimming with excitement about seeing me, his only living relation!
4. SFX: RUSTLING PAPER
5. JOANNA: Those years abroad were a success and time to reunite with what is left of his family! So keen to meet his niece again and her fiancé . . . And, here, missing this city so much with its decent barbers and public houses and its food . . . Yes, here, desperate for a good old-fashioned meat pie in a London pie shop . . . Ha ha! Oh, Stephen, what can have happened . . . ? (Starts to weep)
6. STEPHEN: There, there my dear. We will meet with him – I promise. People don't just disappear in London.
7. JOANNA: But that's exactly what they *can* do! What if someone has taken advantage of him? Look at this letter.
8. SFX: RUSTLING PAPER
9. JOANNA: He says he carried his fortune with him. He owns a string of pearls, perfect in every way.
10. STEPHEN: They'd be worth hundreds.
11. JOANNA: Thousands he says here. He was planning to sell them as soon as he could. Understandable – they'd be attractive to every felon in London if they so much as caught a glimpse of them.
12. STEPHEN: Very well. What shall we do?
13. JOANNA: I think we should read all his letters and follow any clues as to where he might have gone.
14. STEPHEN: That is a good idea.
15. JOANNA: We should visit the shipping office ourselves and retrace his steps.
16. STEPHEN: Ask anyone if they may have seen a gentleman newly arrived from the tropics.
17. JOANNA: Yes. Anyone and everyone.
18. STEPHEN: In London? Ask anyone and everyone?
19. JOANNA: Yes! Do you disagree?
20. STEPHEN: No, no, not at all, my dear.
21. MUSIC: RELENTLESS SEARCH

1. NARRATOR: And so Joanna and her fiancé Stephen read the letters again and again and then they searched and questioned anyone and everyone from the shipping office to the banks and the jewellers, from the alleyways to the street, from the street to the public houses and eventually, to the barbers and the pie shops.
2. MUSIC: FADING AWAY
3. SFX: DOOR OPENS
4. LOVETT: Hello – come in, my dears! Make yourselves comfortable.
5. JOANNA: Thank you, we are in need of a rest.
6. STEPHEN: Indeed we are.
7. LOVETT: Would you care for a pie?
8. STEPHEN: Mm, what an aroma! Mouth-watering! Yes, madam, that would be lovely.
9. LOVETT: And you, my dear?
10. JOANNA: Not for me, thank you.
11. LOVETT: Are you sure? You've no idea what you'd be missing.
12. JOANNA: No, thank you.
13. LOVETT: You don't want to miss out on a treat, do ya? It'd do some good for you, my dear. Put a bit of rosy in your cheeks!
14. JOANNA: No, I'm quite sure.
15. LOVETT: Suit yourself. Your young man knows a good pie when he sniffs one!
16. SFX: PLATES, CUTLERY
17. STEPHEN: I can't wait! I am perishing with hunger!
18. SFX: OVEN DOOR CRASHES
PIE TRAY SLIDES ONTO TABLE
19. LOVETT: Here you are, my lad, straight from the oven, piping hot . . .
20. STEPHEN: Goody, goody!
21. LOVETT: Tuck in! Get the beauty of it hot!
22. STEPHEN: [EATS] Mm, delicious.
23. LOVETT: I like to think so. My own recipe, n'all.
24. JOANNA: You must be Mrs. Lovett, I take it?
25. LOVETT: Yes, this is my shop, I'm proud to say.
26. STEPHEN: [EATS] Quite right too!
27. JOANNA: Could we ask you some questions?
28. LOVETT: My recipe is strictly a secret!
29. JOANNA: No, I don't want to know that.
30. LOVETT: I'm a busy woman.
31. SFX: TIDYING TABLES, PLATES, CUTLERY ETC.
32. STEPHEN: Let me congratulate you on a magnificent pie, Mrs. Lovett.

1. LOVETT: Thank you, young man, you're welcome back any time.
2. JOANNA: Just a few questions.
3. LOVETT: Questions, questions!
4. JOANNA: Do you ever get customers who are back from the tropics or Africa?
5. LOVETT: I get people from all over. Now if you don't mind, I'm very busy . . .
6. JOANNA: Did a Mr. John Clark come here for a pie?
7. SFX: CRASH OF PIE DISHES AND CUTLERY
8. LOVETT: Who sent you here? So many questions! Never heard of him! It's a common name, anyway, isn't it? If you'll excuse me, I'm a busy woman – pies don't make themselves, you know.
9. SFX: OVEN DOOR ETC.
10. JOANNA: (whisper) Stephen, what a reaction!
11. STEPHEN: Yes, I have to agree.
12. JOANNA: She'll say nothing more, I fear, but I will try. Maybe mentioning a string of pearls will jog her memory. While I try, you slip away and go to the barbershop next door. Perhaps the barber may have seen or heard something he can tell you.
13. STEPHEN: Very well.
14. MUSIC
15. SFX: SHOP DOOR AND BELL
16. STEPHEN: Good afternoon.
17. TODD: A shave is it? I was just about to close up the shop.
18. STEPHEN: Sorry to trouble you. Just wanted to ask a few questions, if I may.
19. TODD: Oh yeah, what about?
20. STEPHEN: Strangers returning from the tropics. Such as Mr. John Clark. You see, when we mentioned his name to Mrs. Lovett . . .
21. TODD: Who do you think you are? Get out of here!
22. STEPHEN: A strange reaction, I must say! What is wrong with a few honest questions? Have you something to hide?
23. TODD: Shop's closed. Out you go.
24. STEPHEN: We believe he had a string of pearls . . .
25. TODD: That does it! Maybe I do have time to give you a shave, sir! Ha ha!
26. STEPHEN: You're mad! You demon! You devil! Drop that razor!
27. TODD: I will not! Ha ha!
28. SFX: SWISH OF RAZOR
29. STEPHEN: Keep away! Keep away I tell you!

1. TODD: I will not! You're mine now!
2. SFX: SWISH OF RAZOR AND A RIP
3. STEPHEN: Agh!
4. TODD: Got ya!
5. SFX: SHOP DOOR CRASHES OPEN WITH BELL
6. JOANNA: Stephen!
7. TODD: Get out!
8. LOVETT: I'm sorry, Sweeney, I couldn't stop her!
9. STEPHEN: Joanna, my dear! They're in it together!
10. LOVETT: That's right, my lad! The perfect couple of crime! We get what we want *with never a witness*! Kill 'em, Sweeney! Just like you did with Mr. John Clark!
11. TODD: He he, with pleasure! Ah, sorry, my little lovebirds, my blades are quite blunt today!
12. LOVETT: All the better to hurt 'em with!
13. STEPHEN: Quick, Joanna, make for the door!
14. LOVETT: Oh no, you don't, miss!
15. SFX: HURRIED STEPS THEN A SLIP AND CRASH
16. JOANNA: She's fallen!
17. STEPHEN: She's out cold! Now's our chance!
18. JOANNA: Look out!
19. TODD: I've got you now!
20. STEPHEN: No! I've got you!
21. SFX: SOUND OF STRUGGLE
22. STEPHEN: Help me, Joanna, let's force him away! Into the chair! Find something to tie him down!
23. TODD: I'm gonna kill ya! Let me go! No! *No*!
24. SFX: TRAP DOOR OPENS
SWEENEY TODD SCREAMS
HEAVY WEIGHT OF BODY CRASHES AT DISTANCE
TRAP DOOR CLOSES
25. STEPHEN: My God, Joanna! What happened!?
26. JOANNA: My dress caught on this lever here – and the chair swung back!
27. STEPHEN: I nearly fell in after him. A devilish invention! No poor unwitting fellow would stand a chance.
28. JOANNA: Like my uncle . . . ?
29. STEPHEN: I'm afraid that might be the case, Joanna.
30. JOANNA: Poor Uncle John!
31. STEPHEN: Do not despair. At least that demon barber's down in the cellar now – that fall will have stopped his misdeeds.
32. JOANNA: Stephen, you're bleeding!
33. STEPHEN: I'll be fine. He merely caught my arm with that cursed razor!

1. JOANNA: Look, the steps over there must lead down into the cellar.
2. STEPHEN: Come on, let's ensure that this skulduggery is at an end.
3. MUSIC: DRAMATIC CHORD
4. SFX: FOOTSTEPS DESCENDING ON STONE STEPS
ATMSOPHERE OF ECHOES
RATS SQUEAK
5. STEPHEN: There he is.
6. JOANNA: All those rats!
7. STEPHEN: At his body already. Be off!
8. SFX: RATS PANIC AND DISAPPEAR
9. JOANNA: Oh, Stephen!
10. STEPHEN: Not a pretty sight. His neck quite broken – but I suppose that saved the hangman his labours. But those rats began their work quickly . . .
11. JOANNA: And look all around – clothes, boots.
12. STEPHEN: Including your uncle's, no doubt.
13. JOANNA: How many people have met their end in this demonic barbershop?
14. STEPHEN: And look at this slab. Flesh, meat, blood, saws and knives . . .
15. JOANNA: Oh, my God!
16. STEPHEN: A butcher's slab!
17. JOANNA: And look at those steps.
18. STEPHEN: They're not the ones we came down.
19. JOANNA: Just smell the air – they must lead up to the pie shop! You don't suppose . . . No!
20. MUSIC: DRAMATIC CHORD
21. STEPHEN: Oh dear. Let us call the police.
22. JOANNA: Stephen, what of Mrs. Lovett?
23. STEPHEN: Yes, come on, let's restrain her while we call the authorities.
24. SFX: FOOTSTEPS ASCENDING STONE STEPS
25. JOANNA: Stephen – oh heavens!
26. STEPHEN: What is it?
27. JOANNA: She's gone!
28. MUSIC: SUSTAINED DRAMATIC CHORD
29. NARRATOR: And so ends The Terrifying Tale of Sweeney Todd. Mr. Todd, the demon barber, lies dead, a victim of his own devilish device. And Mrs. Lovett, quite flown the nest. And the string of pearls with her. A grisly job for the police now as they piece together the cold, calculated slaughter and the woeful wickedness of that barbershop and that kitchen. And the whole of the city will be off pies for a little while.

1. NARRATOR (CONT'D): Some tender folk will even worry themselves into food poisoning. And did they catch Mrs. Lovett? No! Not her! Too clever! She got away, changed her name and her identity and, yes, her voice. Wherever could she be?
2. SFX: PEARLS RATTLE
3. NARRATOR: Ah, do you like my pearls, hmm? Fancy a meat pie anyone? Ha ha ha!
4. MUSIC
5. ANNOUNCER: You have been listening to The Terrifying Tale of Sweeney Todd live on GTFM. The cast featured Ruth Majeed as the Narrator and Mrs. Lovett, Geraint D'Arcy as John Clark, David MacDonald as Sweeney Todd, Arielle Tye as Joanna, and Jesse Schwenk as Stephen. The music was composed by Ben Challis and performed by Joe Starr and Liberty Rochford. The sound effects were created by Robert Dean and performed by Rebecca Wilton-Jones, Helena Harrison, Stacey Horton and James Doughty. Technical support was provided by the University of Glamorgan. The play was written and directed by Richard Hand and produced by Mary Traynor. Until next time, thanks for listening.
6. MUSIC ENDS

Appendix

Writing effective radio ad copy: Six steps to successful radio commercials

Rik Ferrell

(1) Determine your radio commercial length

First of all, know the length of the radio spot that you need to write. Most radio stations these days sell 15, 30, and 60 second commercials. You'll need to be precise. Radio adheres to a strict clock, so your 60-second ad likely won't be acceptable as a 62-second ad.

Typically, a radio script format calls for 12-point type in all caps, with double spacing between each line. With this in mind, here is a simple guide to follow:

- 15 seconds = 4 typed lines
- 30 seconds = 7–8 typed lines
- 60 seconds = 12–14 typed lines

And if you're including any pricing figures or your phone number, be sure to write each number as text to give you a more accurate line count.

(2) Plan what you want to say in your radio ad

Before you start, take a few minutes and make a list of the necessary points that you need to have included. These should be key attributes and selling points that sets your business apart from the competition.

Be clear and concise, and try to avoid listing too many different points, as this can lead to confusion on the listener's part. If your company is blessed with multiple key attributes, consider running multiple ads that incorporate the different attributes, but be sure to maintain the same 'feel'. You want your script to have a natural flow, not be crammed full of as many words as you can fit within the time limit.

(3) Use a strong opening statement in your radio ad

Simply put, your commercial's opening line will likely determine whether or not the listener sticks around or changes the station. This really needs to be an attention-grabber. Unless you're a seasoned Hollywood comedy writer, you might want to avoid trying to be too cute or clever here. Instead, consider using a strong, open-ended question that's pertinent to your company and/or industry, which the average listener can relate to. Here are a few examples:

- Are you paying too much for car insurance?
- Is your home as safe as it could be?
- When is the last time you enjoyed a really good burger?

By posing a question like this, right out of the box, the listener could be compelled to want to hear the answer, and the rest of your ad.

(4) Include key attributes and your company personality in your radio ad

The purpose of an ad – any ad – is to arouse enough curiosity that the target is compelled to act upon it. Get that? You don't need your ad to close the deal; you just want it to tease your product or service enough that the target decides to contact you. And that's where you and your staff come in.

With the body of the ad, address the opening question in a clear and concise manner, while working your company's key attributes into the mix. In a 60-second ad, you'll want to include your company's name at least four times. Shoot for three times in a 30-second ad, and at least twice in a 15-second ad. And, unless you have trained voice actors available, keep the script to one person. It's a lot safer.

Also, show your company's personality. Known for having the lowest prices in town? Say it. Environmentally focused? Say it. Sell the only authentic German widgets within a 40-mile radius? Say it. Don't be afraid to brag a little here – just don't overdo it.

(5) Use effective contact info in your radio ad

Just use a phone number, right? Not necessarily. When you consider that a large portion of your audience will be driving, cooking, working out, or engaged in some other activity as they're hearing your ad, most won't have a pen and paper ready to write down your digits. Which means that unless you have a Nursery School-simple number like 1–800-BIG-JOES, you'll have to repeat it, which takes up a lot of script space. And you STILL won't have guaranteed retention. Instead, consider using your web address. Most of the time they're a lot easier to recall, and it gives the listener a 24-hour point of access to your business.

(6) Further suggestions for your radio script

Above all, adhere to the K-I-S-S rule ('Keep It Simple, Stupid!'). The most effective ads usually do. And remember to time your script after you're done. If you don't have a stopwatch available, double-click on the clock on the bottom right of your computer screen and use the pop-up. Ideally, you'd like to bring the script in a few seconds short. This will give the station's production manager time to add a music intro or outro, and allow him or her to not have to rush the read.

Proper utilization of these six points will allow you to take a more seasoned approach with your copywriting, and should garner better end results. Writing a radio script isn't rocket science, but it can be daunting. However, if you can convey a few select points and ideas in a clear and concise manner, and keep your target interested, your radio campaign will indeed pay dividends.

Works cited

Books, articles, interviews

Abbott, W. (1941), *Handbook of Broadcasting (How to Broadcast Effectively)*. New York: McGraw-Hill Book Company.

Accampo, D. (2010), Interview with Richard J. Hand, November 2010.

Adams, J. (2010), Interview with Richard J. Hand, November 2010.

Angelou, M. (1984), *I Know Why the Caged Bird Sings*. London: Virago.

Apte, T. (2005), 'Interactive radio drama', in *Power Tools Series*. London: International Institute for Environment and Development [Online]. Available at: http://www.policy-powertools.org/Tools/Organising/docs/interactive_radio_drama_card_english.pdf (accessed: December 2010).

Arnold, R. (2010), Interview with Richard J. Hand, November 2010.

Augoyard, J-F., and H. Torgue (2005), *Sonic Experience, A Guide To Everyday Sounds*. Montreal: McGill-Queen's University Press.

Barnouw, E. (ed.) (1945), *Radio Drama in Action: Twenty-Five Plays of a Changing World*. New York: Rinehart.

Bartell, H. (1998), *Struts and Frets* [Online]. Available at: http://www.lofcom.com/nostalgia/columns/struts/struts001.php (accessed: January 2010).

Beck, A. (1997), *Radio Acting*. London: A&C Black.

———. (1998), 'Point of Listening in Radio Plays', *Sound Journal* [online]. Available at: http://www.kent.ac.uk/arts/sound-journal/beck981.html (accessed: December 2010).

Bick, A. (2010), 'At the Holcaust Tower', in *Andreas Bick: Composer and Sound Artist* [Online]. Available at: http://www.andreasbick.de/en/downloads/?article=52 (accessed: December 2010).

———. (2011), Interview with Mary Traynor, January 2011.

Blue, H. (2002), *Words at War: World War II Era Radio Drama and the Postwar Broadcasting Blacklist*. Lanham: Scarecrow.

Boal, A. (1996), *Games for Actors and Non Actors*. London: Routledge.

Boardman-Jacobs, Sam (ed.) (2004), *Radio Scriptwriting*. Bridgend, UK: Seren.

Bond, E. (1978), *Plays: 2*. London: Methuen.

Brady, E. (2005), 'C. S. Lewis opposed to a film lion', *USA Today*, 12 February [Online]. Available at: http://www.usatoday.com/life/movies/news/2005-12-02-narnia-lewis_x.htm (accessed: January 2011).

Briggs, A. (1961), *The History Of Broadcasting in the United Kingdom: Volume I: The Birth of Broadcasting*. Oxford: Oxford University Press.

———. (1965), *The History Of Broadcasting in the United Kingdom: Volume II: The Golden Age of Wireless*. Oxford: Oxford University Press.

Brown, M. (2010), Interview with Richard J. Hand, November 2010.

Carlile, J. (1942), *Production and Direction of Radio Programmes*. New York: Prentice-Hall.

Caulfield, A. (2009), *Writing for Radio*. Marlborough: Crowood Press.

Cazeau, C. *Chambers English Dictionary* (7th edn) (1992), New York: Chambers.

———. (2005), 'Phenomenology and radio drama', *British Journal of Aesthetics*, 45(2), 157–73.

Chignell, H. (2009), *Key Concepts in Radio Studies*. London: Sage.

Churchill, W. (1940), 'We Shall Fight Them on the Beaches', on BBC Home Service, 4 June.

Coe, L. (1996), *Wireless Radio: a Brief History*. Jefferson, NC: McFarland.

Conrad, J. (1925), *Nostromo*. London: Routledge.

Corwin, N. (2003), 'An interview with Norman Corwin', in *Crazy Dog Audio Theatre* [Online]. Available at: http://www.crazydogaudiotheatre.com/corwin.php (accessed: January 2011).

Crisell, A. (1994), *Understanding Radio*. London: Routledge.

Crook, T. (1999), *Radio Drama: Theory and Practice*. London: Routledge.

Darnall, S. (1998), 'A nostalgic look at radio's golden age', *Nostalgia Digest* [Online]. Available at: http://www.nostalgiadigest.com/ (accessed: July 2007).

Davies. H. (2003), 'Daphne Oram obituary', *Guardian* 24 January [Online]. Available at: http://www.guardian.co.uk/news/2003/jan/24/guardianobituaries.artsobituaries (accessed: November 2010).

DeBona, G. (2010), *Film Adaptation in the Hollywood Studio Era*. Urbana: University of Illinois Press.

Dickinson, R. (1995), 'Two cultures – one voice? Problems in broadcaster/health educator co-operation', *Health Education Research: Theory & Practice*, 10(4), 421–30.

Douglas, S. J. (1999), *Listening In*. New York: Times Books.

Drakakis, J. (1981), *British Radio Drama*. Cambridge: Cambridge University Press.

Dunning, J. (1998), *On the Air: The Encyclopedia of Old-Time Radio*. Oxford: Oxford University Press.

Eliot, E. (2010), Interview with Richard J. Hand, December 2010.

Fink, H. (1981), 'The sponsor's v. the nation's choice: North American radio drama', in P. Lewis (ed.), *Radio Drama*. New York: Longman, pp. 185–243.

Fisher, S. (2009), 'Case study – Viim Kuunga radio project – Burkina Faso 2009', *The Communication Initiative Network* [Online]. Available at: http://www.comminit.com/en/node/120105 (accessed: December 2010).

de Fossard, E., Riber, J. (2005), *Writing and Producing for Television and Film*. London: Sage.

Friere, P. (2006), *Pedagogy of the Oppressed*. New York: Continuum.

Gleason, J. (2010), Interview with Richard J. Hand, November 2010.

Goldstein, S. (2005), 'Communicating HIV and AIDS, what works? A report on the impact evaluation of Soul City's fourth series', *Journal of Health Communication*, 10, 465–83.

Gray, R. (2006), 'Fireside issues: audience, listener, soundscape', in A. Crisell (ed.), *More than a Music Box*. New York: Berghahn Books, pp. 247–65.

Greig, T. (2010), The Archers: Backstage [Online]. Available at: http://www.bbc.co.uk/radio4/archers/backstage/studio.shtml (accessed: February 2010).

Haining, P. (1993), *Sweeney Todd: The True Story of the Demon Barber of Fleet Street*. London: Robson.

Hale, J. (1975), *Radio Power: Propaganda and International Broadcasting*. London: Paul Elek.

Hand, R. J. (2006), *Terror on the Air! Horror Radio in America, 1931–1952*. Jefferson NC: McFarland.

——. (2009), '"Stay tuned for tricks, treats and terror": Halloween and horror radio in the era of American live broadcasting', in M. Foley and H. O'Donnell (eds), *Treat or Trick? Halloween in a Globalising World*. Cambridge: Cambridge Scholars Press, pp. 214–27.

Harmon, J. (1967), *The Great Radio Heroes*. New York: Doubleday.

Hatley, K. (2010), Interview with Richard J. Hand, November 2010.

Hayley, W. (1946), 'An Introduction by the Director General of the BBC, Sir William Hayley, KCMG to the BBC Third Programme', in *BBC Radio 3 60 Years On* [Online]. Available at: http://www.bbc.co.uk/radio3/classical/thirdprogramme/introduction.shtml (accessed: January 2011).

Heffernan, T. (2010), Interview with Richard J. Hand, November 2010.

Hendy, D. (2007), *A Life on Air: A History of Radio Four*. Oxford: Oxford University Press.

Heong, K. L., Escalada M. M., Huan, N. H., and Mai, V. (1998), 'Use of communication media in changing rice farmers pest management in the Mekong Delta, Vietnam', *Crop Protection*, 17(5), 413–25.

Hickey, S., and Madia, R. (2007), 'Now Fear This: Writing Horror for Audio Theatre', in Mort Castle (ed.), *On Writing Horror* (rev. edn). Cincinnati: Writer's Digest, pp. 209–12.

Hilliard, R. L. (1985), *Radio Broadcasting: An Introduction to the Sound Medium* (3rd edn). New York: Longman.

Hilmes, M. (2002), *Radio Reader: Essays in the Cultural History of Radio*. New York: Routledge.

Hodgson, B. (2010), Presenting at *Fag-ends and Lollypops: The BBC Radiophonic Workshop*. A symposium at the National Media Museum, Bradford, UK, November 2010.

Horstmann, R. (1997), *Writing for Radio* (3rd edn). London: A & C Black.

Hoverson, J. (2011), Interview with Richard J. Hand, January 2011.

Jaker, B. (2010), *Old Time Radio Digest* [Online]. Available at: http://www.oocities.com/emruf7/1922.html?20105#ixzz11TjE3Aki (accessed: December 2010).

Jayaprakash, Y., And Shoesmith, B. (2007), 'Community radio and development: Tribal audiences in South India', in L. Fuller (ed.), *Community Media International Perspectives*. New York: Palgrave Macmillan, pp. 43–5.

Kerr, D. (1998), *Dance, Media Entertainment & Popular Theatre in South East Africa*. Bayreuth: Bayreuth African Studies.

Kingson, W. K. (1950), *Radio Drama Acting and Production*. Cairo: Rinehart.

Knowlson, J. (1996), *Damned to Fame: The Life of Samuel Beckett*. London: Bloomsbury.

Kyagambiddwa, S., and Uwamariya, J. (2004), 'Urunana: creative communication for development', in *Communication Initiative Network* [Online]. Available at: http://www.comminit.com/en/node/69884/3499 (accessed: December 2010).

Lea, G. (1926), *Radio Drama and How to Write It*. London: Allen and Unwin.

Lewis, P. (1981), *Radio Drama*. London: Longman.

MacLoughlin, S. (2008), *Writing for Radio*. Bristol: Soundplay.

Maltin, L. (2000), *The Great American Broadcast*. New York: Penguin Putnam.

Marshall, S. (2008), 'The story of the BBC radiophonic workshop', in *Sound on Sound* [Online]. Available at: http://www.soundonsound.com/sos/apr08/articles/radiophonic.htm (accessed: November 2010).

Mason, R. (1978). *The Revenge*: pre-transmission interview [Radio]. London: BBC Radio 4.

McInerney, V. (2001), *Writing for Radio*. Manchester: Manchester University Press.

McLeod, E. (1998), 'The WGY Players and the Birth of Radio Drama' [Online]. Available at http://www.midcoast.com/~lizmcl/wgy.html (accessed: 30 January 2011).

McPhail, T. (2009), *Development Communication: Reframing the Role of Media*. Chichester: Blackwell Publishing.

McWhinnie, D. (1959), *The Art of Radio*. London: Sage.

Mda, Z. (1993), *When People Play People*. Johannesburg: Witwatersrand University Press.

Melville, H. (1952), *Moby-Dick, or, The Whale*. New York: Hendricks House.

Merrill Squier, S. (2003), *Communities of the Air: Radio Century, Radio Culture*. Durham, NC: Duke University Press.

Mills, D. (2010), Presenting at *Fags and Lollipops: The BBC Radiophonic Workshop*. A symposium at the National Media Museum, Bradford, UK, November 2010.

Morrison, H. (1937), 'The Hindenburg Report' on WLS Chicago, 6 May.

Morton, D. (2000), *Off the Record: The Technology and Culture of Sound Recording in America*. New Brunswick: Rutgers University Press.

Mott, R. L. (1993), *Radio Sound Effects*. Jefferson: McFarland.

Nachman, G. (1998), *Raised on Radio*. Berkeley: University of California Press.

Naremore, J. (1989), *The Magic World of Orson Welles*. Dallas: Southern Methodist University Press.

Oboler, A. (1937), 'The dark', in *Generic Radio Workshop Script Library* [Online]. Available at: http://genericradio.com/library.php (accessed: January 2011).

——. (1939), 'Another world', in *Generic Radio Workshop Script Library* [Online]. Available at: http://genericradio.com/library.php (accessed: January 2011).

Palermo, T. (2011), 'Sound effects for audio theatre', in *Tony Palermo's Ruyasonic Site* [Online]. Available at: http://www.ruyasonic.com/sfx_primer.htm (accessed: January 2011).

Pappas-DeLuca, K. A., Kraft, J. M., Galavotti, C., Warner, L., Mooki, M., Hastings, P., Koppenhaver, T., Roels, T., and Kilmarx, P. (2008), 'Entertainment-Education radio serial drama and outcomes related to HIV testing in Botswana', *AIDS Education and Prevention*, 20(6), 486–503.

Plunkett, J. (2010), 'More than 8m Britons have downloaded podcasts', *Guardian*, December 15 [Online]. Available at: http://www.guardian.co.uk/media/2010/dec/15/rajar-radio-listening-smartphones-podcasts (accessed: January 2011).

Raban, J. (1981), 'Icon or symbol: the writer and the "medium"', in P. Lewis (ed.), *Radio Drama*. London: Longman, pp. 78–90.

Raw, L. (2010), Interview with Richard J. Hand, December 2010.

Reynolds, S. (2009), 'Sorcerers of sounds', *Guardian*, 29 September [Online]. Available at: http://www.guardian.co.uk/culture/2008/sep/20/bbc.doctorwho (accessed: November 2010).

Runacre Temple, M. (2010), Interview with Richard J. Hand, November 2010.

Sachs, A. (1978), '*The Revenge*: pre-transmission interview' [Radio]. London: BBC Radio 4.

Salk, S. (2010), Interview with Richard J. Hand, November 2010.

Schaeffer, P. (1966), 'Acousmatics', in C. Cox and D. Warner (eds), *Audio Culture: Readings in Modern Music*. New York: Continuum.

Schafer, R. Murray (1994), *The Soundscape: Our Sonic Environment and the Tuning of the World*. Rochester: Destinys.

Shingler, M., and Wieringa, C. (1998), *On Air: Methods and Meanings of Radio*. London: Hodder.

Singhal, A., Cody, M., Rogers, E., and Sabido, M. (2004), *Entertainment Education and Social Change: History, Research and Practice*. New Jersey: Lawrence Erlbaum Associates.

Slavik, K. (2010), 'Surround sound systems', in *Surround Sound Broadcasting Stations* [Online]. Available at: http://www.nti-audio.com/Portals/0/Products/Minstruments/DR2/Downloads/NTI_AppNote_Surround_Sound_in_Broadcasting_Stations.pdf (accessed: January 2011).

Stanislavski, C. (1967), *An Actor Prepares*. London: Geoffrey Blers.

Thomas, D. (1962), *Under Milk Wood: A Play for Voices*. London: J. M. Dent.

Thorpe, V. (2010), 'Finest hour for actor who was Churchill's radio voice', *Observer*, October 29 [Online]. Available at: http://www.guardian.co.uk/media/2000/oct/29/uknews.theobserver (accessed: October 2010).

Watson, S. (2010), [Online]. 'Epic sound: the guide to sound effects' [Online]. Available at: http://www.epicsound.com/sfx/#a (accessed: January 2010).

Wayland, Kc. (2010), Interview with Richard J. Hand, November 2010.

Weiss, A. (1995), *Phantasmic Radio*. Durham, NC: Duke University Press.

Welles, O. (1938), Interview for Universal Newsreel, October 1938.

———. (1970), Interview with NBC's Dean Martin Show, 1970.

Wells, H. G. (2008), *The War of the Worlds*. Charleston, SC: Forgotten Books.

West, S. (2007), 'Fathers and sons', *Guardian*, March 17 [Online]. Available at: http://www.guardian.co.uk/books/2007/mar/17/featuresreviews.guardianreview13 (accessed: January 2011).

White, R. (2001), 'Musique concrète', in *Greater London Industrial Archaeology Society* [Online]. Available at: http://www.glias.org.uk/glias/rws/pgs/rx01.htm (accessed: November 2010).

Young, F. (1933), *Shall I Listen: Studies in the Adventure and Technique of Broadcasting*. London: Constable.

Websites

19 Nocturne Boulevard (2011). Available at http://19nocturneboulevard.net/ (accessed: January 2011)

3dHorrorfi (2011) [Online]. Available at http://www.3dhorrorfi.com/ (accessed: January 2011).

About NPR (2010). Available at: http://www.npr.org/about/aboutnpr/history.html#history (accessed: November 2010).

About The Archers (2010). Available at: http://www.bbc.co.uk/radio4/features/the-archers/about (accessed: November 2010).

About the BBC (2010). Available at: http://www.bbc.co.uk/aboutthebbc/purpose/ (accessed: November 2010).

AMARC World Association of Community Radio Broadcasters (2010). *What is Community Radio*? Available at: http://www.amarc.org/index.php?p=What_is_Community_radio?&l=EN (accessed: December 2010).

The Archers 60th Tweetalong (2011). Available at: http://www.bbc.co.uk/radio4/features/the-archers/content/social/b00x3q7c/ (accessed: January 2011).

BBC (2010). *The Royal Wedding*. Available at: http://www.bbc.co.uk/news/uk-11767495 (accessed: January 2011).

BBC Radio 4: Writing for Radio 4 (2011). Available at: http://www.bbc.co.uk/radio4/arts/commissioning_briefs.shtml#drama (accessed: January 2011).

BBC World Service History (2010). Available at: http://www.bbc.co.uk/worldservice/history/timeline.shtml (accessed: November 2010).

Chatterbox Audio Theatre (2011). Available at: http://chatterboxtheater.org/ (accessed: January 2011).

Communications Initiative Network (2010). *Soul City Television Series*. Available at: http://www.comminit.com/en/print/122775 (accessed: November 2010).

Crazy Dog Audio Theatre (2011). Available at: http://www.crazydogaudiotheatre.com/about.php (accessed: January 2011).

Daphne Oram (2010). *Daphne Oram: An Electronic Music Pioneer*. Available at: http://daphneoram.org/oramarchive/bbc/ (accessed: November 2010).

Department for Children, Schools and Families (2009). *DCSF Launches UK's First Interactive Mobile Drama*. Available at: http://www.coi.gov.uk/press.php?release=266 (accessed: December 2010).

The Drama Pod (2010). Available at: www.thedramapod.com (accessed: January 2011).

English Wordplay (2010). *Radio Drama and Documentaries in Prison.* Available at: http://englishwordplay.com/prison.html (accessed: December 2010).

The Freesound Project (2010). Available at: http://www.freesound.org/ (accessed: December 2010).

The Generic Radio Workshop (2011). *Vintage Radio Script Library.* Available at: http://genericradio.com/ (accessed: January 2011).

Icebox Radio Theater (2010). Available at: http://www.iceboxradio.org/Info.html (accessed: January 2011).

Radio Conventions (2010). *Haiti's Signal FM radio honored at NABEF's service to America awards.* Available at: http://www.radioconventions.com/radio-industry-interest/haiti-signal-fm-radio-honored/ (accessed: January 2011).

Radio Drama Reviews Online (2010). Available at: http://www.radiodramareviews.com/index.html (accessed: January 2011).

Realtime Associates (2009). 'Soul Trapper: Episode 1'. Available at: http://itunes.apple.com/us/app/soul-trapper-episode-1-ollie/id292616556?mt=8# (accessed: January 2011).

SilenceRadio (2010). Available at: http://www.silenceradio.org/ (accessed and translated by Mary Traynor: December 2010).

Soul City Institute for Health Development Communication (2007). *HIV/AIDS Impacts of Soul City Series 7.* Available at: http://www.soulcity.org.za/research/evaluations/soul-city-its-real-evaluation-report-2007/evaluation-report-2007/view (accessed: November 2010).

Soundsnap (2010). Available at: http://www.soundsnap.com (accessed: December 2010).

Story Workshop (2010). *Our Approach.* Available at: http://www.storyworkshop.org/our_approach/community_dialogue/index.html (accessed: December 2010).

UN Data (2009). *UNSD Statistical Databases.* Available at: http://unstats.un.org/unsd/databases.htm (accessed: January 2011).

We're Alive: A Story of Survival (2010). Available at: http://www.zombiepodcast.com (accessed: January 2011).

We're Alive Forum (2010). Available at: http://werealive.hyperboards.com/ (accessed: December 2010).

We're Not Dead (2011). Available at: http://www.facebook.com/pages/Were-Not-Dead-Official-Were-Alive-Community-Podcast/193315070695125 (accessed: January 2011).

Wireless Theatre company (2011). Available at: http://www.wirelesstheatrecompany.co.uk/ (accessed: January 2011).

Radio and audio plays: A selection

The Archers (1951 onwards) [online]. Available at: http://www.bbc.co.uk/radio4/features/the- archers/ (accessed: January 2011).

The Chair (2000), BBC Radio 4.

A Comedy of Danger (1924), BBC.

Dark House (2004), BBC Radio 4.

The Darkness of Wallis Simpson (2010), BBC Radio 4.

Don't Let Go (2010) [online]. Available at: http://www.spotify.com/int/new-user/ (accessed: January 2011).

The Dreams (1964), BBC Third Programme.

Embers (1959), BBC Third Programme.

Escape (1947), CBS.

The Hound of the Baskervilles (1998), BBC Radio 7.

Medusa on the Beach (2009) [online]. Wireless Radio Theatre. Available at: http://www.wirelesstheatrecompany.co.uk/ (accessed: January 2011).

Moby Dick (2010), BBC Radio 4.

Old Harry's Game (2009) [DVD]. Available at: http://www.bbc.co.uk/programmes/b007jvj6 (accessed: January 2011).

One Eighteen: Migration (2008) [online]. Available at: http://oneeighteen.libsyn.com/ (accessed: January 2011).

A Pot Calling the Kettle Black (2010) [online]. Available at: http://www.andreasbick.de/en/music/radio_art/?article=10 (accessed: December 2010).

Quiet, Please (1947), Mutual.

Red Cross emergency (2009) [online]. Available at: http://www.rab.co.uk/rab2009/showContent.aspx?id=398 (accessed: January 2011).

The Revenge (1978), BBC Radio 4.

Sorry, Wrong Number (1943), CBS.

Soul Trapper (2009) [online]. Available at: http://itunes.apple.com/us/app/soul-trapper-episode-1-ollie/id292616556?mt=8# (accessed: January 2011).

Staring into the Fridge (2010), BBC Radio 4.

This Gun That I Have in My Right Hand is Loaded (1972), BBC training.

Under Milk Wood (1954), BBC Third Programme.

The Unfortunates (2010), BBC Radio 3.

The Voyage of the Dawn Treader (2005) [DVD]. Available at: http://family.christianbook.com/Christian/Books/easy_find?Ntt=narnia&N=0&Ntk=keywords&action=Search&Ne=0&event=ESRCN&nav_search=1&cms=1&search= (accessed: January 2011).

War of the Worlds (1938), CBS.

We're Alive (2009 onwards) [online]. Available at: http://www.zombiepodcast.com/The_Zombie_Podcast/WereAliveMain.html (accessed: January 2011).

The Witch's Tale (1931–38), WOR.

Wormwood (2007–2010) [online]. Available at http://wormwoodshow.com/ (accessed: November 2010).

Filmography

Here are some films that feature radio:

Annie (John Huston, 1982)
Betrayed (Costa Gavras, 1988)
The Boat that Rocked (Richard Curtis, 2009)
Dead Air (Corbin Bernsen, 2009)
Eight Legged Freaks (Ellory Elkayem, 2002)
Haunted Honeymoon (Gene Wilder, 1986)
The King's Speech (Tom Hooper, 2010)
Me and Orson Welles (Richard Linklater, 2008)
O Brother, Where Art Thou? (Joel Coen, 2000)
Pontypool (Bruce McDonald, 2009)
A Prairie Home Companion (Robert Altman, 2006)
Radio Days (Woody Allen, 1987)
Radioland Murders (Mel Smith, 1994)
Resident Evil: Afterlife (Paul W. S. Anderson, 2010)
Talk Radio (Oliver Stone, 1989)
Terminator Salvation (McG, 2009)
White Noise (Geoffrey Sax, 2005)
White Noise: The Light (Patrick Lussier, 2007)

Index

Printed in Great Britain
by Amazon